The Battered Woman Syndrome

2nd Edition

Lenore E. A. Walker, Ed.D., A.B.P.P., is a clinical and forensic psychologist who first named the Battered Woman Syndrome from the landmark research program she conducted with battered women in the early 1980's. During the intervening years she has developed a new therapy technique for working with battered women called Survivor Therapy and testified on behalf of hundreds of women who survived abusive situations. Dr. Walker, who received her bachelor degree from Hunter College of the City University of New York (CUNY), her master degree from City College of CUNY, and her doctorate from Rutgers, The State University of New Jersey, is currently a professor of psychology at Nova Southeastern University in Ft. lauderdale, Florida and coordinator of the Forensic Psychology concentration in the doctoral psychology program at the Center for Psychological Studies. She is Executive Director of the Domestic Violence Institute with affiliate centers all over the world. A frequently sought out keynote speaker and workshop leader, Dr. Walker travels all over the United States and the world to assist others working together with battered and abused women through education and training, facilitating research and public policy initiatives. Gathering knowledge from these different areas, she has integrated the current status of the field together with the previous research findings to produce the second edition of *The Battered Woman Syndrome.* An active member of the American Psychological Association's governance, she chaired the APA Task Force on Violence and the Family that produced a report in 1996. Called the "mother of the Battered Woman Syndrome," Dr. Walker remains a leading figure in the psychology of domestic violence. She can be reached on email at Drlewalker@aol.com or through the Domestic Violence Institute's web page www.dviworld.org.

The Battered Woman Syndrome

2nd Edition

Lenore E. A. Walker, EdD

SPRINGER PUBLISHING COMPANY

Springer Publishing Company, Inc.
11 West 42nd Street
New York, NY 10036-8002
www.springerpub.com

Acquisitions Editor: Bill Tucker
Production Editor: Helen Song
Cover design by James Scotto-Lavino

05 06 07/9

Library of Congress Cataloging-in-Publication-Data

Walker, Lenore E.
    The battered woman syndrome / Lenore E. A. Walker. — 2nd ed.
        p.   cm. — (Springer series, focus on women)
    Includes bibliographical references and index.
    ISBN 0-8261-4322-9 (hardcover)
    1. Wife abuse—United States.   2. Abused wives—United Sates—
Psychology.   I. Title.   II. Series: Springer series, focus on
women (Unnumbered)
HV6626.2.W33   1999
362.82'92—dc21   99-43559
                                                                           CIP

Printed in the United States of America

Contents

Appendixes

Acknowledgments

lthough I cannot individually thank each of the 435 women who volunteered to let us scrutinize their private lives, I want to take this opportunity to publicly say thank you and to acknowledge our debt to them. They were courageous, articulate, and caring people whose strengths always seemed to come through despite their pain. I admire and applaud all those women who were able to make the difficult decision to terminate an abusive relationship, knowing the risk they took that the violence would get even worse. Also, I hope our interaction helped give those women still living in violence some extra courage to leave.

My sincere thanks also goes to our National Institute of Mental Health project officer, Thomas Lalley, Deputy Director of the Center for Criminal and Violent Behavior. Tom encouraged me from the beginning, and he and Elizabeth Reed, our Grants Management Officer, guided us to completion even when adverse financial conditions at Colorado Women's College threatened a premature end to the project. A special thanks goes to Charles Corriere, who donated so much of his own time, staff time, and equipment at Estimatics Corporation, to print our questionnaires at a cost we could afford. The Denver area media were especially helpful in publicizing our project, which encouraged a steady flow of subjects.

This project flourished with the capable work of many people. At its height, we had approximately 30 women conducting interviews and compiling data. So many work-study students, volunteers, and staff have helped us that it would be difficult to name them all. Majorie Leidig, Kathy Jens, Gayle Costello, Denise Murray, and Phil Shaver were invaluable and supportive, as well as competent at their jobs. Others whose contributions I want to acknowledge include: Phyllis Buck, Barbara Cohen, Cathie Cox, Marilyn David, Patricia Eberle, Annelle Griggsmiller, Carol Hathaway-Clark, Daphne Heritage, Betsy House, Diana Huston, Lou Isaacson, Nancy Lemnitzer Kaser-Boyd, Linda Kastelowitz, Miriam Latorre, Ruth Larsen, Renee Lewin, Robin Lopez,

Madalyn Millensifer, Donna Stringer-Moore, Joyce Nielsen, Flo Phillips, Elaine Sage, Charelle Schillo, Cassandra Smoot, Nancy Thoennes, Shirley Waterman, Barbara Welsh-Osga, and Marilyn Wright. Mary McCurry, my friend and accountant, provided invaluable support during the financially disastrous last year.   (

A special thanks goes to my associates Angela Browne and Roberta Thyfault, who continued working as hard as they could right up to the very end. Without their capable assistance and deep friendship, this project could not have been completed.

The second edition of this book was completed with the help of Monica Beer, my excellent research assistance at Nova Southeastern University. I also want to thank Erna Beerheide and Ross Seligson, for all their loving support. Ursula Springer and Bill Tucker at Springer Publishing never gave up on me and special thanks go to them for their patience and wonderful assistance.

LENORE E. A. WALKER, ED.D.

Introduction to the Research Study

From July 1978 through June 1981, the Battered Women Research Center at Colorado Women's College in Denver, Colorado, undertook a study of over 400 battered women in the Rocky Mountain region. The purpose of the study was to learn about domestic violence from the battered woman's perspective. From preliminary investigations, it was believed that women develop a cluster of psychological symptoms from living in a violent relationship that could be called "The Battered Woman Syndrome." At the time this study was conceived, there was little funded research in this area. During the past 15 years much more data has become available. Rapid dissemination of this new knowledge has been necessary in order to have an impact on the public policy. Our results have been presented at various professional conferences and meetings as well as in journal articles and book chapters. I have been invited to share my professional opinions by testifying before several Congressional committees, the U.S. Commission on Civil Rights, the Surgeon General's conference on family violence, and the Attorney General's Task Force on Violence and the Family. I have chaired task forces on child abuse policy and violence in the family for the American Psychological Association. My testimony on behalf of violence victims has been accepted in the courts in over 40 states and Federal court. The first edition of this book was written to present an integration of the final analysis from this research project into the body of literature specializing in understanding spouse abuse that was available at that time. Today, the body of literature on domestic violence is huge. This second edition attempts to analyze the original study results in light of the new clinical and empirical research and determine if the original conclusions still hold true today. They do!

The goals of the research project were to identify key psychological and sociological factors that compose the battered woman syndrome, test specific theories about battered women, and collect comprehensive data on battered women. The data were analyzed in order to clarify the psychological and sociological factors involved in the battered woman syndrome. The two specific theories that were tested were the learned helplessness theory and the cycle theory of battering. Both of these theories were formulated from my previous work (Walker, 1979).

It was hypothesized that early social influences on women facilitate a psychological condition called "learned helplessness," first described by psychologist Martin Seligman, which causes women to feel powerless to effect positive control over their lives. It was suggested that "learned helplessness" is responsible for the apparent emotional cognitive and behavioral deficits observed in the battered woman that negatively influence her from leaving a relationship after the battering occurs.

It was also hypothesized that further victimization occurs by the nature of the cycle of violence. The theory tested was that battering is neither random nor constant but rather occurs in repeated cycles each having three phases. The first phase is a period of tension-building that leads up to phase two, or the acute battering incident. The third phase consists of kind, loving, and contrite behavior displayed by the batterer toward the woman, which provides the reinforcement for the cycle. Our research indicates that the third phase may also be characterized by an absence of tension or violence, which then takes on a positive value.

In previous knowledge about domestic violence investigators proposed other theories to account for men's inability to control their violent behavior toward women. They include the belief that these men perceive they have few resources other than physical coercion to get what they need and one or both partner's abuse of alcohol and drugs and his or her major psychopathology. Situational factors such as the presence of children and economic distress have also been explored. Child abuse literature has supported the theory that intrafamily violence is learned behavior that is passed down from one generation to the next.

The socialization process of assigning male and female sex role behavior is also seen as contributing to violence against women. It is suggested that battered women are more rigidly socialized into the female sex role stereotype. It is also suggested that batterers are more rigidly socialized into the male sex role expectations. Thus another objective of this research was to examine the data to learn more about the impact of the sex role socialization process on the battering relationship. None of these factors were viewed as mutually exclusive and it was anticipated that a number of theoretical concepts may be found to interact that explain this complex behavioral syndrome.

This study has been concerned primarily with the woman's perceptions in the battering relationship. It studied the woman's role within the family from her vantage point and examined how abuse impacted on her and on the family unit. The possibility that violence in a family may have mutual causation or that women may batter men was not negated, but was not the focus of this study. A major objective of this research was to add a different view, the woman's, to the total understanding of the problem of intrafamily violence. We found that the women's descriptions of the violence were the most accurate, even though they tended to minimize, deny, and forget many incidents. Thus, it is suggested that no exploration of the problems within the field of domestic violence be considered accurately completed without including the women's perspectives.

When the project began, there had been little other data systematically collected from a wide spectrum within the population of battered women. Previously, most data had come from subsamples such as those who called the police, those who sought help at a shelter or agency, or those who used the court to try to find relief. Thus, we wanted to attract as broad a sample as possible.

Specific topics in this study that investigated psychological and sociological characteristics of these battered women were:

1. Family origin demographics: history of intrafamily abuse, sex role socialization, and child raising patterns for both the woman's and the man's parental homes.
2. Current family demographics: history of abuse, sex role socialization, and child-raising patterns.
3. Other relationships the woman may have had, including demographics, history of abuse, if any, sex role socialization, and child-raising patterns.
4. The woman's educational history, paid or volunteer work history, community activities, and direct measures of self-esteem.
5. Battered women's views of the battering relationship as compared to other nonviolent relationships they may have had.
6. The woman's current attribution of locus of control for her life events.
7. The woman's current psychological functioning including history of treatment for her emotional difficulties. Her perception of the batterer's psychological functioning during the relationship was also investigated.
8. The battered woman's tolerance for physical stress, including psychophysiological generalized stress reaction symptoms, medical history, and injuries received.

These topics have continued to fascinate researchers during the intervening 15 years. Their results aren't much different than ours.

Battered women come from all walks of life and the only fact that brings them together is their victimization by an intimate male partner. The one answer that continues to elude researchers, clinicians and the general public alike is to the question, *"Why doesn't she leave."* Hopefully the data in this book will provide the multiple answers, but most simply put: *Leaving does not stop the abuse and may even make it worse.*

PART ONE

The Battered Woman Syndrome Study

Overview of the Battered Woman Syndrome Study

Over the years it has been found that the best way to understand violence in the home comes from listening to the descriptions obtained from those who experience it—whether victims, perpetrators, children or observers. Until the study reported here, obtaining accurate descriptions of the violence had been difficult to obtain from women as well as men, partly due to the effects of the experience, as well as feelings of shame and fear of further harm. This particular study pioneered in using methods that were rarely used by researchers 20 years ago, although these methods are more common today. Women were given the opportunity to fully describe their experiences in context, using what researchers call an "open-ended" technique combined together with "forced-choice" responses that prompted their memories and went beyond the denial and minimization that were the typical first responses. As a result, the study collected ground-breaking data that had never before been totally heard by anyone, including mental health and health professionals.

The understanding of domestic violence reported here has been taken from the perceptions of the courageous battered women who were willing to share intimate details of their lives. It must be remembered that this study was conducted almost 20 years ago, during the late 1970s and early 1980s, before victimization was popular to talk about. These data indicated that events that occurred in the woman's childhood as well as other factors in the relationship, interacted with the violence she experienced by the batterer and impacted upon the woman to produce her current mental state. The research demonstrated that psychologists could reliably identify these various events and relationship factors and then measure their impact on the woman's psychological status. Although the data we obtained supported the theories that I proposed at the time, it has become even more relevant today, almost 20 years later, to recognize the robust nature of these findings that continue to be reaffirmed in subsequent research.

After analyzing reported details about past and present feelings, thoughts, and actions of the women and the violent and nonviolent men, the data led me to conclude that there are no specific personality traits that would suggest a victim-prone personality for the women (see also Brown, 1992; Root, 1992), although there may be an identifiable violence-prone personality for the abusive men (Dutton, 1995; Holtzworth-Monroe & Stuart, 1994; Jacobson & Gottman, 1998; Sonkin, 1995). From the woman's point of view, the batterer initiated the violence pattern that occurred in the relationship because of his inability to control his behavior when he got angry. There is still an ongoing debate in the field about whether the batterer is really unable to control his anger, as was perceived by the woman, or if he chooses to abuse her and therefore, is very much in control of where and when he uses violence. The women's reports of the man's previous life experiences indicated that engaging in such violent behavior had been learned and rewarded over a long period of time. The women who reported details contrasting the batterer's behavior with their experience with a nonviolent man further supported this view. Information about the batterer's childhood and his other life experiences follow the psychological principles consistent with him having learned to respond to emotionally distressing cues with anger and violent behavior. The high incidence of other violent behavior correlates, such as child abuse, violence toward others, destruction of property, and a high percentage of arrests and convictions support a learning theory explanation for domestic violence.

These data compelled me to conclude then, as well as now, that from the woman's point of view, the initiation of the violence pattern in the battering relationships studied came from the man's learned violent behavior. The connections between violence against women, violence against children, violence against the elderly, and street/community violence have been demonstrated in subsequent research (APA, 1996a; Walker, 1994). Patterns of one form of violence in the home create a high risk factor for other abuse. Alcohol and other drugs appear to exacerbate the risk for greater injury or death. Men continue to use physical, sexual, and psychological abuse to obtain and maintain power and control over women and children, often viewed as his "property" even as we move into the next century! Thus, we must continue to study the impact of violence on the women in the total context of our lives, to better understand its social and interpersonal etiology as an aid to prevent and stop violence. If this mostly male to female violence is learned behavior, and all the psychological research to date supports this view (APA, 1996a; Koss et al., 1994), we must understand how men learn to use violence, what maintains it despite social, financial and legal consequences, and how to help them unlearn the behavior.

NEW RESEARCH ON ETIOLOGY OF VIOLENCE IN THE HOME

Since the original battered woman syndrome research was completed in 1982, the field has become one that is most often studied by social policy, health and mental health scientists, students and professionals. In 1994, I was asked by the President of the American Psychological Association to convene a special task force composed of some of the most respected psychology experts in the area of family violence to review the research and clinical programs to determine what psychology has contributed to the understanding of violence and the family, including battered woman. Our goal was to prepare materials for policymakers to aid them as they created social policy to stop and prevent all forms of interpersonal violence. This anti-violence initiative is still ongoing in the Public Interest Directorate of the APA, continuing to publish materials (APA, 1995, 1996a, 1996b, 1997).

Although we have much more data on the topic today, in fact, the conclusions I reached and stated in the 1984 edition of *The Battered Woman Syndrome*, still hold up today, over 15 years later. Partner violence (as battering of women, wives, or other intimate relationships is sometimes called) is still considered learned behavior that is used to obtain and maintain power and control over a woman. Although lesbians and gay men also engage in violence against their partners, the limited available research suggests that there may be some differences including less physical harm in lesbian relationships (Lobel, 1986; Renzetti, 1992) and more physical harm in brief but not long-term gay male relationships (Island & Letelier, 1991). Our findings were that although racial and cultural issues might impact on the availability of resources for the victim, they do not determine incidence or prevalence of domestic violence (Browne, 1993; Browne & Williams, 1989; Gelles & Straus, 1988). Many factors appear to interact that determine the level of violence experienced and the access to resources and other help to end to violence. Although there are some who have designed intervention programs to help save the relationship while still stopping the violence (see below and chapters 4 and 12), it remains a daunting and difficult task with only limited success (Harrell, 1991).

One of the most important facts we have learned about domestic violence is that it not only cuts across every demographic group we study, but also that both batterers and battered women are very different when they first come into the relationship than when they leave. Although there are "risk-markers" for both men and women, increasing the probability of each group becoming involved in a violent relationship, the most common risk-marker is still the same one that the battered woman syndrome research study found; exposure to violence in their childhood home (Hotaling & Sugarman, 1986). Other studies have found that poverty, immigration status, and prior abuse, are also risk factors for women to become battered, although they are not predictive (Walker, 1994).

New research on batterers suggests that there are several types of abusers. Most common is the "power and control" batterer who uses violence against his partner in order to get her to do what he wants without regard for her rights in the situation. Much has been written about this type of batterer as he fits the theoretical descriptions that feminist analysis supports (Lindsey et al., 1992; Pence & Paymar, 1993). However, most of the data that supports this analysis comes from those who have been court ordered into treatment programs and actually attend them, estimated to be a small percentage of the total number of batterers by others (Dutton, 1995; Hamberger, 1997; Walker, 1999).

The second most common type is the mentally ill batterer, who may also have distorted power and control needs but his mental illness interacts with his aggressive behavior (Dutton, 1995). Those with an abuse disorder may also have coexisting paranoid and schizophrenic disorders, affective disorders including bipolar types and depression, borderline personality traits, obsessive compulsive disorders. Also, those with substance abuse disorders may have a coexisting abuse disorder (Sonkin, 1995). Multiple disorders make it necessary to treat each one in order for the violent behavior to stop. As the intervention methods may be different and possibly incompatible, it is an individual decision whether to treat them simultaneously or one at a time. Usually, different types of treatment programs are necessary for maximum benefit whether or not the intervention occurs at the same time.

A third type of batterer is the "antisocial personality disordered" abuser who displays what used to be called psychopathic character flaws that are difficult to change. Many of these men commit other criminal acts including violence against other people making them dangerous to treat unless they are incarcerated. Dutton (1995) suggests that this type of batterer is a variant of men with an attachment disorder that produces borderline personality traits. Jacobson and Gottman (1998) suggest that there are actually two subtypes within this group. They call them "pit bulls" and "cobras." Pit bulls are the more common type who demonstrate the typical signs of rage as they become more angry. Cobras, on the other hand, become more calm, lower their heart rate, and actually appear to be more deliberate in their extremely dangerous actions. Women whose partners exhibit cobra-like behavior are less likely to be taken seriously as their partners do not appear to be as dangerous to others.

Understanding the motivation of the batterer appears to be quite complex, especially when consequences do not appear to stop his abusive behavior. Information gained from new research suggest that there may well be structural changes in the midbrain structures from the biochemicals that the autonomic nervous system secretes when a person is in danger or other high levels of stress. Fascinating studies of "cell memories" (Goleman, 1996; van der Kolk, 1988, 1994), changes in the noradrenalin and adrenalin levels, glucocorticoids, and serotonin levels (Charney, Deutch, Krystal, Southwick, & Davis, 1993; Rossman, 1998) all may mediate emotions and subsequent interpersonal relationships. The precise impact of these biochemicals on the developing brain of the child who is exposed to violence in his or her home has yet to be definitely studied. Obviously, this research is critical to our understanding of the etiology of violence and aggression.

SUSCEPTIBILITY (HIGH RISK) FACTORS

Some reported events in the battered women's past occurred with sufficient regularity to warrant further study as they point to a possible susceptibility factor that interferes with their ability to successfully stop the batterers' violence toward them once he initiates it. It was originally postulated that such a susceptibility potential could come from rigid sex role socialization patterns that leave adult women with a sense of "learned helplessness" so that they do not develop appropriate skills to escape from being further battered. This theory does not negate the important coping skills that battered women do develop that protect most of them from being more seriously harmed and killed. However, it does demonstrate the psychological pattern that the impact from experiencing abuse can take and helps understand how some situations do escalate without intervention. While our data support this hypothesis, it appears to be more complicated than originally viewed. This viewpoint also assumes that there are appropriate skills to be learned that can stop the battering, other than terminating the relationship. In fact, the data from the study did not support the theory that doing anything other than leaving would be effective, and in some cases, the women must leave town and hide from the man in order to be safe. Later, it was found that even leaving did not protect many women from further abuse. Many men used the legal system to continue abusing the woman by forcing her into court and continuing to maintain control over her finances and children.

It was expected that battered women who were overly influenced by the sex role demands just because of being a woman would be traditional in their own attitudes toward the roles of women. Instead, the data surprisingly indicated the women in our study perceived themselves as more liberal than most in such attitudes. They did perceive their batterers held very traditional attitudes toward women, which probably produced some of the disparity and conflict in the man's or woman's set of expectations for their respective roles in their relationship. The women saw their batterer's and their father's attitudes toward women as similar, their mother's and nonbatterer's attitudes as more liberal than the others, but less so than their own. The limitation of an attitude measure is that we still do not know how they actually behave despite these attitudes. It is probably safe to assume that the batterer's control forces the battered women to behave in a more traditional way than they state they would prefer. From a psychologist's viewpoint, this removes power and control from the woman and gives it to the man, causing the woman to perceive herself as a victim. It also can create a dependency in both the woman and the man, so that neither of them feel empowered to take care of oneself.

Other events reported by the women that put them at high risk included early and repeated sexual molestation and assault, high levels of violence by members in their childhood families, perceptions of critical or uncontrollable events in childhood, and the experience of other conditions, which placed them at high risk for depression. These are discussed in greater detail in the next few chapters. At the time of the research, we were surprised at the high percentage of women in the study who reported prior sexual molestation or abuse. Although the impact of having experienced sexual assault and molestation was consistent with reports of other studies, we, like other investigators at the time, tended to view victims by the event that had victimized them, rather than look at the impact of the entire experience of various forms of abuse. Since that time it is clear that there is a common thread among the various forms of violence against women, especially when studying the commonality of the psychological impact on women (Walker, 1994; Koss et al., 1994).

Finkelhor's (1979) caution that seriousness of impact of sexual abuse on the child cannot be determined by only evaluating the actual sex act performed was supported by our data. Trauma symptoms were reportedly caused by many different reported sex acts, attempted or completed, that then negatively influenced the woman's later sexuality, and perhaps influenced her perceptions of her own vulnerability to continued abuse. Incest victims learned how to gain the love and affection they needed through sexual activity (Butler, 1978). Perhaps some of our battered women did, too (Thyfault, 1980a, 1980b). These findings were consistent with reports of battering in dating couples studied on college campuses (Levy, 1991; White & Koss, 1991). The critical factor reported for those cases was the level of sexual intimacy that had begun in the dating couples. At the very least, the fear of losing parental affection and disruption of their home-life status quo seen in sexually abused children (MacFarlane, 1978) was similar to the battered women's fears of loss of the batterer's affection and disruption of their relationship's status quo.

The impact of physical abuse reported in the women's childhood was not clear from these data. Part of this difficulty was due to definitional problems that remain a barrier to better understanding of violence in the family. The women in this study were required to conform to our definitions of what constituted battering behavior, so we know that their responses about the impact of the violence were based on that definition. But, we do not know the specific details of more than four of the battering incidents they experienced. This makes it difficult to compare our results with other researchers such as Straus, Gelles, and Steinmetz (1980) who used different definitions of conflict behavior without putting events into the context in which they occurred. However, we do have details of over 1,600 battering incidents, four for each of the 403 final sample. Our data indicate the women perceived male family members as more likely to engage in battering behavior that is directed against women. They perceived the highest level of whatever behavior they defined as battering to have occurred in the batterer's home (usually their home, too), and the least amount of abuse to have occurred in the nonbatterer's home. Interestingly, if the other man really was nonviolent, then the relationship should have had no abuse reported, not just the comparatively lower amount. This suggests the need to be extremely precise in collecting details of what women consider abusive or battering acts.

The opportunity for modeling effective responses to cope with surviving the violent attacks but not for either terminating or escaping them occurred in those homes where the women described witnessing or experiencing abusive behavior. Certainly, the institutionalized acceptance of violence against women further reinforced this learned response of acceptance of a certain level of battering, provided it was defined as occurring for socially acceptable reasons, like punishment. Even today, those who work with batterers report that the men who do take responsibility for their violent behavior often rationalize their abuse as being done in the name of teaching their women a "lesson" (Dutton, 1995; Ewing, Lindsey, & Pomerantz, 1984; Jacobson & Gottman, 1998; Sonkin, Martin, & Walker, 1985; Sonkin & Durphy, 1982). This is dangerously close to the message that parents give children when they physically punish them "for their own good" or to teach them a "lesson." In fact, although the psychological data are clear that spanking children does more harm than good, the fact that it remains a popular method of discipline is one of the more interesting dilemmas (APA, 1995).

LEARNED HELPLESSNESS

Learned helplessness theory predicts that the ability to perceive your effectiveness in being able to control what happens to you can be damaged by some aversive experiences that occur with trauma. The perception of personal helplessness can be learned during childhood from experiences of uncontrollability or noncontingency between response and outcome. Critical events that were perceived as occurring without their control were reported by the battered women and were found to have had an impact upon the women's currently measured state. Other factors such as a large family size also may be predictive of less perception of control. It seems reasonable to conclude that the perception of learned helplessness could be reversed and that the greater the strengths the women gained from their childhood experiences, the more resilient they were in reversing the effects from their battering, after termination of the relationship. Those who have developed learned helplessness have a reduced ability to predict that their actions will produce a result that can protect them from adversity. As the learned helplessness is developing, the person (a woman in the case of battered women) chooses responses to the perceived danger that are most likely to work to reduce the pain from trauma. Sometimes those responses become stereotyped and repetitive, foregoing the possibility of finding more effective responses. In classical learned helplessness theory, motivation to respond is impacted by the perception of global and specific attitudes that may also guide their behavior.

It is important to recognize that their perceptions of danger are accurate; however, the more pessimistic they are, the less likely they will choose an effective response, should such a response be available.

Interestingly, psychologist Martin Seligman who first studied learned helplessness in the laboratory (1975) has now looked at the resiliency factor of "learned optimism" as a possible preventive for development of depression and other mental disorders (1991, 1994). When I first used the construct of learned helplessness to help explain the psychological state of mind of the battered woman, it was with the understanding that what had been learned could be unlearned. Although many advocates who worked with battered women did not like the implications of the term "learned helplessness," because they felt it suggested that battered women were helpless and passive and therefore, invalidated all the many brave and protective actions they do take to cope as best they can with the man's violent behavior, once the concept of learned helplessness is really understood, battered women themselves and others see the usefulness of it. It also makes good sense to train high-risk children and adults to become more optimistic as a way to resist the detrimental psychological impact from exposure to trauma. Seligman (1994) has developed just such a treatment program called "posture psychology."

Although certain childhood experiences seemed to leave the woman with a potential to be susceptible to experiencing the maximum effects from a violent relationship, this did not necessarily affect areas of the battered women's lives other than her family life. Most of the women interviewed were intelligent, well-educated, competent people who held responsible jobs. Approximately one-quarter of them were in professional occupations. In fact, they were quite successful in appearing to be just like other people, when the batterers' possessiveness and need for control was contained. Once we got to know them, we learned how to recognize the signs that this outward appearance was being maintained with great psychological cost. But battered women adopt behaviors in order to cover up the violence in their lives. The women who had terminated the relationship and were not still being harassed by the batterer spoke of the sense of relief and peacefulness in their lives now that he was gone. The others still faced the high-tension situations on a regular basis. For most it seemed that severing the batterer's influence was one of the most difficult tasks for them to do. Unfortunately, separation and divorce usually did not end the man's attempts at continued power, control, and influence over the woman. In fact, the most dangerous point in the domestic violence relationship is at the point of separation.

VIOLENCE-PRONE PERSONALITY OF MEN WHO BATTER

Although the patriarchal organization of society facilitates and may even reward wife abuse, some men live up to their violent potential while others do not. Violence does not come from the interaction of the partners in the relationship, nor from provocation caused by possibly irritating personality traits of the battered women; rather, the violence comes from the batterers' learned behavioral responses. We attempted to find perceived characteristics that would make the occurrence of such violence more predictable. While a number of such perceived characteristics were identified, the best prediction of future violence was a history of past violent behavior. This included witnessing, receiving, and committing violent acts in their childhood home; violent acts toward pets, inanimate objects, other people; previous criminal record; longer time in the military service; and previous expression of aggressive behavior toward women. If these items are added to a history of temper tantrums, insecurity, need to keep the environment stable, easily threatened by minor upsets, jealousy, possessiveness, and the ability to be charming, manipulative, and seductive to get what he wants, and hostile, nasty, and mean when he doesn't succeed, the risk for battering becomes very high. If alcohol abuse problems are included, the pattern becomes classic.

Many of the men were reported to have experienced similar patterns of discipline in their childhood home. The most commonly reported pattern was a strict father and an inconsistent mother. Their mothers were said to have alternated between being lenient—sometimes in a collusive way to avoid upsetting her own potentially violent husband—and strict in applying her own standards of discipline. Although we did not collect such data, it is reasonable to speculate that if we had, it could have revealed a pattern of the batterer's mother's smoothing everything over for the batterer so as to make-up for or protect him from his father's potential brutality. Like the battered woman, the batterer's mother before her may have inadvertently conditioned him to expect someone else to make his life less stressful. Thus, batterers rarely learn how to soothe themselves when emotionally upset. Often they are unable to differentiate between different negative emotions. Feeling bad, sad, upset, hurt, rejected, and so on gets perceived as the same and quickly changes into anger and then, triggers abusive behavior (Ganley, 1981a, 1981b; Sonkin, 1994, 1995). The impact of the strict, punitive and violent father is better known today—exposure to him creates the greatest risk for a boy to use violence as an adult. Although we called for further study into these areas with the batterers and their fathers themselves over 15 years ago, such research is still not available.

RELATIONSHIP ISSUES

There seems to be certain combinations of factors that would strongly indicate a high-risk potential for battering to occur in a relationship. One factor that has been mentioned by other researchers (Berk, Berk, Loeske, & Rauma, 1983; Straus et al., 1980) is the difference on sociodemographic variables between the batterers and the battered women. Batterers in some studies have seemed to be less educated than their wives, from a lower socioeconomic class, and from a different ethnic, religious, or racial group. In this study, while there was some indication that his earning level wasn't consistent and was below his potential, we felt that the factor was not as important a variable as others in domestic violence relationships. We looked at the different earning abilities between men and women, but since we didn't account for the difference in value of dollar income for different years, these data could not be statistically evaluated. We concluded that it is probable that these issues are other measures reflective of the fundamental sexist biases in these men that indicates their inability to tolerate a disparity in status between themselves and their wives. Perhaps they used violence as a way to lower the perceived status difference.

Marrying a man who is much more traditional than the woman in his attitudes toward women's roles is also a high risk for future abuse in the relationship. Traditional attitudes go along with the patriarchal sex role stereotyped patterns that rigidly assign tasks according to gender. These men seem to evaluate a woman's feelings for them by how well she fulfills these traditional expectations. Thus, if she does not have his dinner on the table when he returns home from work, even if she also has worked outside the home, he believes she does not care for him. Women who perceive themselves as liberal in their attitudes toward women's roles clash with men who cling to the traditional sex role stereotyped values. They want to be evaluated by various ways that they express their love and affection, not just if they keep the house clean. If the man also has a violence prone personality pattern, the conflict raised by the different sex-role expectations may well be expressed by wife abuse.

Men who are insecure often need a great amount of nurturance and are very possessive of the women's time. These men are at high risk for violence, especially if they report a history of other abusive incidents.

Most of the women in this study reported enjoying the extra attention they received initially, only to resent the intrusiveness that it eventually became. Uncontrollable jealousy by the batterer was reported by almost all of the battered women, suggesting this is another critical risk factor. Again, enjoyment of the extra attention and flattery masked these early warning signs for many women. There is a kind of bonding during the courtship period that was reported which has not yet been quantified. The frequency with which the women, men, and professionals report this bonding phenomenon leads me to speculate that it is a critical factor. Each does have an uncanny ability to know how the other would think or feel about many things. The women need to pay close attention to the batterer's emotional cues to protect themselves against another beating. Batterers benefit from the women's ability to be sensitive to cues in the environment. At the same time they view the battered women as highly suggestible and fear outside influence that may support removal of their own influence and control over the women's lives.

Another factor that has a negative impact on relationships and increases the violence risk is sexual intimacy early in relationships. Batterers are reported to be seductive and charming, when they are not being violent, and the women fall for their short-lived but sincere promises. It seemed unusual to have one-third of the sample pregnant at the time of their marriage to the batterer, although we had no comparison data then. We did not control for pre- and post-liberalization of abortion to determine how battered women felt about the alternatives to marriage, including abortion or giving the child up for adoption. Thus, then as now, we were unable to analyze these data further.

Finally, the abuse of alcohol and perhaps some drugs is another area that would predict violent behavior. They are similar forms of addiction type behavior, with the resulting family problems that can arise from them. The clue to observe is the increase in alcohol consumption. The more the drinking continues, the more likely it seems violence will escalate. Yet, the pattern is not consistent for most of our sample, with only 20% reportedly abusing alcohol across all four acute battering incidents. It is important to note that the women who reported the heaviest drinking patterns for themselves were in relationships with men who also abused alcohol. Thus, while there is not a cause and effect between alcohol abuse and violence, this relationship needs more careful study. When looking at alcohol and other drug abusing women, there is a high relationship with a history of abuse. Kilpatrick et al. (1990) suggests that prior abuse is the single most important predictive factor in those who later have substance abuse problems. Mothers of infants who are substance abusing, especially during pregnancy, are almost all abuse victims (Walker, 1991).

SUMMARY

It is interesting that we reported the findings from this study as risk factors long before the recent categorization of family violence in similar terms. Once it was established that family violence and violence against women was at epidemic proportions by U.S. Surgeon General C. Everett Koop (1986), violence began to be conceptualized as a public health problem that would be best understood through epidemiological community standards. Planning intervention and prevention programs could use the criteria of risk and resiliency factors rather than thinking in more pathology terms of illness and cure.

One of the most interesting analogies comes from the public health initiative to eradicate malaria. It was found that people would be less likely to become sick from malaria if they were given quinine as a preventive measure. So, strengthening the potential victims by prescribing quinine tablets was an important way to keep safe those who could not stay out of the malaria-infested area. Once it was learned that diseased mosquitoes carried the malaria germs, it became possible to kill the mosquito. However, unless the swamps that bred the malaria germs that infected the mosquito were drained and cleaned up, all the work in strengthening the host and killing the germ-carrier, would not have eliminated malaria—it will return!

So, too for domestic violence. We can strengthen girls and women so they are more resistant to the effects of the abusive behavior directed toward them and we can change the attitudes of known batterers so they stop beating women. However, unless we also change the social conditions that breed, facilitate and maintain all forms of violence against women, we will not eradicate domestic and other violence—it will return!

Our data support the demand for a war against violence inside and outside of the home. The United Nations has placed this goal as one of the highest priorities for its member nations in order to foster the full development of women and children around the world (Walker, 1999). It is a goal worthy of the attention of all who read this book.

Psychosocial Characteristics of Battered Women, Batterers, and Non-Batterers

T he prevailing viewpoint in the early 1970s, prior to the Battered Woman Syndrome Study was that battered women were poor, uneducated, unable to get a job to support themselves and their children, and from the disenfranchised, minority groups in society. However, once services were established, it became clear that battered women came from all classes and demographic groups—just like we found in this study. Wealthy Euro-American educated women got beat up just as did poor, young, women from the disenfranchised classes. But, those who were marginalized in society needed to use government-sponsored resources where available, and therefore, became easier to notice. Women with greater economic and personal resources were better able to hide their physical and mental bruises. Their partners rarely got arrested and taken to jail. Rather, they were the men who law enforcement officers took for a walk around the block to help them cool-off! But, these were clinical findings and those who conducted empirical studies kept insisting poor women were more likely to be battered (see Gelles & Straus, 1988).

This research helped to document the extent of battering across all sociodemographic groups. As an empirical study, a stratified but not randomly selected population was studied. We created certain criteria (listed in Appendix B) that a woman had to meet to be accepted as a participant in the study and then kept track of who fell into the various demographic categories reported here. We planned to control the stratification so that there would not be an imbalance in any one particular category that could skew the data, but that turned out not to be necessary as the women fell into the classification groups naturally. This gives even more power to the opinion that battered women are everywhere!

The demographic variables examined during the research program were then analyzed to provide frequency information about our sample and are reported here as psychosocial characteristics that come from typical social science classification categories. These frequencies are based on all 403 cases unless otherwise noted. Where data on nonbatterers are reported, they are based on the 203 cases where the woman gave information on both battering and nonbattering relationships.

SOCIODEMOGRAPHIC PROFILE OF BATTERED WOMEN, BATTERERS, AND NONBATTERERS AS REPORTED BY THE WOMEN

As reported in Table 1, the battered women in this sample were similar in characteristics to the general population from which they were selected in all areas for which comparison data were available. These results are reported for the woman's current status at the time of the interview. This finding is important as it confirms the belief that battered women come from every walk of life and no particular characteristic in a woman leads her to become an abuse victim.

At the time of the relationship, batterers differed from battered women and from nonbatterers in a number of areas. These comparisons are reported in Table 2. All 403 women reported details about a battering relationship, as that was the criteria for inclusion in the sample, while 203 of those women also had a nonbattering relationship to report. The inclusion of retrospective self-report data on nonbatterers partially controls for each individual woman's possible idiosyncratic selection pattern of a mate. Like all retrospective self-report data, the information and all comparisons based on the data need to be interpreted with caution. They are interesting, however, and are included in this discussion because they give one of the few measures of comparison for battered women using these kinds of data.

The height and weight of all three groups—batterers, nonbatterers, and battered women—were examined because of the common belief that batterers use their greater *size and strength* to intimidate, bully and abuse the woman. Not surprisingly, the size of the women and their reports on the men were distributed across the range of possibilities. Men were usually larger than the women in both height and weight. While there may be large size disparities between some individual couples, for the whole group those differences were similar to what would be expected between men and women in general.

As many of the women in the research study were no longer living together with the batterer, *current partner status* was of interest. The batterers reportedly differed from the battered women in current marital status. About two times as many men were currently married or living together in another relationship as compared to the women. If the number still married to the batterer at the time of the interview are subtracted from these results (about 25%), it seems that very few women remarried, as compared to the men. These data contradict the popular myth that battered women go from one battering relationship to another, which was also found by others (Pagelow, 1982). Rather, it seems more likely to be the pattern for the men. Frank and Houghton (1981) also found that the batterer will frequently transfer their dependency from one woman to another and the battering will ultimately begin again. Ganley's (1981a, 1981b) reports on batterers treated at a Veteran's hospital also support the revictimization by a batterer of women with whom he is in a new relationship as did Sonkin's experience with the men who were court ordered to his groups in San Francisco (Sonkin, Walker, & Martin, 1985). D. Dutton (1995) has since found similar patterns among batterers who do not complete treatment programs. Others have found that a significant number of those men who use battering as a way of gaining more power and control in their relationships repeat the abuse pattern without treatment (Hamberger & Hastings, 1986; Lindsay, McBride, & Platt, 1992; Pence & Paymar, 1993). In reviewing results of the more popular intervention programs, Harell (1991) found that even with treatment many batterers who stopped their physical abuse became more psychologically abusive. Thus, the findings here that these men went on to other partners and were more likely to repeat their violent behavior there, continue to be a significant factor in the focus on stopping the batterer's violent behavior rather than concentrating on changing the dynamics of any one particular relationship. These data further suggest that family therapists who focus on changing the family system rather than on changing the batterer's violence may well put their clients in greater danger for further harm.

There was no direct link between unemployment and violent behavior for our sample. Less than 15% of the batterers and 10% of the nonbatterers were unemployed at the time of the relationship for which the woman was reporting. These are not significant differences, and batterers and nonbatterers could be said to be alike in this area. Other researchers have reported such a relationship (Gelles, 1972; Straus et al.,

1980) but it is not known who was their informant. Recent data from other countries (Steiner, 1999) support these findings, also. Perhaps, like alcohol, stress from unemployment is being used as a means to rationalize undesirable behavior rather than its being an element in cause and effect in the relationship. Unemployment of the male in the family may also be predictive of an increase in frequency and severity of abuse in an already abusive relationship. Our data on income levels could not be analyzed separately because we were unable to adjust for inflation factors when asking about income during relationships that could have existed any time over the past 20 or so years. Other demographic information suggests that batterers as a group might demonstrate an erratic earning capacity—or one that is below expectations for the man's occupation and training.

Educational levels differ significantly for batterers, battered women, and nonbattering men. The results of significance tests are reported in Table 3. Here nonbatterers and battered women were more alike with a mean educational level of 12.7 years of schooling as compared to the batterers' mean of 12.1. A higher percentage of batterers did not complete high school (24%) as compared to 12% for the women and 17% for the nonbatterers. In comparing the battered women with the batterers, a chi-square indicated significantly higher levels of education for the women $\chi^2 > (9) = 118.34$, $p < .001$). When comparing the woman to the nonbatterer she was also significantly better educated $\chi^2 > (9) = 22.36$, $p < .01$). And when comparing the batterer with the nonbatterer, the nonbatterer was significantly better educated $\chi^2 > (9) = 20.95$, $p < .013$). Similar differences in educational levels have been reported in the URSA Institute study commissioned by the L.E.A.A. (Law Enforcement Assistance Agency) in 1980 to evaluate the comprehensive domestic violence centers they funded (Fagan, Stewart, & Hansen, 1983). Later research continues to indicate an educational and class difference with women holding higher status than their abusive partners. This difference extends to women who are immigrants and have obtained their legal status in the United States through their husbands. In fact, the 1996 U.S. Violence Against Women Act gives these women the right to apply for special immigration status should they divorce their husbands because of the abuse.

Gelles (1983; 1993a) proposed a resource-exchange theory to help explain the complex behavior displayed by batterers. He suggested that batterers resort to violent acts as a way of competing with women's superior abilities and resources, particularly the well-known belief that women in general have greater verbal skills than do men. Our findings here, however, suggest a more complicated explanation. Typically, traditional men cannot tolerate a disparity in social, educational, or economic status in their wives' favor. The Archie Bunker mentality calls for the woman to use her skills to provide the assistance she intuits that her man needs, without him knowing she has done so. His ego is pictured as so fragile that disclosure of her talents would cause him embarrassment because it implies that he is not doing his job to protect her. Such marital relationships based on this stereotyped view of men's and women's roles force the deception and dependency that can lead to mistrust, low self-esteem, isolation, jealousy, exclusive need for mate's emotional gratification and finally, a strong need to control and reassure self of partner's exclusive loyalty. These are the conditions that accompany battering relationships. Thus, sex role stereotyping rather than lack of competitive resources may be why the higher educational levels found in the women we studied were related to battering.

FAMILY BACKGROUND FOR BATTERED WOMEN, BATTERERS, AND NONBATTERERS AS REPORTED BY THE WOMEN

Selected characteristics from the family backgrounds of the women and men with whom they have had relationships are reported in Tables 4 and 5.

In comparing social class for family of origin, more batterers come from lower- and working-class homes (67%) than the women (48%) or the nonbattering men (51%). Although these differences were not significant, National Opinion Research Center (NORC) data would place 50% of both men and women in that category who live in the region that was sampled. Thus, our sample has higher numbers of lower- and working-class men than would be expected. While 6% of the women were from upper-class homes, only 1% would have been expected for our region. There were 7% of the batterers who came from upper-class homes and 11% of the nonbatterers. The reasons for these differences are not understood. It cannot be inferred from these data that upper classes have more battering. It is possible that more well-educated women from a higher social class would volunteer for this type of a research program.

The nonbatterers, in general, were more similar to the women in all the background data. Since women are said to tend to marry above their family of origin's status, and the men typically marry at or below theirs, these relationships are obviously different. The trend for those women who reported on both violent and nonviolent relationships was in the direction of the violent pairs being less equal on those demographic variables that sociologists suggest are important in establishing stable marriages (Gelles, 1983, 1993a).

Both the battered women and batterers came from families with a larger number of people than usual. The women reported 4.2 siblings in their childhood home, compared with 4.5 for the batterer and 3.2 for the nonbatterers. Seligman (1975) suggested that the number of siblings might be a factor in producing helplessness because each individual then has less potential to exercise contingent control to get what is needed. It is interesting that three-quarters of the women came from two-parent homes. Similar data were not obtained for the men. Also interesting is that these women tended to leave their parental homes earlier than would be expected. While the average age they left home was 17.78, 42% of our subjects had already left home by the age of 17.

We explored the women's health and other potential stress factors while growing up. Almost 90% of the women stated that their physical health was average or above during childhood, although about one-quarter reported problems with eating, menstruation, sleep, and weight, and two-thirds reported suffering from depression. This inconsistency in reporting the presence of symptoms indicative of less than adequate health, yet labeling their childhood health as average or better, was a constant problem in interpreting our results. This is a case where the population needed to be asked more structured questions, with specific response choices, rather than to assume that they responded consistently to a general definition. Obviously, this is a problem with qualitative data collected in a context-specific method. While we anticipated definitional problems in many areas, we did not hypothesize the importance of prior health issues emerging as a factor in determining the impact of abuse or occurrence of battered woman syndrome.

We also looked at the frequency of critical periods in the women's childhood as a factor to produce learned helplessness. The critical periods were self-defined and included events perceived as uncontrollable like moving a lot, early parent loss from death or divorce, school failure, shame or humiliation because of poverty or other reasons, one or both parents as substance abusers, sexual assault, family disruptions, and so on. Over 91% of the women in our sample reported experiencing such critical periods, with the mean number of critical periods experienced being 2.1. This is further discussed in the learned helplessness theory section. We concluded that it was the impact of the uncontrollability and unpredictability of response-outcome at an early age that we measured, rather than simply the outcome from the individual events themselves, that formed the factor we measured.

It was predicted that battered women and batterers came from homes where traditional attitudes toward sex roles were held, and that they would also hold such traditional attitudes. Using the AWS (Attitudes Toward Women Scale) as a measure, we found that the women reported that the batterers and their fathers held very traditional values. Their own attitudes toward women's sex roles were self-reported as more liberal than 81% of the normative population, while the scores of their mothers and the nonbatterers were reported at about the average level. The implications of these results are discussed later. It is evident that the women perceived their family members as less liberal in their attitudes toward women's roles than themselves.

CORRELATES OF CURRENT VIOLENCE

It has been suggested that wife abuse is related to other types of family violence, such as child abuse and sexual assault (APA, 1996a, 1996b; Walker, 1979; Straus et al., 1980; MacFarlane, 1978; Finkelhor, 1979) and other forms of violence against women (Farley & Barker, 1998; Koss et al., 1994; Walker, 1994). Studies on aggression strongly suggest that violence is learned behavior (Bandura, 1973; Patterson, 1982). The family home is the place where this behavior is best learned, using both direct and indirect modeling techniques. Hotaling and Sugarman (1986) found that the single most important risk marker for batterers is exposure to violence in their family homes. Straus et al. (1980) and Kalamus (1990) using the Straus et al. data, found that the risk factor for boys who are exposed to domestic violence in their own homes to use violence later in life is 700 times greater than the average population. This risk factor is raised to 1,000 times the nonexposed boys, if they also have been abused. Obviously, exposure to abuse as a child has the most devastating consequences for boys who later become involved in aggressive, violent and criminal behavior. Thus, an important area we carefully examined was the battering history in their childhood homes. As expected, there were differences in the battering history reported by the women for the batterers and nonbatterers as well as in their own childhood homes. We also carefully inquired about any forms of sexual molestation and assault the women might have experienced as children. The high incidence of childhood sexual assault data for the women was quite surprising at that time. Other instances of the man's violent behavior, such as his criminal arrest and military history, were also reported by the woman. Some men possibly learned to be violent in the military or in prison, although for most, it apparently simply reinforced already established patterns learned in their childhood homes.

ABUSE HISTORIES

Battering and other forms of abuse were reported to have been present in 67% of the battered women's homes, 81% of the batterers', and only 24% of the nonbatterers. This finding is consistent with our theoretical assumption that violence is learned behavior. It supported data from Straus et al. (1980) and Washburn and Frieze's (1980) studies as well as later studies by Egeland (1993), Gelles and Straus (1988) and others. We had some difficulties with our subjects' inconsistencies in definitions of battering in their childhood homes. Some were highly sensitive to any form of physical punishment and labeled it "battering," while others felt spanking with an object was not, and labeled it appropriate discipline. Further analysis of these details are in Table 6. This area became an important part of the learned helplessness theory and these data are part of the scale suggested in Chapter 9.

It is interesting to note that while the battered women indicate they were equally battered by their mothers and fathers, batterers were one-third more likely to have been battered by their fathers. The role of fathers in perpetuating their own abusiveness through their sons is an interesting area to explore. Punishment in those homes where violence was reported may have served to teach battering behavior to the next generation. When we hit a child in order to teach him or her a lesson, we may suppress the negative behavior temporarily, but it returns with greater frequency than before once the external controls are removed. Learning theory tells us that we also teach the child that the person who loves you the most has the right to physically hit you, under some circumstances—usually with the admonition that it is "for your own good," "to teach you a lesson" or "because you must realize that you did something wrong." These are the messages remembered, which make it possible for batterers to rationalize and justify their behavior without feeling a need to change. If they can justify their aggressiveness by believing in the socially acceptable rationale that it was to teach the child or woman a lesson or somehow rationalize that it was for the other person's benefit, then their violence is not only justifiable, it is necessary! Battered women often believe this type of rationalization— especially when they feel guilty for not taking better precautions. One often heard lament from the women was, "Why didn't I just keep my mouth shut!" Obviously, such rationalizations make it easier for the woman to minimize the man's actions and forgive him for the damage he has caused by his violence.

For 63% of the batterers, their fathers reportedly battered their mothers. This also occurred in 44% of the women's homes and 27% of the nonbatterers'. In 35% of the cases, the batterers' mother reportedly battered their fathers as compared with 29% of the women's mothers and 13% of the nonbatterers'. About 20% of the women's mothers battered their sisters and brothers, while one-third of the batterers' mothers and only 6% of the nonbatterers' mothers reportedly battered siblings. This is compared with about one-third of the battered women's fathers battering sisters and brothers, one-sixth of the nonbatterers' and one-half of the batterers' fathers reportedly battering siblings. While it is difficult to evaluate all of the battering that went on in these family homes, it is clear that there was more violence than the stereotyped image of a family.

Fathers were more likely to batter other family members than mothers. Differences in discipline in the batterers' and nonbatterers' home were also interesting. The women reported that the batterers were more likely to have received discipline that was "too lenient" or "too strict," while nonbatterers were more likely to have received discipline that was "fair" and "consistent." A large number (65%) of batterers' fathers are reported as using strict discipline, as compared with 44% of nonbatterers'. More of their fathers are reported to have been "strict" than either "fair" or "lenient." Nonbatterers' mothers are more often seen as "fair." This is consistent with the reports that the women were more likely to view their fathers as batterers. These results suggest that fathers' behavior has an important impact on men who become violent. Further study is needed on the relationship between such behavior and the batterers' subsequent use of violence.

Since batterers reportedly become dependent upon the battered women, their dependency on their parents was also questioned. Approximately 50% of the batterers, as compared to 25% of the nonbatterers, were reportedly dependent upon their mothers. While smaller numbers—30% of the batterers and 15% of the nonbatterers—were dependent upon their fathers, it was again a two-to-one ratio of batterers to nonbatterers who could be said to have been dependent in their family homes. Unfortunately, we did not ask these questions for the woman, although we did ask her other questions relating to her perception of control in her home, and these are reported in the discussion of learned helplessness.

CHILDHOOD SEXUAL ABUSE

Incidents of sexual assault as a child were investigated by a series of questions asked of the women. The items called for responses to whether or not specified acts occurred with specific persons, because we found in the pilot instrument that interviewers were as likely as our subjects to avoid hearing details, especially in cases of incest. These data are reported in Tables 7, 8 and 9.

Almost one-half of our sample (48%) reported that they were the victims of a sexual assault as children. While this seemed like a very high percentage, there were few data on incidence levels of childhood sexual assault in the general population at that time. We analyzed for racial and ethnic composition of the subsample and the results are in Table 7. The percentage of those assaulted varied with the highest likelihood of childhood sexual abuse for the Hispanic women (68%), followed by the African-American women (56.9%), and then Caucasian (white) women (45%). There were too few Asian and Native American women in the sample to rely on those percentages for generalization to the entire group.

In analyzing the racial and ethnic composition of those 192 women reporting childhood sexual assault, three-quarters of them were white, which is similar to the number of white women in our sample. These results refute the stereotype that it is usually the minority women who are subjected to such violent behavior. All ethnic and racial groups had about one out of two chances to have been sexually assaulted as a child in this sample.

These data raised the question of whether or not the families of origin for our sample were more violence-prone and troubled than others. Without a control group, this question could not be accurately answered. However, others studying incidence rates of incest in our population suggest it may occur more frequently than previously expected (Finkelhor, Hotaling, Lewis, & Smith, 1990; Peters, Wyatt, & Finkelhor, 1986; Russell, 1986; Sedlak, 1991). It is interesting that in the 20 years since then, the controversy on the incidence and prevalence of child sexual abuse has deepened rather than become resolved (Besharov, 1993; Finkelhor, 1993). Other syndromes to account for the large number of reports have been proposed, without any empirical data to support them, such as Parental Alienation Syndrome by Gardner (1987) or Psychological Munchausen by Proxy Syndrome by Parnell and Day (1998). Not surprisingly, the proponents of these new entities find that mothers are invariably the perpetrators while the fathers who are accused of abuse are innocent victims of women's misguided anger. Groups such as the False Memory Syndrome Foundation (1992) with headquarters in Philadelphia hold training conferences to help mental health professionals identify cases where adults have had false memories of child sexual abuse implanted by unscrupulous or misinformed therapists. There is major conflict in the field between the clinicians and researchers. Yet, the data speak for themselves. High numbers of adult women continue to report having been sexually molested and abused as a child and they show up in populations where other forms of abuse are also reported (Courtois, 1995, 1997; Pope & Brown, 1996).

We analyzed our data to determine the frequencies of the specified sex acts. These results are reported in Table 8. There were fewer attempts and single incidents reported in any category, which suggests that when our women were sexually assaulted as a child, it was a repeated occurrence. Fondling was the most frequently reported sex act. Male relatives were reported as the most frequent perpetrators, as can be seen in Table 9. These data indicate that childhood sexual assaults by fathers, brothers, stepfathers, uncles, grandfathers, and family friends occurred repeatedly in our samples' lives. Further discussion can be found in Chapter 5.

OTHER VIOLENCE HISTORY

Another area that had been suggested as providing both the opportunity to learn violent responses and reinforce already learned ones is the military (Martin, 1976). About one-half of both the batterers and nonbatterers served in the military. There were no significant differences between those who were drafted or those who had combat experience, as shown in Table 10. However, there was a significant difference ($p < .01$) in the number of years served in the military, with the batterers spending an average of 3.2 years as compared to the nonbatterers' 1.9 years. Perhaps the batterers felt the military stance of aggression more compatible with their own violent response pattern, or, it may simply reflect a difference in branch of service chosen. Equally possible is that batterers find security in the structured military experience. Since this research was completed, all branches of the United States military have undertaken studies leading to the conclusion that there was a sufficiently high incidence of family violence in the homes of the service members to warrant specialized prevention and intervention programs.

It was surprising to find a high arrest and conviction rate for batterers as previous data had not uncovered such a pattern (Walker, 1979).

However, these data are consistent with others such as Fagan et al. (1983). Since those studying prediction of dangerousness include these indices of different violent acts (Monahan, 1981) our information leads us to predict the batterers' overall dangerousness. Since then researchers in this area have found that there is a separate group of batterers who are also violent criminals (Dutton, 1995; Jacobson & Gottman, 1998).

In our sample, the women reported that 71% of the batterers had been arrested as compared to 34% of the nonbatterers. These results are shown in Table 10. The arrest data were not separated into offense categories, but they represent diverse criminal offenses such as driving under the influence of alcohol, rape, assault, and homicide. In addition 44% of those batterers arrested, as compared with 19% of the nonbatterers, were convicted of the charges filed against them. While no comparison data were available, this seems like a disproportionately high rate of convictions. These results support the belief that there is a group of batterers who come from an otherwise violent population. This is further discussed in Chapter 4 on lethality and dangerousness.

CHAPTER THREE

Behavioral Descriptions of Violence

Over the years we have learned that the richest source of information about women abuse comes from the analysis of the details of battering incidents themselves. Typically, behavioral descriptions of violent acts tend to be omitted from discussions of battering behavior for several reasons. First, the recall of the details of a violent incident brings with it an internal reexperiencing of the emotions felt during the time of the abuse. Thus, battered women and batterers are more likely to repress or deny the violence or, as happens frequently with batterers, rationalize it by concentrating on describing why it occurred rather than focus on what actually happened. Second, most battered women do not think anyone will believe the actual level of violence experienced. Indeed, when preparing legal cases attorneys often suggest highlighting only a few battering incidents for fear the judge or jury might not believe that so much violence could occur without beginning to question the credibility and stability of the woman. Batterers, described as having Dr. Jekyll and Mr. Hyde personalities, often show their violent side only to the woman, further reinforcing her thoughts that no one would believe he could do such things. Thus, battered women do not automatically describe the details because they don't want to be disbelieved or thought to be crazy or guilty of causing their own abuse.

Third, most listeners have trouble hearing about the terrible ordeals that these women survive. It is difficult to listen to stories of brutality told by the victim. It taps our own vulnerabilities. If the listener has experienced trauma, memories that may have been previously buried can be triggered by hearing about similar details. If the listener must hear numerous similar stories during job performance, it is now known that a secondary post traumatic stress syndrome may develop with similar properties as the acute trauma reaction or Post Traumatic Stress Disorder (PTSD) that frequently develops after direct experience of trauma. This may cause the listener to tune out so that the details are not heard accurately, be unable to concentrate and focus so that the information is not remembered, or give out other signals that stop the woman's report. In some cases, the listener may become emotionally over-involved with the woman and lose professional boundaries while in other cases, the attempt to distance from the woman may be perceived by her as negative and hostile (APA, 1996a; Figley, 1995; Perlman & Saakvitne, 1995).

Women's own omission of details, like so many other behaviors adopted by battered women, helps them survive while coping with the violent acts on their own. Their fear is that talking about the violence in too much detail will upset the precarious situation and cause further harm. These perceptions are probably accurate. Nevertheless, battered women often do remember the details of the violent behavior and can relate it when asked direct and specific questions. We collected such information about the details of violent acts in a systematic way by asking a series of forced choice as well as open-ended questions. Our definition of a battering incident included the time leading up to the abuse, the acute period of violence, and a short period of time afterward. Most women did report the acute battering incidents as though they were reexperiencing it.

The emotional pain the women exhibited as they told us their stories was both real and compelling. It was not uncommon to find both the interviewer and interviewee crying together after the telling of a gruesome incident. More recent research on traumatic memories suggest that these women had not cognitively processed many of the memories so when they retold their stories, they were indeed reexperiencing the emotions together with the information (Courtois, 1997, 1995). This new research indicates that trauma memories are first experienced in the midbrain area where the emotion center is located before it is cognitively experienced. Often there is no language to describe the feelings of terror that occurred at the time of the incident. This explains why so many of the women we interviewed appeared to be in a dissociative state as they recounted the incident, often appearing to be repeating what they saw in a "movie-in-their-minds" as they described it. The inability to stop the story once they began to tell it, the high level of fear and terror as they were talking, and the changes in their appearance and in tone and quality of their voices all spoke to a similar clinical dissociative state. Since this was a research project, it was not appropriate to conduct therapy but many of the women told us afterwards that they felt the retelling of their stories in a safe place with a trained interviewer was therapeutic for them. Acknowledging the emotional trauma in an appropriate way allowed all of us to remain human without sacrificing accurate data. However, the interviewer then brought the situation back to task by asking a series of questions designed to help the woman distance herself from the emotional pain by recognizing the commonalties to batterer's violent acts.

PROFILE OF BATTERING INCIDENTS

One of the most unique data sets from this project was the detail collected from four specific battering incidents per woman. As was expected, we found that battered women have amazingly accurate recall of such details. We asked a series of discrete questions for four incidents: the first incident that occurred, the second incident, one of the worst, and the last incident prior to their interview. The questions covered antecedents to the incident, the acute battering itself and the consequent results for both the women and the men. Time of day, where the battering occurred, weapons used, violent acts committed by both parties, help sought, and other correlates were examined. The results are reported in Table 11.

TIME OF DAY

The time each battering incident occurred was distributed across the possible categories. Slightly more incidents occurred in the warm summer months, which is consistent with other data on violent crimes. The day of the week most likely for a battering incident to occur was on the weekend (Saturday or Sunday), especially if it was one of the worst battering incidents. It is possible that the more time the couple spent together, as is often the case on a nonwork day, the more the risk of a violent incident increased. For our sample, the most likely time of day for an abusive incident was from 6 P.M. to 12 midnight. The second most likely time for battering to occur was from 12 noon to 6 P.M. This 12-hour period accounted for over three-quarters of the battering incidents reported, with the remainder divided between 12 midnight and 6 A.M. (about 15%) and 6 A.M. to 12 noon (about 10%). This is important information for domestic violence units in police departments—it would seem sensible to have sufficient domestic violence detectives on the 4 P.M. to 12-midnight shift. It would also be expected to be the peak time period for crisis shelters to expect to receive new women.

PLACE OF BATTERING

If at home, where about 80% of the battering incidents started, the abuse was most likely to begin and end in the living room or in the bedroom. Less than 20% of the reported incidents began in the kitchen, and even fewer ended there. This is interesting as almost every battered woman reports some fights over her partner's expectations of her meal preparation. It may be that the woman has more control in her kitchen or the man believes she does as per the traditional image of a homemaker. If the violence didn't begin at home, it was most likely to occur in the car, in a public setting, or at a relative's or a friend's home. The first incident was most likely to end where it began, except if that was in a public place. Later incidents were more likely to end at home, or in a public place, regardless of where they started.

MEDICAL ATTENTION

In our sample, the need for medical attention increased from about one-fifth of the women after the first incident to almost half after one of the worst incidents. Despite that need, only about two-thirds of the women who needed it, actually went for medical treatment. This was consistent with other reports at the time of the original study that battered women were less likely to seek the medical treatment they required (Stark, Flitcraft, & Frazier, 1979; Walker, 1979). Others had found that even when medical treatment was sought out, doctors were unlikely to ask patients about the origin of their injuries. This made it even more likely that if they did seek treatment, they didn't tell the doctor about the abuse. During the 1990s, the American Medical Association and other doctor's groups began an education campaign for their members, teaching them how to ask women who appeared to be battered the appropriate questions. The most recent data suggests that battered women are more likely to talk to their doctors about the abuse they experience if they seek out treatment, although it is still unclear about how many battered women never go for medical treatment.

Doctors describe those women who do seek treatment as having a greater tolerance for the pain usually associated with their injuries. Two things appear to account for this observation. First, it is quite probable that, like our interviewers, they are observing the woman in a process of dissociation, whereby the battered woman perceives her mental state separate from her physical body. Descriptions and observations of the battered woman's disassociation suggest it is similar to a form of self-hypnosis with intense focus on surviving the physical and emotional trauma. The second explanation is in the more recent studies of biochemical changes in the autonomic nervous system that lower the pain threshold during the experience of trauma (Cotton, 1990; Goleman, 1996). Changes in the glucocorticoids that are secreted in the midbrain structures lower the perception of pain at the time of the trauma. This is obviously an adaptive response helpful to the organism for survival in crisis situations.

ESCALATION OF VIOLENCE

These results also support the finding that the violence escalates in seriousness over time, with about double the number of women receiving serious injuries in later rather than earlier incidents. The batterer's use of weapons also reportedly increased over time, with 9% using a household item or other weapon during the first incident, 14% during the second, 24% during one of the worst, and 20% during the last battering. Interestingly, O'Leary (1993) has found that battering does not necessarily increase on a continuum from verbal aggression to pushing, shoving and hitting, to more serious forms of physical abuse. Rather, his data shows that many batters who are verbally aggressive and abuse power and control in other ways in the relationship remain psychologically abusive and do not move to physical abuse without some external precipitant such as environmental stress. Other data suggest that there is also a point where the violence remains stable and nonhomicidal or suicidal unless there is some external circumstance that causes it to rise even further (Walker, 1996a). In any case, the more we learn about the details of violence in the family, the more apparent it becomes that violence begets more violence over time, similar to these results.

WOMEN'S REACTIONS

As the violence escalated, so did the probability that the battered women would seek help. While only 14% sought help after the first battering incident, 22% did after the second, 31% after one of the worst, and 49% sought help after the last incident. About one-quarter of the women left temporarily immediately after each battering incident, although these were not necessarily the same women each time. When the women told someone about the battering, it was most likely to be relatives or friends. They were twice as likely to discuss the violence after the last incident than following the first one. This is important information for service providers who should assume that by the time a woman starts to talk about the battering, she has probably experienced more than one acute battering incident.

In comparing the batterers' behaviors in the first assault with one-of-the worst incidents (third one reported), it is evident that the violent acts increase over time and in some categories, dramatically so. About two-thirds of the incidents included pushing, shoving, slapping, hitting, spanking, wrestling, and twisting arms. Punching and throwing her bodily occurred in over half of the beatings. Twice as many women were hit with an object during the worst battering as compared with the first one and about one-third of the women reported being choked or strangled. A small percent were burned, attempts made to drown them, hurt with a knife, or hurt with a gun. Almost 10% were hurt with a car. We do not know whether these motor vehicle accidents involved injuries to other persons, also. In over 80% of the battering incidents reported, verbal abuse accompanied the physical assault. Thus, we concluded that physical abuse rarely occurs without psychological abuse. This is consistent with more recent statements of the American Psychological Association that domestic violence is a pattern of abuse that includes physical and sexual violence as well as psychological maltreatment and abuse (APA, 1996a). The women repeated throughout the interview that the psychological degradation and humiliation was the most painful abuse they suffered.

There was a smaller range of violent acts committed by the women during these acute battering incidents, mostly as defensive acts. About one-quarter of the women pushed or shoved the batterer and one-fifth clawed or scratched him during the worst incident. About one-third of the women said they verbally abused the batterer. None tried to drown him or burn him and less than 1% said they used weapons like guns and knives on him. With 6% hitting him with an object, 2% throwing him bodily, and 1% choking or strangling him, it is apparent that the women's life-threatening behaviors toward the man were minimal. These data are consistent with the reports that approximately 5 to 10% of those arrested and convicted for domestic violence are women, although there are also reports that many plead guilty to using violence even when it is in self-defense, in order to be released and go home to their children who otherwise might be placed in foster care while the woman awaits trial.

The violent part of these battering incidents averaged several hours in length, with the most intensely violent part averaging 15 to 30 minutes. Most of the severe bodily injuries occurred during the intensely violent part although some reported a pattern of alternating intense periods with a temporary "cool down" phase. The women who strike back in self-defense sometimes do so during the temporary "cool down" phase, understanding that the batterer will probably get up shortly and repeat the violence again. If the woman's defensive action results in his being seriously injured or killed at that time, it is critical for the defense to understand the cyclical pattern to their battering incidents. Another point during the violence when the woman may use strong force to repel an impending attack is right before an acute battering incident erupts. Further discussion on the legal implications can be found later on.

PSYCHOLOGICAL ABUSE

The details for the psychological abuse were never quantifiably measured very well in this study, even though the women's qualitative reports were that it caused them the most pain. The physically abusive incidents were so compelling and overwhelming in the amount of overt violent behavior that the psychological components got less attention. Further, it is easier to measure and count discrete units of physically violent acts than it is to quantify the subjective pain from psychological abuse. Eventually, we settled on using the definition from Amnesty International as the most encompassing way to categorize the qualitative data obtained. Another problem with classifying psychological abuse in battering relationships is the sequencing of the pattern of abuse. In Patterson's (1982) study of coercive behavior in aggressive children's family interactions, it was found that the psychologically abusive acts occurred in a pattern with negative behaviors being chained one after another followed by positive acts in the same chaining sequence. This created what Patterson labeled, "chaining and fogging" behavior that was extremely difficult to respond to. Our study supported this view, understanding that it was the sequence and timing of the psychological abuse that impacted the women as well as the nature of the acts themselves. This is discussed further below.

The two areas of psychological abuse, other than verbal harassment, that we were able to directly measure were social and financial isolation.

AMNESTY INTERNATIONAL DEFINITION
OF PSYCHOLOGICAL TORTURE

The definition of psychological torture used by Amnesty International to understand the impact on prisoners of war and hostages was the best objective measure of the reported psychological abuse and has since been used as a measurement standard in clinical assessment cases by others (Sonkin, 1995; Walker, 1994). It includes eight areas of abuse. They are: (1) isolation of the victims; (2) induced debility producing exhaustion such as limited food or interrupted sleep patterns; (3) monopolization of perception including obsessiveness and possessiveness; (4) threats such as death of self, death of family and friends, sham executions, and other indirect threats; (5) degradation including humiliation, denial of victim's powers, and verbal name calling; (6) drug or alcohol administration; (7) altered states of consciousness produced through hypnotic states; and (8) occasional indulgences which, when they occur at random and variable times, keep hope alive that the torture will cease. As is evident from the following discussion, the battered women in the study reported being subjected to these eight forms of psychological torture.

Social isolation of battered women has been written about in the literature as occurring both as a part of and a result of the violence. It has been suggested that the batterer systematically isolates the woman from others, and that she also withdraws to protect herself from further embarrassment and others from potential harm (Walker, 1979, 1994; Jones, 1994; Martin, 1976). The results of our questions about social isolation are in Table 12.

Battered women appeared to be more isolated when living with the batterer, as compared to the nonbatterer. Twice as many frequently got together with neighbors when living with the nonbatterer (53%) than with the batterer (26%). Although there was no difference in whether our sample owned or rented their homes, they moved on the average of 6.2 times with the batterer and 2.2 times with the nonbatterer. Our subjects were not likely to be involved in voluntary organizations or recreational activities in either relationship. Since this study, it has been found that the quality of interpersonal relationships also changes when a woman is battered. She is less likely to trust family or friends, often because the batterer has heightened her belief in the importance of small misunderstandings and petty jealousy. It is also now know that battered women, like other trauma victims, lose the ability to perceive neutrality or objectivity in relationships. She must perceive that someone is supportive of her or that person is seen as potentially dangerous to her survival. Clinically, this finding is critical in providing appropriate interventions where the therapist is supportive and not neutral as is appropriate in other clinical treatment.

Financial isolation is also reported in Table 12, with three times as many (27%) indicating that they had no access to cash with the batterer, as compared to 8% with the nonbatterer. Thirty-four (34%) percent said they did not have access to a checking account, and 51% did not have access to charge accounts with the batterer, as compared to 26% with no checking account and 53% with no charge accounts in the nonbattering relationship. These data are reminders that it is important to have a comparison standard for these women, especially when over half didn't have access to credit cards in either relationship. Obviously, it was not the abuse in the relationship but other factors that entered into this result. It is interesting to note that many of these women were well-educated, held responsible jobs, and came from financially stable families. Twenty-two (22%) percent of the women in a battering relationship, and only 13% of those in a nonbattering relationship, did not have access to an automobile. These results supported the prediction that the battering relationship negatively impacts on the social and financial independence of the women. It was likely that the batterer had the power in social and financial areas, whether or not the woman had her own access to money.

BEHAVIORAL CONTROLS

The conceptualization of domestic violence as an abuse of power and control by the batterer made it especially important to measure the types of behavioral control that were commonly reported in battering relationships. It was expected that the techniques used to control one another's behavior would be different in relationships in which the man's violence against the woman had been used as the ultimate weapon of control. Table 13 shows the answers to some of the questions we asked to compare various areas within a relationship where behavioral control could be asserted.

In general, there were substantial differences in the kinds of control techniques used in battering and nonbattering relationships. The women reported that while the batterer knew where she was almost all of the time, she only knew where he was less than half the time. This is in contrast to each partner reportedly knowing where the other was about three-quarters of the time in nonbattering relationships. It was reported that about three-quarters of the time the women didn't get to go places they wanted, because of the batterer. This only happened about one-quarter of the time in nonbattering relationships. The women reported using more indirect techniques to get what they wanted or needed while with the batterer, including the use of physical force, than with the nonbatterer. They perceived the batterer as having won 73% of their major disagreements compared to 16% of disagreements being won by the nonbatterer. In nonviolent relationships, the women perceived that there was an equal chance of winning an argument at least 60% of the time.

Women reported feeling more anger when living with a batterer, though they didn't always express that anger directly. While 26% said they did not show anger and 73% sulked or didn't speak, 52% shouted or cursed, and 35% directed the anger at objects. Three times as many women were likely to show their anger by using physical violence toward their partner while in the battering relationship than in the nonbattering relationship, while eight times as many may use physical violence against the children when with the batterer as with the non-batterer. This is an important factor to consider when studying child abuse. It confirms the reports of battered women shelter staff that women seem less likely to use physical violence toward their children after leaving the shelter, particularly if they remain outside of the batterer's influence.

MUTUAL COMBAT AND VIOLENT WOMEN

The issue of women's use of violence in relationships has been a highly visible one during the past 15 years. Straus (1993) reviewed a number of studies and concluded that women used violent acts at or above the frequency of men. When the data from which this article was generated were reanalyzed, it was apparent that the authors' misinterpreted or miscited the relevant data. Interestingly, the data from this study were included as being supportive of their conclusions, certainly untrue from this author's perspective. Straus (1993a) has perpetuated the argument by his belief that feminists may not be reporting data appropriately. Given the inadequacy of the research due to the poor quality of retrospective data, it is important to recognize that this is more a political rather than a scientific argument.

The small percent of women who admitted directing physical violence at the nonbatterer (5%), and the batterer (15%), may represent the small subsample for whom the "mutually-combatant" couple or even the "battered man" designation applies. Straus et al. (1980); Berk et al. (1983); and Frieze et al. (1980) also found a small percentage of battered women who struck back at the men, usually in self-defense. While a control group would help clarify whether this is unusual behavior for women in general, our data allow comparisons to be made for the individual in two different situations, one violent and one nonviolent.

The significant differences in the women's reported behavior for when they were in a battering relationship and when they lived with a nonviolent man raise certain questions about their role in precipitating and maintaining the abuse. While it is popular to support the notion that "it takes two to make a fight," causation for these violent acts cannot be equally assigned to the men and women. These data strongly point to the social learning theory explanation that when the women use violence, they are reacting to the man's violent aggression. When they did not live with a violent man, then they were less angry, less manipulative, and less likely to use violent behavior themselves. Violence does seem to beget more violence in these people's lives.

Berk's et al. (1983) work supports our findings that, while there is a small percentage of women who use violence, the notion of "mutual combat" cannot be supported by the data. These researchers were also unsuccessful in finding incidents of mutual violence to support Straus et al. (1980), finding that equal numbers of violent acts were committed by women as by men, though it is the women who suffer most injuries. The media sensationalized Steinmetz's (1978) interpretation of her preliminary data showing 4 battered men out of 60. Unfortunately, by the time Steinmetz corrected the error in interpretation, reported at a U.S. Congressional Hearing (1978), the media were no longer interested. The idea of violent women intrigues and frightens people, and the image of women abusing men has been firmly rooted in the public's mind.

Straus' Conflict Tactics Scale (CTS) further exacerbated this spurious notion by only measuring reported violent acts rather than including a measure of severity of injury, intended action, and other antecedents or consequences to the conflict. Straus has accepted the limitations of the CTS but insists it is a legitimate measure of actual violent acts. Our data demonstrate that its very simplicity, which appeals to Straus and other researchers, is what makes the CTS an inaccurate measurement device as it cannot account for the complexity of such violence. Women may react to men's violence against them by striking back, but their actions are generally ineffective at hurting or stopping the men. However, they may be effective in controlling the level of the man's violence against them. Thus, it is not surprising that Straus' category of "biting" was the most frequent act women engaged in. While we did not use a separate category for measuring "biting," our category for "scratch or claw" probably measures the same kind of defensive, close contact behavior.

Our data indicate, as it did in their study, that "scratch or claw" and "push and shove" are the most frequent physically violent acts made by the women. It is probably safe to assume that the woman usually strikes the man as a way to break out of a hold rather than strike in offense. If the CTS were able to separate defensive from offensive violent acts, I suspect even Straus' data would support these findings.

CHAINING AND FOGGING EFFECT

Patterson (1982) and his colleagues Reid, Taplin, and Lorber (1981) at the Oregon Social Learning Center found some interesting parallels to our behavioral descriptions of violent acts in families of the aggressive boys they've studied. Their research included an elaborate behavioral observation and coding scheme designed to measure the types of behaviors emitted in families where there was an identified aggressive boy. The original design suggested two types of families to study, one with behavioral patterns approximating the average family and the other suggesting a dysfunctional family unit. The dysfunctional family unit they studied tended to have a larger ratio of negative to positive behaviors expressed. Early into the study, they found a third distinct pattern, that of the abusive family. They measured the relationship between the aggressive acts and other events in terms of conditional probabilities of social interactions using mathematical psychology and probability theory. Patterson suggests that the most accurate measurement paradigm to be used is: *given that one event occurs, what is the likelihood that it was preceded by a particular behavior of another person?* Thus, behavioral events can be studied in sequence, like beads on a string or chain (Patterson, 1982, p. 5). What seemed to distinguish the abusive family pattern from the dysfunctional one was not simply the number of negative behavioral acts but also the sequencing of such stimuli. They found that there seemed to be a "chaining" of nasty acts together creating what they called a "fogging" effect that seemed to make choosing an effective response to stop the aggression highly improbable. While their observers rarely saw actual physically violent acts between parents or children, they did observe psychologically abusive behaviors and received reports of the physical abuse. Thus, in the coercion theory they have developed, there is a set of statements about pain control techniques employed by one or both members of the dyadic interaction that affects their performance.

There is an excellent possibility that the "chaining" and "fogging" observed by Patterson and his colleagues is the essence of the abusive behavior pattern described by our sample of battered women. Some women reported that the distinguishing difference between tension-building behaviors they felt better able to cope with and those exhibited during the acute battering incident phase was how rapidly one aversive act followed another, the essence of the chaining process. Control techniques developed during the less intense periods were not available nor able to be used successfully by the women during the more dangerous acute battering stage. This may explain why our women found the psychological abuse the most devastating. Some may perceive that the only way to break up the "fog" created by the "chaining" pattern and defend themselves against further harm is to bite, kick, scratch, shove, or push back. Thus, mutual combat in these situations might be better expressed in terms of reciprocal pain control techniques.

The battered women we interviewed do not perceive such acts as violent in the same way they would perceive it if the man did it to them. We asked questions designed to measure the women's physical and emotional response to each of the four acute battering incidents. These results can be found in Table 14. A special analysis was performed to compare the responses to the first and third significant (one of the worst) battering incidents reported (Browne, 1980). As was expected, most emotional reactions intensified over time with fear, anxiety, depression, anger, and hostility being reported at higher levels after the third incident. In fact, as is shown in Table 14, the percentage of women experiencing these emotions as "overwhelming" doubled after repeated violence. Only reported levels of shock decreased.

Few women reported that they made any attempt to take offensive action against the batterer after having been beaten. After the first incident 8% reported some kind of offensive action (which may or may not have been self-defined as physical violence directed toward him) and 15% did so following repeated abuse signified by the third battering incident reported.

SURVIVAL OR COPING SKILLS

The issue of the woman's response to violent attacks by the man who loves her has been further clouded by the mythology that she behaves in a manner that is either extremely passive or mutually aggressive. Rather, these data suggest that battered women develop survival or coping skills that keep them alive with minimal injuries. There is also some evidence that such skills are developed at the expense of escape skills. This concept is further discussed in connection with the learned helplessness theory as it is consistent with that theory to narrow one's perceptions and focus only on survival, causing misperception of other important information.

In order to evaluate the battered woman's response to battering, we had the interviewers note her behavior before and after the incident on a five-point Likert-type scale ranging from very passive to very active. Results can be found in Table 15.

The activity level of women after the first abusive incident shows a decrease, with 61% of the women being rated as "more active than passive" or "very active" before the incident and only 22% after the incident. Also, after repeated battering, only 48% still remained "more active" or "very active" while 40% did something active following the third significant beating. We did not analyze for severity or frequency of battering which may account for the variance of battered women's reported response to violence. Obviously, these are subjective ratings given by our trained interviewers and despite our attempts to do reliability ratings, their accuracy can and should be cautiously accepted. Nevertheless, they demonstrate that even when most seriously battered, about one-half of the women still took some action to survive.

These results are consistent with the learned helplessness theory in that they took this action without any belief that it would contingently stop the battering. I interpret their behavior as a basic coping mechanism, much like Seligman's (1975) dogs, who used passivity as their way to stay alive. The analogy is in the failure for both the dogs and the battered woman to develop adequate escape skills. Failure to develop such adequate problem-solving skills can be seen in Seligman's (1975) later human subjects caused by experimentally produced learned helplessness. Thus, Straus' et al. (1980) simple counting of aggressive acts distorts rather than aids the understanding of violence in the family by misleading others into accepting a mutual expression of violence notion. Rather, our data suggest evaluating the men's violent acts for power and control differently than the women's, who strike back in self-defense, to stay alive or minimize their possible injuries.

The Lethal Potential

T he amount of violent behavior expressed in abusive families is enormous. Those of us in this research project were continually surprised by what we heard and we never habituated to the high level of brutality. However, our amazement and respect grew for the battered woman's strength, which permitted her to survive such terrifying abuse. Today the amount of violence in these relationships is less surprising to the general public, especially since we now know that most homicide/suicides that are reported take place in domestic violence families. And, we are much more aware of the fact that from the point of separation until about two years afterward is the most dangerous time for a battered woman and her children.

Although we did not have these facts at the time we collected our research data, it seemed as if either the man or woman or both of them could have died any number of times, given the lethal level of some of the acts and threats against the woman. We wondered if the women knew how close to death they actually were. Women were asked directly about their perception of danger with the batterers. Their responses are reported in Table 16.

These results indicate the women's perception of the high risk of lethality, or of someone dying in battering relationships. The women believed the batterer could or would kill them in three-quarters of those relationships; and in almost half, that they might kill him. Only 11% said that they had ever tried to kill the batterer, and 87% believe that they (the women) would be the one to die if someone was killed. Half of the batterers and about one-third of the women had threatened to commit suicide. We did not ask if either had made an actual suicide attempt. However, from the literature on suicide, we can assume that it is likely actual attempts followed at least some of the threats in a number of these high-risk relationships. Jens (1980) points out the ease with which batterers move from being suicidal to homicidal in violent relationships, as does Boyd (1978), Ganley (1981a, 1981b), Jacobson and Gottman (1998), Kaslow (1997), Sonkin and Durphy (1982), Walker (1979, 1989a, 1989b) and others. From this we conclude that suicide threats by the batterer should also be taken as a warning of homicidal tendencies.

Over 60% of the sample reported that they never felt they really had control over the batterer's behavior, over three-quarters believed he would continue to be a batterer, and four-fifths believed he would batter another woman. What is even more surprising is that despite the women's perception of danger, 17% still believed the batterer would eventually change, and not batter any longer. Perhaps they were in the group that was still living with the batterer at the time of the interview.

BATTERER'S VIOLENCE-PRONE PERSONALITY PATTERN

The women reported attitudes and behavior patterns in the men that strongly suggest the men have violence-prone personalities. While I previously estimated that only about 20% of the population of batterers exhibited other forms of violent behavior (Walker, 1979), these data cause me to reverse those statistics and estimate that only 20% limit their abuse toward their wives. The other 80% may also engage in other violent behaviors, such as child and parent abuse, incest, hurting pets and other animals, destroying inanimate objects, and responding abusively to other people.

The high number of arrests (71%) and convictions (44%) of batterers as compared to arrests (34%) and convictions (19%) for nonbatterers also indicates a generalized pattern of violence-prone behaviors. Table 17 shows these comparisons between batterers and nonbatterers, as reported by the women. These numbers may be expected to be even higher today, especially where the special domestic violence courts exists.

The women reported that these men have always lived in an atmosphere of familial or domestic violence. Spouse or child abuse occurred in 81% of the batterers' childhood homes as compared to 24% of the nonviolent men's homes. In 63% of the men's families, their fathers beat their mothers; this is in contrast to abuse in only 27% of the nonbatterers' homes. In 61% of the men's childhood homes, they told the women that their fathers battered them and in 44%, they told the women that they were battered by their mothers. In some cases, they were battered by both. These data become even more significant when compared to the 23% of nonbatterers beaten by their fathers and 13% beaten by their mothers. And, perpetuating the high level of violence in the family, over one-half of the batterers (53%) reportedly battered their children.

Other research and clinical reports support these data reported by the women in our study. Clinical experience has shown that batterers will volunteer little detailed information about the violent acts that they commit. However, once in effective offender-specific treatment programs, the men's information corroborates the women's reports of their dangerousness (Dutton, 1988, 1995; Hamberger, 1997; Jacobson & Gottman, 1998; Lindsay, McBride, & Platt, 1992; Sonkin & Durphy, 1982). Orders of protection were sought by 39% of the women when living with a batterer as compared to 1% when with a nonbatterer. The issue of the effectiveness of restraining orders will be discussed later. Also see Meloy et al. (1997). In any event, battered women said they felt stronger if they are armed with such an order.

These findings are consistent with other research. In one of the few studies at the time of our research that actually questioned the batterers, Hanneke and Shields (1981) found they exhibited three general patterns of violence. The three groups were: (1) men who were violent against family members only, (2) men who were violent against nonfamily members only, and (3) men who were generally violent against both family and nonfamily members. They found that men in groups 2 and 3 used the most severe forms of violent behavior and showed more similar characteristics than men in group 1 who were only violent with family members. Yet, despite important differences between these three groups, including groups 2 and 3 using violence as a general interpersonal strategy, they found no significant differences between them in use of life-threatening behaviors against the women they battered. This is supported by our data indicating that almost all of our subjects thought the batterer was capable of killing them.

While others have looked to some form of psychopathology to predispose men to become batterers, most of the literature suggests that they learn to be violent because such coercive behavior works (Meloy, 1988, 1992, 1995, 1998). They usually get what they want with very few negative consequences. Exposure as a child to the use of violence as an interpersonal strategy seems to be a common pattern for batterers as found in our study and by Hampton and Gelles (1994), Hanneke and Shields (1981), Fagan et al. (1983), Hilberman (1980), Straus et al. (1980), Frieze et al. (1980), Frieze and Browne (1989), Gelles (1983), Patterson (1982), Reid et al. (1981), and others. However, such socialization alone is not enough to create a batterer. Certain environmental situations must also occur and the combination then creates a man who uses coercion (physical, sexual, or psychological) as his primary means to obtain his needs.

Hanneke and Shields (1981) suggest that all three of their groups of violent men started out being generally violent as adolescents, perhaps similar to Patterson's (1982) and Reid's et al. (1981) aggressive children. Their group 1 men, who were only violent with their families, tended to have higher levels of education and careers. They were more law-abiding in general than men in groups 2 and 3. The researchers suggest that the more middle-class the man, the more likely his violent behavior will remain in the family only. This serves to keep his violent behavior invisible so that it doesn't threaten his social status.

But, at the same time, Hanneke and Shields found that about one-half of the group 2 men were never violent towards family members despite their generally deviant lifestyle. The researchers suggest that perhaps there are some factors in those relationships that stopped them. Our data suggest that the men themselves may set such limits, which they can keep only if they never do express physical violence directly towards their wives. One slap can change it.

Reinforcement of violence as a strategy occurs at all levels in our society. It is particularly evident in some of our child-raising practices. When we teach children that it is appropriate to hit them for disciplinary purposes, we also teach them that the people who love them the most have the right to physically hurt them if they do something wrong. It should not be a surprise, then, that male batterers say they have the right to physically hit the women they love if they do something wrong. The women accept such minor abuse in the name of discipline. However, unlike most cases of child discipline, physically punishing an adult woman rapidly escalates into violent abuse. Considering that there are many more effective methods of disciplining children, such as time-out procedures, I strongly urge adopting no-hitting rules for all members of families.

Men's dominance over women in a patriarchal society is an important factor in spouse abuse, as is discussed in this book. Our data, as well as those of Straus et al. (1980), Berk et al. (1983), and Fagan et al. (1983), demonstrate that in homes where the man is more dominant, the woman is more likely to suffer serious battery. The Berk study found that white men married to Hispanic women tended to be the most brutal in their sample. Martin (1976) has found that Asian women married to American servicemen tend to be brutally beaten. Friedman (1992) found high rates of domestic violence and rape among refugee women.

It is also interesting that in the many countries where I have traveled, the domestic violence problem is always ascribed to whatever group occupies the lowest status there. For example, in Israel, at first it was those who immigrated from Arab lands, then Ethiopian immigrants, and then the Russian immigrants who supposedly had the most violent relationships; in China, it was those who lived in rural areas; in England, it was the Indians and Pakistanis; in Latin America, the poor, unmarried women; in Africa, the tribal cultures; and in the United States, poor people of color. While most of the women who use battered woman shelters all over the world are indeed economically poor minority women, often with young children, in my travels, I have met battered women from all social strata. Battering is not a class issue as seen by our data reported in Chapter 2. But, again like the middle-class men reported by Hanneke and Shields (1981), violence in the family can more easily remain invisible in the dominant class.

This is important information for other researchers to pay attention to. When studying domestic violence, it is of critical importance to the findings to carefully select from where the population is to be gathered. If the sample to be studied is gathered from the criminal justice population only, it will skew the data towards the overrepresentation of the poor and marginalized classes. So too, if social service populations or battered woman shelter populations are used, poor and marginalized groups are overrepresented using these services. On the other hand, in university clinics and counseling centers, mental health centers and private practice populations, more of the so-called advantaged or educated populations will be found. Divorcing populations would probably give a good cross-section from which to sample although many states that do not require a reason for divorce other than "irreconcilable differences" would not have the necessary data to provide access to large numbers of those who seek dissolution of their marriages and thus, only those with problems such as custody disputes will become known to the court.

HOMICIDE

Occasionally, the violence between the man and woman escalates beyond control and someone dies. Most of the time, it is the woman; her batterer either kills her or she commits suicide as a result of his abusive behavior. Sometimes they both die; he kills her and then himself. And, in a smaller number of cases, the woman strikes back with a deadly blow and kills the batterer. While statistics vary, just reading the newspaper gives a good estimate of the number of such deaths. The 1994 FBI Uniform Crime Report indicated that approximately one-quarter of all homicides in the United States occur within the family. Wolfgang (1978), studying homicides in Philadelphia, found that one-quarter of those homicides occurred within the family and one-half of those were between spouses. Of those, only 11% of the homicides were committed by women.

Jacqueline Campbell (1981), in her study of homicides in Dayton, Ohio, found that 91% of the murderers of women during an eleven-year period (1968–1979) were men. She also reports that in 1977, of the 2,740 American female homicide victims, 2,447 of the perpetrators were men. Of the 8,565 male victims, 1,780 of the offenders (21%) were women. In her Dayton sample, 19% of the perpetrators who killed men were women. Campbell notes that the homicide rate in the U.S. occurs at a base rate of 9 in 100,000 and the homicide rate where there is known family violence is 16,000 in 100,000. Another way to look at the risk is in percentages; the Bureau of Justice Statistics (1994b) indicates that 16% of all murder victims in large urban courts in 1988 were members of the defendant's family. The remainder were killed by friends or acquaintances (64%) or strangers (20%). Among Black partners, women were about equally responsible for killing their partners as were men, but among white partners, 38% of the victims were men killed by women and 62% of the victims were women killed by their male partner. Women were more likely to be murdered within the family (45%) than by nonfamily members (18%). Campbell (1981, 1995) concludes that the predominance of men killing women results from the misogyny created by our patriarchial society. Certainly, it doesn't appear to be accidental.

Ann Jones (1980) has found that, historically, the rate of women committing homicide has remained around 15%. However, today we know that it is more likely that the women who kill men are doing so in self-defense after a period of having been victims of violence. An Italian psychiatrist, who studied thirty men in prison for killing their wives, found that almost all had been seriously abusing the women prior to their deaths (Neschi, personal communication, 1981). Charles Ewing's (1987) studies have similar findings. However, although 74% of all defendants on trial for murder had a prior criminal record of arrest or conviction for a crime, a substantial percentage of victims (44%) also had a prior criminal record. Only 19% of family murder victims had a prior record as compared to 51% of nonfamily murder victims and only 56% of family murder defendants as compared to 77% of other murder defendants had a prior record (Bureau of Justic Statistics, 1994a, 1994b, 1995, 1997).

Interspousal homicide is rarely unexpected. Battered women in our sample recognized the potential for lethality, even though they often denied it would really happen. Almost all of the women (92%) believed that the batterer could or would kill them and 87% of the women believed if someone would die during a battering incident, it would be them. About one-half said they could never kill the batterer, no matter what the circumstances, while the other half said they possibly could kill him. Only 11% said they had tried to kill him and nine women out of the 403 actually had been successful. Several men had killed themselves while the woman was involved with our project and others had done so earlier. Relationships that have a high risk for lethality can be recognized retrospectively, but prediction is still difficult given the large number of high-risk battering relationships that do not result in homicide. In fact, the number of women who are killed by men with whom they have been in a violent relationship (50% of all female murder victims) is about the same for those who do not have any earlier abuse history. Reports indicate that these figures further break down into 40% of women who live in suburbia and 60% of those in urban areas who are killed by former or present partners (BJC, 1994a).

Angela Browne (1987) analyzed the data from our research study for lethality patterns and found that there were a number of high-risk factors to look for when attempting to protect women from being killed. Some characteristics of relationships at high risk for interspousal homicide include an intense level of involvement between the two parties, a history of physical and psychological battering, and threats of further violence, or even death. Pathological jealousy, sexual assault, violence correlates such as child abuse, injury to pets and animals, threats and actual violence against others, and alcohol and/or drug abuse are also part of the highly lethal relationship.

Sonkin and Walker (1995) reviewed several of the studies of homicides. There are approximately 15 factors that stand out as adding to the high risk of lethality:

LETHALITY CHECKLIST

- Frequency of violent incidents is escalating
- Frequency of severity of violence is escalating
- Man threatens to kill woman or others
- Frequency of alcohol and other drug abuse is increasing
- Man threatens to kidnap or harm children
- Man forces or threatens sex acts
- Suicide attempts
- Weapons at home or easily accessible
- Psychiatric impairment of man or woman
- Close to each other at work and at home

- Man's need for control around children
- Current life stresses
- Man's prior criminal history
- Man's attitude towards violence
- New relationship for man or woman

In Chimbos' (1978) study of Canadian spousal homicides, 70% previously reported repeated physical abuse and 83% reported a physical fight within four months of the fatal incident. In many of our cases, there is also a longer period of loving contrition behavior and then a gradual escalation of the abuse again. In the Chimbos study, over half of the survivors reported threats to kill made either by the offender or victim, prior to the fatal incident. The threat, which had occurred many times before, was taken or given more seriously this last time, and someone died. These data have continued to hold steady in more recent studies also (APA, 1996a). A Kansas City study found that there had been a domestic disturbance call at least one time prior to the homicide in 85% of the cases, and in 50% the police had been involved at least five times (Gates, 1978). It was not uncommon for the women in our study to report that neither the police, nor others they had told, took the threats of further violence or death seriously. The problem caused by a police officer's inability to understand the high risk of lethality in responding to domestic disturbance calls will be discussed later. However, in the intervening years, there have been significant changes in how police respond to domestic violence calls, helping to keep women safer.

Several factors are common in the life histories of individuals where an abusive relationship ends in the death of one or both partners. Some of these factors, such as a high degree of social isolation, long-standing battering histories, use of coercion as the major form of communication in resolving interpersonal conflicts, and a high degree of withdrawal through the abuse of alcohol and drugs have been confirmed by the major researchers in this field, to date (Chimbos, 1978; Totman, 1978; Gelles, 1972, 1993a, 1993b; Straus et al., 1980; Jones, 1980, 1994; Berk et al., 1983; Fagan et al., 1983).

WOMEN WHO KILL IN SELF-DEFENSE

In our work at Walker & Associates since the research project, we have had the opportunity to evaluate over 350 battered women, in addition to the original nine, who have struck back in self-defense with deadly force. The data on the first 100 cases were reported in another book (Walker, 1989a). These interviews, similar to those done with the 403 subjects in the research projects, have provided a rare glimpse into the escalation of violent behavior to its ultimate conclusion, death and destruction of human lives. In each case there were numerous points when some intervention might have prevented the tragic outcome. The women felt that no one took them seriously, that they alone had to protect themselves against brutal attacks, and that they knew by observable changes in the man's physical or mental state that this time he really would kill them. Most of the time the women killed the men with a gun; usually one of several that belonged to him. Many of the men actually dared or demanded the woman use the gun on him first, or else he said he'd kill her with it. Other men seemed to set up their own death in other ways, similar to the group Wolfgang (1968) studied.

Some women, who had made suicide attempts previously, at the last second before killing themselves this time, turned their rage against their tormentor. Most women who killed their batterers have limited memory of any cognitive processes other than an intense focus on their own survival. Although, retrospectively, it can be seen where her defenses against denial of her anger at being an abuse victim are unraveling, the women do not have any conscious awareness of those feelings. Their descriptions of the final incident indicate that they separate those angry feelings by the psychological process of a dissociative state and thus, do not perceive them. This desperate attempt at remaining unaware of their own unacceptable feelings is a measure of just how dangerous they perceive their situation. They fear showing anger will cause their own death, and indeed it could, as batterers cannot tolerate the woman's expression of anger.

In less lethal situations, the battered woman might deal with the high level of appropriate anger at being abused in other ways. Our data showed that going "crazy," becoming physically ill, abusing prescription drugs and alcohol, becoming passive and servile, and expressing anger in safe, public situations all helped lower the immediate risk of homicide or suicide, but only for a time. The women all told of ways they learned to keep control of their own minds, recognizing that the batterer had the ability to control their bodies. They let the batterers think they were stupid or suggestible and appeared to conform to his wishes. Sometimes, despite these efforts at only making believe, his mind control techniques were successful. For some of the women who kill, however, their violence is a desperate attempt to keep him from gaining total control of their minds, too. For example, several told us of how the men managed to convince doctors to prescribe major psychotropic drugs for the women and began supervising their taking them.

Although our data indicate that the women kill their abusers for different reasons, they all resorted to using such violence as their last attempt at protecting themselves from further physical and mental harm. These findings are similar to others who have also concluded that women don't kill unless it is their last resort (Browne, 1987; Browne & Dutton, 1990; Browne & Williams, 1989; Ewing, 1987; Hart, 1988; Jones, 1980; Walker, 1989a, 1994, 1996). They don't want the batterer to die, but rather, they just want him to stop hurting them. Thus, to predict the risk of lethality, it is important to assess the level of the victim's coping skills. If she is feeling terrified, overwhelmed, angry, or trapped, and perceives a high level of dangerousness in the man's behavior, then, in certain situations, she could respond in self-defense with deadly force. I compiled the stories of many of the battered women who killed in self-defense and published them in *Terrifying Love* (Walker, 1989a).

Children in the home increase stress and opportunity for more violent behavior, although their presence is not sufficient to add to the risk factor unless they are involved in the violence. This involvement can include protection of their mother from abuse or the woman's attempt at protection of the children from the father's abuse. Several women shot their husbands rather than let them physically or sexually abuse their children. Others acted with adolescent or adult children for protection with one or the other or both administering the fatal blow to the man who had abused them. In several cases, the presence of adult children in the home served as a deterrent; once they left, the batterer's violent behavior escalated.

Another high risk situation which increases the potential for a lethal incident is the occurrence of threats to kill made by the batterer. In the research sample, over half of the women (57%) reported that the batterer had threatened to kill someone else besides herself, and half reported that he had threatened to commit suicide. Women who killed in self-defense recognized that something changed in the final incident and he was going to act out his threat this time. Only 11% of the women studied said they had ever threatened to kill anyone other than themselves. Very few of the women who actually killed the batterer had threatened to do so earlier, although overzealous prosecutors often try to use a general kind of statement, like, "I'm gonna kill him for that," as evidence of premeditation. This is consistent with the Browne (1987), Ewing (1987), Jones (1980), Pleck (1979), and Bende (1980) reports of actual homicides committed by women.

Over one-third of the women told us about having made suicide attempts while living with a batterer. There is no way to know how many women who successfully commit suicide were driven to it by abusive men. We do know from suicide studies that the threat of death from a terminal illness raises the likelihood that a person will choose to die at his or her own hands. Perhaps, battered women believe that batterers will inevitably kill them and choose to kill themselves instead. Since the original study, clinical reports indicate that many women feel that the only way to take back control over their lives is to choose when to end it, especially if they believe that they have a foreshortened future, as is common in trauma victims.

The presence of weapons in the home also seems to increase the risk for a lethal incident to occur. While about 10% of the battered women in the research study reported being threatened by a dangerous weapon during an acute battering incident, many more indicated that the presence of guns in their homes constituted a constant threat to their lives. In contrast, in the sample of 50 women who did kill their batterers, almost all of the men reportedly seemed fascinated by weapons and frequently threatened the woman with a weapon during abusive incidents. For that sample, of the 38 women who killed the batterer with a gun, 76% used the same weapon with which he had previously threatened her. Each of them believed he was prepared to make good on his threat to use it against her. In the later samples we found a similar proportion of homicides committed with the same gun that the batterer had used to threaten to kill the woman.

Threats of retaliation made by the batterer also raise the risk for lethality. Women commonly reported phrases such as, "If I can't have you, no one will"; "If you leave, I'll find you wherever you go"; "Just do that and you'll see how mean I can really be." Threats of bodily mutilation such as cutting up her face, sewing up her vagina, breaking her kneecaps, and knocking her unconscious also served to terrify women and confirm their fears of receiving lethal blows. They often isolate themselves from family and friends who could help because of the batterer's threats to hurt, mutilate, and/or kill them. Many of the women said that they learned not to let him know how much someone meant to them, simply to protect that person from being threatened by the batterer. The more isolation, however, the higher the risk for a lethal incident. In fact, one of the main hints for families and friends of battered women is to keep hanging in with contact, as the more the isolation can be broken, the more likely the woman will be rescued from serious or fatal injuries.

The presence of the man's excessive jealously has been described as a major component in battering relationships. Campbell (1981) cites data to support jealousy as the predominant reason given by men who kill their wives or lovers. Hilberman and Munson (1978) found pathological jealousy to be a cornerstone to homicidal rage in their study of family violence in North Carolina. Based on our data, this jealousy is most often unfounded; the abused women in our research were not that interested in another sexual relationship. However, the batterers' need to control their women leads them to be suspicious and intrusive. Sometimes their very possessiveness drives some women briefly to another man. But, more often, it is the batterers who are involved in other sexual liaisons. Some of the battered women were unable to control their jealous feelings, especially when the men flaunted the other women. A few of the women killed the man when he set up the situation to be "caught." For these women, the defenses to control their anger were no longer adequate, and their rage exploded. The jealousy seems to be used as a catalyst for the women while it provides the entire rationale for the men who kill. Nevertheless, despite the differences in men and women, the presence of excessive jealousy is a high risk factor for prediction of lethality.

Alcohol and drug abuse are other high risk factors for potential lethality. While the exact relationship between alcohol intoxication and battering is not clear, excessive drinking is often present in those relationships in which there is a fatality. None of the research, to date, including ours, finds a direct cause and effect relationship between chemical substance abuse and aggressive behavior. Nonetheless, it cannot be ignored that 88% of the men and 48% of the women were frequently intoxicated in the 50 homicide cases from our data studied by Browne (1987), as compared to 67% of the men and 20% of the women in the research study. Although getting high or drunk is not a cause of abusive behavior, it may facilitate it. An offender may become intoxicated to excuse or escalate the violence, or the altered state of consciousness may cause poor judgment in dealing with the aggression. A full discussion on the findings concerning alcohol can be found in Chapter 7.

In our study we found that both the frequency and severity of the abuse escalated over time. Two-thirds (66%) of the women said that the battering incidents became more frequent, 65% said that the physical abuse worsened, and 73% reported that the psychological abuse became more severe. Table 18 reports these results.

It is often helpful to contrast the violent acts reported in first battering incidents with more recent incidents. Higher lethality risk is predicted when the first incident starts out with life-threatening or severe violent acts or injuries. Sharp escalation rates are also a predictor. In working with battered women, it is useful to graphically demonstrate how the violence is increasing so she can recognize its dangerousness and her need for greater protection.

MEASURING SEVERITY OF VIOLENCE: THE BATTERING QUOTIENT

Neither the violent acts or the resultant injuries alone can measure the severity of the battering relationship. Rather, a combination of both must be used. To predict lethality, two other factors must be included: The frequency with which the beatings occur and the total length of time in the relationship. The latter variables were measured directly in the questionnaire, while the first two variables require interpretation, since perceptions of seriousness or severity were not directly assessed.

One of the goals, following completion of this research, has been to develop a Battering Quotient to assess severity and predict lethality in a battering relationship. This task was begun, with hopes of further funding, by having both battered women and staff rate their perceptions of severity of injuries and violent acts on a 1 to 100 scale. The battered women living in shelters who completed these ratings turned out to be "unreliable" because they tended to give rating scores of 100 to acts or injuries they themselves had experienced, regardless of a more "objective" standard of seriousness or severity. This has become a more important finding today than we initially thought at the time because of the difficulty in identifying those women who are more likely to heal from their experiences and become survivors and those who remain caught up in a victim lifestyle. There appears to be several stages of healing that take place for those who go on to become survivors including an intense self-focus without the ability to discriminate protective actions, which is then supplanted by a more generalized view of violence against women from which there is no effective protection, and then the development of some ability to protect from some violence even if it is not complete protection. I have developed a new treatment approach that deals with these natural stages of healing called Survivor Therapy (Walker, 1994), and videotapes that demonstrate the application of the theory (Walker, 1996, 1998).

Consequently, in order to proceed with the development of a Battering Quotient, we had the acts and injuries rated by 20 shelter staff and project interviewers. Each act was rated under three headings: threatened but not committed, committed briefly, and committed repeatedly. Table 19 shows those rating scores; the higher the score, the more serious or severe the act. The severity of injuries was also given rat-ings from 1 to 100; the higher the score, the more severe the injuries were thought to be, in general. The results are shown in Table 20.

These ratings have a lower variability than would have been expect-ed given their range of "objective" seriousness. Our raters were not able to use the bottom third of the scale for acts threatened or bottom half of the scale for rating injuries. Most of the severity ratings for the acts and injuries specified clustered in the top third of the scales. And, when the battered women rated their seriousness, almost all clustered in the top 10% of the scale. It is possible that once people are involved in understanding the extent of violence that occurs in battering rela-tionships, there is little tolerance for any kind of abusive behavior. For example, in my work as a forensic psychologist, I am often questioned by prosecutors who trivialize slaps, punches, and bruises that do not necessitate emergency medical care. Many of those same state attor-neys have great difficulty prosecuting cases unless they have broken bones or injuries requiring stitches to repair them.

This attitude can be understood by looking at the addictions field where former victims also provide many of the services to those cur-rent victims who are trying to become survivors. Recovered alcoholics in the AA program would rate one drink with a higher seriousness than would those who have not been involved in alcohol abuse. Probably, so would alcohol counselors who have seen first hand its destructive impact on people. Thus, a standard of battering severity or serious-ness must take into account that high upper range, too. In finalizing the ranked orders of acts and injuries, it would be useful to add the opinions of those not directly involved with the syndrome. We have not done so at this time but report our work-to-date as encouragement for those who are interested in finding new directions for their own studies.

The categories of acts and injuries that we used in this preliminary exercise were taken from the acts and injuries most frequently report-ed and therefore measured in the interview. We planned the analysis from the data already collected in this research study. Given what we have learned from our results, I would change some of the categories if new data were being gathered. Delineating areas of the body struck and psychological acts and injuries more carefully seems to be a nec-essary addition if this scale is to be more useful. I would also add a measure of the Patterson (1982) and Reid et al. (1981) component of "fogging" or "chaining" of acts that our headings of "briefly" and "repeatedly" committed tried to tap. Sonkin (1998) has attempted to be more specific in his rating scale that is used by many domestic vio-lence workers. In addition, I would add some categories that we did not measure in the research but now find important in looking at potential long-term neurological injuries that occur from head-banging, head and shoulder-shaking, and hair pulling, all of which are more frequently associated with closed-head injuries and neurological demyelinization disorders.

Had funds continued to be made available, we would have attempted to develop the Battering Quotient (BQ) using two different methods of computation. The first method is based on standard scale construction techniques. The four variables are inter-correlated, and the BQ is computed using either an equally-weighted or factor-weighted sum, depending upon the correlations obtained. The second method is one that relies more on stronger assumptions. Logically, overall battering severity would seem to be a multiplicative (rather than additive) function of duration frequency, and average severity of acts and injuries. If a woman is battered once a week for two years, for example, the number of incidents would be 104 (52 x 2); each incident (or the typical incident) can be weighted by the average severity of acts and injuries, determined as described above. Therefore, the two severity variables are combined (again, in a way based on their inter-correlation) and multiplied by duration and frequency. The relative power of these two battered women variables will determine which computation method is more accurate and useful.

The usefulness of the BQ is obvious in predicting lethality. Violent couples could learn their BQ scores, much like learning other medical high risk factor scores, such as their blood pressure, which indicates the life-threatening nature of hypertension. Perhaps translating the lethality potential of domestic violence to a numerical value might help people take it more seriously. Spouse abuse is a life-threatening disorder that is "catching." It can be prevented, by changing individual life-style behaviors and, thus, societal norms. But it is causing an enormous loss of life, now. Our data indicate that it can be stopped.

Sexual Issues for Battered Women

While the definition of a battering relationship has always included sexual abuse as part of physical abuse, not until the data from this research were collected, it was not known precisely how the sexual abuse in the battering relationship differed from other forms of sexual abuse. Perhaps the most significant fact was the realization that sexual abuse in intimate relationships is more like incest than stranger rape that is more violent. It is not unusual for batterers to use sexual coercion to shame and humiliate women, making it easier for them to gain their desired psychological control. Battered women often use sex to barter for their safety—if they give in to sex, even when they do not desire it, then perhaps they will not be as badly physically or psychologically harmed. Therefore, one of the interesting areas that we studied in this research was the impact of repeated sexual coercion and assault by someone who is capable of tender lovemaking at other times (Finkelhor & Yllo, 1985; Walker, 1979, 1994).

Rape within marriage or marriage-like relationships has been found to occur far more frequently than previously estimated (Laura X, 1981; Martin, 1982; Russell, 1975, 1982). Part of the difficulty in measuring incidence and prevalence rates is that of confusing definitions. Since marital partners are presumed to engage in sexual relations, such consent given automatically along with the marriage vows, it is difficult for many to conceive of either partner having the right to say, "no." Sexual assault statutes used to exclude marital rape but due mostly to the untiring work of Laura X, at the National Clearinghouse for the Study of Marital Rape, all states in the United States now permit some form of criminal prosecution (Laura X, 1981). Even so, as long as the couple is living together, unless the forced sex includes physical assault that can be prosecuted under the regular assault or domestic violence laws, it may not be considered criminal behavior and its effects are usually discounted. Even when they are no longer living together, it is difficult to persuade prosecutors to take on these cases.

Occasionally a civil tort action may be filed for damages from sexual abuse within the intimate relationship but unless the damage is obvious and severe, such as transmitting a sexual disease or preventing the ability to bear a child, it is difficult to persuade others of the damage. Some cases have been successful, however, such as *Curtis v. Curtis,* a 1988 Idaho case. In this case, Sandra Curtis claimed that her common law husband, Carl Curtis had sexually abused her for the 10 years they lived together by using cocaine and coercing her into all-night sex that included pornography. Mr. Curtis attempted to show videotapes that he took during sex to prove that Ms. Curtis was enjoying herself. Ms. Curtis countered by stating she perceived more danger if she didn't give in to his demands. The jury agreed and she won 1.2 million dollars in actual and punitive damages. Mr. Curtis appealed both the decision and the amount of the award but the Idaho Supreme Court affirmed both. In a Colorado case, the amount won by a woman was considerably less, but the precedent was set. This case is used for a mock trial conducted by University of Colorado law school professors teaching future lawyers the important issues of both personal injury torts and battered woman syndrome.

Given the difficulties in reaching a common definition of marital rape, our research project decided to measure the woman's perception of their entire sexual relationship with the abusive partner. Questions about sexual abuse were embedded in the section that asked other questions about sex. We decided to use a broad definition of sexual abuse that included any kind of forced oral, anal or vaginal penetration. Washburne and Frieze (1980) found that women were more likely to discuss sexual abuse in their relationships if they were asked in a more indirect way. They found that they gained more reliable and valid information by asking questions like, "Is sex with your batterer ever unpleasant for you?" and then giving her several answers from which to choose, such as, "Yes, because he forces me to have sex when I don't want to." A more direct question, and perhaps more threatening one for the women: "Did he ever force you to have sex?" We included some questions worded the same way as Frieze and her colleagues did as well as some that asked for the information in a more direct way. This also helped us better understand the contradictions often seen when battered women answer questions differently from one interviewer to another.

We did not use the term "rape" in the questions we asked as other researchers had reported that it is such an emotionally loaded term that women will be less likely to use it to describe what their husbands do to them (Russell, 1982; Doron, 1980). The questions regarding sexual abuse were placed at different parts of the interview rather than in just one section to both reduce the stress around these emotionally charged questions and provide a reliability check. While many of our questions required a forced-choice response, some allowed the woman to respond with open-ended answers. An entire set of questions were asked about the woman's relationship with both the batterer and the nonbatterer in the 200 cases where such data were collected. The specific incidents described support the contention that sex can and is used as a way to dominate, control, and hurt them even if there is no physical abuse. Table 21 discusses the results.

Of our sample, 59% said that they were forced to have sex with the batterer as compared to 7% with the nonbatterer. Of course, the men who were described by those 7% were not actually nonbatterers by definition of the behavior described here, but the women perceived them as such obviously not defining forced sex as battering behavior by itself. With the batterer, 41% were asked to perform what they described as unusual sex acts, as compared to 5% of the nonbatterer. Women reported being forced to insert objects in their vaginas, engage in group sex, have sex with animals, and partake in bondage and various other sadomasochistic activities. A large variety of uncommon sexual practices were reported similar to that which were told to me during my previous research (Walker, 1979).

When asked if sex was unpleasant, 85% said "yes" with the batterers and 29% with the nonbatterers. Of these, 43% of them said that the sex was unpleasant because he forced her when she didn't want it. Interestingly, about one-half thought that sex with her was unpleasant for the batterer but only 12% thought it was unpleasant for the nonbatterer. As we shall see later, a large number of battered women were also incest survivors for whom any sex may have been seen as traumatic. This may explain those who reported sex with nonbatterers as unpleasant also.

Almost two-thirds of the women reported that batterers almost always initiated their sex, while both initiated sex with one-half of the nonbatterers. This is an important finding to refute the often-held notion that battered women are frigid and cause their marriages to fail (Snell, Rosenwald, & Robey, 1964). Two times as many women felt guilt and shame about the sex that they had with the batterer. No specific questions were asked to determine how many women perceived non-violent sex as rape although they were clear that they did not want it at the time. The open-ended responses to the question of why sex was unpleasant, for those 85% who said it was, indicated that they gave in to his coercive demands so that it would calm down the batterer.

These women believed the men were in total control of their sexual interactions. Some of the reasons given were as follows: initiating sex to avoid a beating, having sex after a beating to calm him down, having sex after he beat the baby for fear he would do it again. For some women, refusing sex meant they didn't get money for groceries or other essentials for their survival.

Couples in an abusive relationship often withheld sex from one another as a means of getting what they want. Forty-six percent (46%) of the women said they had stopped having sex with the batterer to get what they wanted from him. Forty-five percent (45%) of them said the men stopped having sex with them. In contrast, 16% of the women said they stopped having sex with the nonbatterer and 11% of the non-batterers did the same. Although these percentages are similar to those who said that sex with the batterer was unpleasant for them, our analysis did not permit us to see if they were the same responders. A small number of women said that the batterer refused to have sex with them, especially as the violence escalated. These women were psychologically devastated by this rejection and felt that the pain experienced from the psychological humiliation and cold anger demonstrated by these men was as cruel and abusive as were the other psychological and physical abuse they experienced. Jacobson and Gottman (1998) in their study found this behavior was consistent with the type of batterer they called a "cobra." They found this type of batterer used a lack of sexual passion and withholding of sex as a deliberate control technique.

Our finding that over half of the battered women in this research study reported forced sex is consistent with that of other researchers on violence against women. Frieze (1980) found that 34% of the battered women in her sample were victims of at least one incident of marital rape with 11% stating it occurred several times or often. Finkelhor and Yllo (1985) report that Spektor's study of 10 Minneapolis battered women shelters found that 36% and Pagelow's (1982) study found 37% said their husbands or cohabiting partner raped them. This compares to 59% in our sample, a figure that is almost twice as high as the others. None of these studies used a random sampling technique due to the difficulties in obtaining a sufficiently large population of women who had only experienced partner abuse. One explanation for our larger number is that our questions were more carefully worded due to the experience of underreporting that the other researchers had previously reported.

Diana Russell (1986, 1987) surveyed a large-sized (930) random sample of women in the San Francisco area to learn more about their experiences with various forms of sexual assault. Of the approximately two-thirds who were married, 12% said that they had been sexually assaulted by their husbands at least one time. She found that sexual assaults by marital partners were twice as common as sexual assaults by strangers. Interestingly, she used a conservative definition of marital rape that had to include forced intercourse with penetration. If these data can be generalized to the population at large, then battered women have three to five times the risk of being sexually assaulted by their partners than do nonbattered women.

Yllo (1981) discusses two types of marital rape in addition to the violent type that she found in her research. They were, (1) those that occur in what she defines as relationships with little or no physical abuse, and (2) those that occur in relationships where the man is apparently obsessed with sex. Our data didn't support such distinct categories although my clinical evaluations of battered women who are involved in litigation do. In fact, it is not unusual for men obsessed with sex, demanding vaginal intercourse, oral and anal sex several times daily, to also physically and psychologically abuse their partners. A subsection of these men also have a history of abusing other women and children. Whether this is a subtype of batterer or a combination of a batterer and a sex-offender is not clear at this time. Our findings are consistent with Yllo's conclusions that forced sex occurs more frequently as a form of violent power and control rather than the more common stereotype of the sexually deprived husband who must use force to get his sexual needs met. Her women report, as do ours, that they would be delighted to engage in warm, tender, love-making with their partners who are more frequently hostile than lustful, interested in their own pleasure!

SEXUAL JEALOUSY

Sexual jealousy is one of the most frequently reported features of violent relationships (Browne & Williams, 1993; Frieze, 1980; Koss et al., 1994; Dutton & Goodman, 1994; Hilberman & Munson, 1978; Martin, 1976; Pagelow, 1982; Roy, 1978; Straus et al., 1980; Walker, 1979). This earlier finding was confirmed by our data and continues to be found in later research. When asked if the batterer was ever jealous of her having an affair with another man, almost every woman said "yes" with over one-half saying such jealousy "always" occurred. Of those women reporting on a nonviolent relationship, about one-quarter said the batterer was sometimes jealous, and only 6% said it "always" occurred. Almost one-quarter of the sample said the batterer was also jealous of her

having an affair with another woman as compared to 3% of the nonbatterers. As we did not inquire if the woman was actually having an affair,
these findings cannot be analyzed for accuracy of his jealous perceptions. In most cases, the women described battering incidents that
were triggered by unfounded jealous accusations. Women said they'd
learned to walk with their eyes downcast, to not speak to others in
public, to not smile too much or dance too long with others at a party.
Sometimes jealousy was responsible for them being kept as prisoners
in their own homes, resulting in further social isolation.

The women reported on their own feelings of jealousy with batterers
and nonbatterers. In 67% of the cases, the women were jealous of the
man having an affair with another woman and in 12%, with another
man. This contrasts with one-half of them being jealous of the nonbatterers having an affair with another woman and 1% with another man.
About one-half of the women said the men actually had an affair at
least once to their knowledge and another 14% suspected it but
weren't sure. These data support our conclusions that sexual jealousy
is often part of the battering relationship and like sexual assault is part
of the battered woman syndrome. In essence, what we have observed
is a breach in the kind of trust and the boundaries expected in an intimate relationship. Insecurity about the relationship was apparent no
matter how the woman tried to reassure the batterer.

ABUSE DURING PREGNANCY

A large number of women stated they became romantically involved with
the batterer rather quickly. This involvement usually involved sexual
intimacy and as can be seen in Table 22, over one-third of the women
were not married when they first became pregnant. Our subjects had
an average of two pregnancies and 1.53 children while in the battering
relationship. Battering took place in each of the three trimesters. It is
probably accurate to assume that many of those pregnancies that
ended in a miscarriage, were terminated by the batterers' violent acts.

Our sample, like Gelles' (1975) reported that a high degree of battering occurred during each pregnancy with 59% reporting battering
occurred during the first pregnancy, 63% during the second, and 55%
during the third pregnancy. These data were further analyzed to see if
there was a difference in which time period during the pregnancy the
woman was battered, and the results indicated that if it occurred, it
was likely to happen across all three trimesters. Over 50% of the batterers reportedly were happy about the pregnancy, at least initially,

even though she was later battered, so the women did not perceive the men's unhappiness about the pregnancy as the violence trigger.

We looked for differences in birth control methods in battering and nonbattering relationships, but as the results in Table 23 indicate, no major differences were seen. In about two-thirds of the cases, the women assumed responsibility for the use of birth control, with the most popular methods being the pill and the IUD. Surprisingly, about one-fifth of the women used no birth control at all. Most of the women did not report religious reasons, but rather, because the batterer would not permit her to use any birth control. Although we didn't inquire in this study, because it was too early to be aware of the dangers, it has later been shown that batterers also do not permit women to protect themselves from the possibility of HIV transmission by making them use condoms so that they are at high risk for the transmission of the virus that causes AIDS (Seligson & Bernas, 1997).

In many cases, the batterer kept detailed records of the woman's menstrual cycle and may have known more about her body than she did. The women did not regularly report abortion as a birth control option. One-quarter of the women interviewed had no pregnancies, and there was a relatively small number of pregnancies and live births for the rest. Again, this may be explained by the battering relationships, as many women said they did not want to bring a child into a domestic violence family, but it wouldn't explain the nonbatterers' relationships. However, some women may have been beyond the childbearing years and others may not have been in a relationship with a nonbatterer long enough to have a child with him.

SEXUAL ABUSE OF CHILDREN

The two areas of sexual abuse of children that were studied here included the sexual abuse of the children living in the home with the batterer and the prior sexual abuse of the battered women interviewed when they were children. Although we had to compromise the data we collected on sexual abuse of children living in the home because of the conflict with the mandatory child abuse report laws in Colorado at the time of the study, we were able to get information that supported the findings of other researchers who were specifically studying child sexual abuse and report these results in the next Chapter (6).

Reports on child sexual assault by victims of battering in their adult homes is quite different from the typical rape victim report because of the complicated nature of the relationship between the father and child. Most of the sexual assaults were incest committed by fathers against daughters although some were brothers, uncles and other family members. Incest is more similar to marital rape and sexual coercion not only because of the complicated relationship with the perpetrator, but also because the goal is to use coercion and force to gain affection from the child. It is dissimilar to physical child abuse in that it includes some kind of genital behavior and its primary goal is usually not to inflict pain on the victim. It is dissimilar to other forms of coerced genital behavior like in sexual assault as the young victim often perceives the perpetrator as needing love and affection from her as she does from him. Obviously, incest—whether or not overt violence is involved—has serious psychological ramifications for the victim. Although we suggested that our results be interpreted cautiously at the time they were collected, we realize today that we only touched the tip of the iceberg. It is clear that incest occurs far more often than previously thought in battering homes especially, and the impact is more far-reaching than we suspected (Briere, 1992, 1995; Courtois, 1988, 1997; Herman, 1992; Farley & Balkan, 1998; Goodman et al., 1993; Koss et al., 1994; Walker, 1994).

It is interesting to speculate on the relationship between being molested as a child and subsequent physical and sexual abuse later in life as an adult. As previously described, almost one-half of these battered women reported they had been repeatedly sexually victimized as a child. This is two and one-half times (2½) the number expected from other survey data available at the time of our study (Finkelhor, 1979). In his study of 795 college students, Finkelhor found that 19% of college women reported such early sexual victimization. He was also surprised to find that 9% of the college men reported childhood sexual experiences. In almost all cases, the aggressor was an adult male in the family—similar to our data. Finkelhor concluded from his data that the vulnerability for such sexual experiences could be created in the family, particularly where there are unhappy marriages. Our data suggests that the risk for sexual victimization of children increases if there is also violence in these families with poor boundaries between its members.

The knowledge of the impact on the child of early sexual molestation, with or without physical violence as part of the coercion, has expanded over the last 15 years. Most believe that such behavior is always coercive because of the adult's greater size, strength, and position of power over the child. However, there always have been some who question the actual harm to a child, especially if there is no physical violence or if there is fondling and no genital penetration. It is true that definitions keep changing even since our research. We were less conservative than Diana Russell who use the classic definition of rape that only includes penile-vaginal penetration with our definition of a broader array of sexual behaviors as described above.

In fact, no reports of child sexual abuse are totally free from the emotions of the reporter. It is abhorrent to think of an adult having sex with a child for most people, even its defenders. That may be why today, it is more common for the general public to not want to believe that child sexual abuse, and particularly incest, really happens. There is a whole entire industry that has sprung up to deny its existence by claiming that there is an epidemic of mental health professionals whose business depends on the epidemic of child sexual abuse reports (Loftus, 1993) or the mother is using false reports to alienate the child from the father (Gardner, 1992). Pope (1996, 1997) has demonstrated that using very little relevant empirical data these advocates for a false memory syndrome are obscuring the clinical field so that children who may report truthfully are disbelieved. Unfortunately, this group of alarmists include many of the former defenders of child sexual abuse who used to claim that it wasn't harmful to the child if it was done with loving intentions on the part of the perpetrator.

The most recent controversy, around an article published by the APA in its journal, *Psychological Bulletin* by authors Rind, Tromovich, and Bauserman (1998) has brought this issue before the general public when radio talk show host, Laura Schlesinger sharply criticized the APA for publishing an article that appeared to support adult sex with children, especially men having sex with supposedly willing boys. The public outcry against the APA spread quickly to the U.S. Congress and was continued by other media, finally prompting a statement issued by the APA reiterating psychology's stance that "sex between children and adults is never appropriate" and apologizing for the lack of sufficient vigilance in preventing the publication of this article in its present "inflammatory form." However, while promising to close loopholes in the current process that permitted this contradiction between alleged science and policy, the APA also reaffirmed its policy to continue to publish rigorous scientific findings even if they are unpopular. In recognizing the misinterpretation of the conclusions of the Rind et al. (1998) article by organizations that support pedophiles, one of which already was calling for the decriminalization of man/boy voluntary sex encounters, the APA legal affairs office was directed to prepare documents that could be used in court to defend against these unsubstantiated claims. Interestingly, it wasn't discovered until the controversy erupted publicly that one of the authors also published a treatise on the positive aspects of man-boy sex (Bauserman, 1989, 1997). Ironically, at about the same time, *Journal of the American Medical Association (JAMA)*, the respected medical journal published by the AMA, printed another review article that documented the long-term harm from adult sexual contact with children (Holmes & Slap, 1998). Obviously, politics, personal beliefs, and emotions all impact on science, making it imperative that these factors are clarified before making pronouncements that can become misinterpreted and harmful.

Courtois (1988, 1995, 1997), Gold, Hughes, and Honecker (1994), Pope and Brown (1996), among others have demonstrated that the memory of adults who experienced sexual abuse as a child is far more stable than otherwise believed although from time to time certain facts are remembered and forgotten. Freyd (1994, 1996) suggests that the betrayal of the parent is a significant cognitive trauma that also must be assessed along with the actual physical, sexual and other psychological behavior. Obviously, this debate makes the understanding of child sexual abuse even more complex than it already has been. See the next Chapter (6) for a further discussion on this topic.

Children who experience early sexual molestation have been found to develop certain personality characteristics that assist their adaptation to an uncontrollable and frightening situation (Brown, 1992; Butler, 1978; Courtois, 1997; Finkelhor, 1979; Herman, 1992; Leidig, 1981; MacFarlane, 1979; Walker, 1994). Little girls learn they can control their mother and father by being seductive and cute especially since this behavior is reinforced and rewarded. They also learn how important it is for them to keep this behavior a secret (see Courtois, 1997; Walker, 1988; Walker, Gold, & Lucenko, in preparation). Most incest survivors learn to equate sexuality with intimacy as they never fully experience the developmental stages of adolescence that encourage the growth of psychological intimacy. Their need for secrecy gets in the way of developing close friendships with girls in early adolescence. They also perceive, perhaps accurately, that other girls may not understand their feelings about boys and sex. Some report that they view nonsexually experienced girls as more naïve and less mature than themselves. These feelings are similar to our sample of battered women, at least as measured by their responses on the self-esteem scales. In essence, they report they missed out on teenage companionship and fun. But they also report they feel more experienced in other areas of their life, particularly in sexual matters. Monica Lewinsky, the woman who had a sexual affair with President Clinton, is a good example of such a person. Some incest victims report that they develop a sexual relationship with a boy closer to their own age, often as a way of terminating the sexual molestation. They rarely report platonic friendships with adolescent boys either. This may promote different social skills that can leave the woman more isolated than if she had been able to develop more variety in her friendships during adolescence.

Terminating incest is usually accomplished by the victim, often during middle adolescence by using a variety of methods (Finkelhor, 1979). Usually they seek assistance from a supportive peer or adult indirectly; that is they don't ask directly for help but they do give enough hints or actually talk about the sexual molestation so that help is received. Sometimes they threaten the offender that they will disclose if it doesn't stop immediately. Depending on the offender, this may be sufficient to stop it, which helps reempower the girl. Victims hint that they might have dropped hints to their mothers but rarely do they tell her openly, perhaps recognizing the mother's own vulnerability to the batterer's abuse. The whole issue of complicity in mothers in permitting incest to continue has been one that has been given much attention in feminist analysis (Cammaert, 1988; Yllo, 1993). Given women's lack of power in some marital relationships, they may not have the ability to protect their daughters. In incest families where there is also spouse abuse, the girls perceive their mothers' inability to deal with the violence against themselves, too. While some girls harbor deep resentment against their mothers, usually for not being strong enough, they also report that they protected them from the knowledge and they believed that giving in to their father's demands protected their mothers and the rest of the family from his violent behavior. This is an interesting perception as it includes some sense of power and purpose for these young women that may provide them with some resilience to a more severe impact from the abuse.

Some specialists in incest and child abuse have blamed the mother for encouraging the father's incestuous behavior as a way to escape from what they named as the mother's own obligations and "wifely duties" (Helfer & Kempe, 1974). Using this analysis, however, does not permit the man's sexual misconduct to be accurately understood. The data indicates that he is more likely to be attracted to the daughter precisely because she is a young girl who can be more easily coerced. Abel, Becker, Murphy, and Flanagan (1981) have found that despite reports to the contrary, the incest fathers they evaluated demonstrated physiological arousal patterns in the laboratory similar to other child molesters. This occurred when they viewed slides of young girls and adult women in erotic poses. A penile-tumescence-measuring device recorded their responses sexual arousal to the pictures of young girls. Thus, it appears that many family members who molest young children are more sexually aroused by children than by adult women. This empirical evidence certainly supports the victims' and their mothers' retrospective incest accounts. It has serious implications for reevaluating family treatment modalities and creating new treatment programs for offenders that follows the protocols that have been developed for other pedophiles (Becker, 1990).

The impact of child sexual abuse including incest, like battering and other interpersonal trauma, seems to be based on a multidimensional model that includes intervening contextual or mediating variables together with the acts that occurred, who did them, and over what time span. Finkelhor (1979) for example, found that some reported long-term and repeated occurrences had the same psychological impact as did some short-term behavior. Some reported encounters that involved exhibitionism and/or fondling as equally as traumatic as some where intercourse was completed. These findings have been responsible for the broadening of the definition of child sexual abuse so that it is understood that the impact must be studied from the child's perspective and not just the arbitrary assignment of severity to acts committed by the perpetrator. Father–daughter incest was reported as the most devastating for the child, perhaps because it robs the child of her right to have a father and a mother in her life. Sex with other family members was seen as devastating as sex with a stranger in our population. Finkelhor's study, like ours, found that sexual abuse accompanied with violent force reportedly were the most seriously psychologically traumatized. Often these children run away from home at an early age and may become caught up in a life of drugs, sex, and violence (James, 1978; Farley & Barkan, 1998). In our sample, over half left home before the age of 17. Obviously, it is critical to try to prevent the toll that this kind of violence takes on the family and especially the future lives of these girls.

BATTERED WOMEN, SEX AND INTIMACY

Many of the behaviors described by our battered women were similarly described by those who work with sexually molested children. They include "manipulativeness" that is important to help "keep the peace," the unrealistic sense of power achieved through the use of seduction, the intense concentration on self-survival, the willingness to become dependent upon a man who can be both loving and violent at times, the fear of attempting survival alone, the knowledge of how to decrease a man's violence by demonstrating love to him, and the joy from experiencing intense intimacy. It is quite possible that early exposure to sexual abuse, with or without accompanying violence, creates a dependency upon the positive aspects of the intense intimacy experienced prior to the beginning of the battering behavior and maintained throughout the third phase of loving contrition.

This raises some questions about these battered women's ability to make distinctions between sexual and emotional intimacy. It seems as if both the violent man and the battered woman confuse their need for emotional intimacy with sex, thinking they have met both needs through their intensely sexual relationships. However, the men cannot sustain such intimacy without becoming intensely frightened of their growing dependency on the women, the women become frightened by their dependency on the men as well as their own, and both begin to pull away from each other. Then, needing the intimacy to lessen the violence, both come back together again. Although the women do not need or like the violence that is part of this cycle, they often accept it as part of what they have to put up with in order to get all the other benefits of this relationship. Only when the costs of the relationship outweigh the benefits will a battered woman take steps to terminate it. If the man permits her to leave, then it is over like so many other relationships. But if his dependency needs, possessiveness, and vindictiveness get in the way, he will not let her go even after the ties may be legally severed. Stalking and continued harassment of battered women by their current and former abusive partners is better understood now than it was 15 years ago (Burgess et al., 1997; Walker & Meloy, 1998). Some of the reports we had during the research are similar to the attachment theories proposed by Meloy (1998) and for those where there is also sexual abuse, Meloy's construct of erotomania may also apply. Of course, the issue of stalking in domestic relationships is broader as is described in Chapter 4, but in relationships where sexual abuse is a featured component, it is important to assess for these issues, too.

BATTERED WOMEN AND SEXUALLY TRANSMITTED DISEASES

Although this research asked many different questions about sexuality, we did not inquire into the issue of sexually transmitted diseases, especially HIV and AIDS. However, new data since our study inform that there is a higher risk for battered women to be unprotected during sexual intercourse with an abusive partner (APA, 1996a, 1996b; Koss et al., 1994; Koss & Haslet, 1992; Seligson & Bernas, 1997). Both the coercive nature of the sexual relationship together with the need for the batterer to have control over the woman makes it difficult if not impossible for her to demand that her partner use condoms and other protection during sex. Women who have been sexually abused previously are also known to be more likely to have unprotected sex (APA, 1996) although it is not known if it is a lack of assertiveness especially around sexual matters or a naïve belief that their partner is not sexual with anyone else unless he tells them so. It is interesting that battered women shelters do not ask for this information while women live in shelter, perhaps because they would not know what to do with the women should they turn out to be HIV positive. Therefore, they are exposing the other women and children to high risk when taking simple precautions would permit an HIV positive woman to live in the communal home.

Those who have become prostitutes also have a much higher risk of contracting a sexually transmitted disease including HIV and AIDS. Although many young women who have escaped from abusive homes do go into prostitution, often to support drug habits they have developed, for a short period of time, if they do not use protection during sexual contact, they may not be able to get out of that life as they often plan to do. In any case, the need for good education and training for professionals as well as battered women in this area is critical.

PORNOGRAPHY

The issue of pornography and sexual abuse is one that has divided feminists for many years; not in their collective understanding that there is a relationship with those who frequently use pornography, particularly to stimulate themselves to orgasms but, rather, in what to do about it (Mackinnon, 1983). Many feminists, particularly those who have contributed to the scholarship in feminist psychology (Brown, 1994) and feminist jurisprudence (MacKinnon, 1983) debate the civil rights issue of freedom of speech and other First Amendment rights while acknowledging the inherent dangers of access to the brutal violent images of defiled women often seen in popular pornography. Men interested in changing gender role stereotypes believe that pornography contributes to the maintenance of the "macho-man" image (Brooks, 1996; Levant, 1997; Levant & Pollack, 1993).

Lederer (1980), Rave (1985) and others have written about how pornography is a negative leveler by men against women, permitting them to see women as sex objects. Brooks (1996, 1998) supports this feminist position and details how men permit themselves to shut off their real feelings and violate women by numbing themselves to the full range of sexual expression while focusing on pornographic and centerfold images. These men are much less likely to feel empathy, sympathy or support for women who then can more easily become their victims. We still don't know if there is a direct behavioral connection although the studies point to trends in that direction.

DATING VIOLENCE

Young women have been found to be at risk for abuse in their dating relationships especially if they become sexually active with the man (Levy, 1991). Studies have shown that maybe as many as 25% of teens are abused by their boyfriends on a regular basis (Makepeace, 1981; White & Koss, 1991). Often these girls come from homes where they have witnessed abuse of their mothers by their fathers. It is not unusual for the abuse to begin after sexual intimacy occurs in a battering relationship, often starting with jealousy, possessiveness and attempts to isolate the woman. Many teenage girls who want the security of a boyfriend are uncomfortable with the abusers' attempt to isolate her from high school activities and other friends. Monopolizing her perceptions before she has a chance to learn how to think for herself is a typical way dating violence starts. In a number of cases, the women reported that the first sexual encounter was really a battering incident and a rape where the men refused to stop sex when she asked him to. The women stated that they thought they were just kissing and fooling around with no intentions of having sexual intercourse when all of the sudden, they realized the men were gratifying themselves without communicating with or showing concern for the women.

Sometimes the young women went on to marry the men hoping that this would prove to them that they really loved them and wanted the relationship to work out. Some of the women described themselves as very religious or from other cultures where their virginity was essential to get a good husband to marry. These women felt that they had no choice but to marry this man, speaking as though the die were already cast for them and there was now no going back!

Table 24 indicates the different types of intimate relationships that these women described in the interviews. On average they had 2.1 intimate relationships with one-half married to the man and one-half in significant relationships with other living arrangements. Interestingly, they had been dating less than 6 months when they moved in or married. The average age of the women in our sample when the relationship became intimate was 22 years old for battering and 24 years old for nonbattering relationships. Our data suggest that sexual intimacy may occur sooner in the dating period of battering than nonbattering relationships. No apparent differences were found in where in the life relationship history sequence was the battering relationship. It could have been the first, second, or in another sequence.

SEX AND AGGRESSION

Researchers have postulated a connection between sex and aggression in some individuals, usually men, that appears to have been conditioned in an earlier stage of development (Abel, Becker, & Skinner, 1980; Donnerstein, 1982; Feshback & Malamuth, 1978; Malamuth, in press; Malamuth & Check, in press). In several studies, average male college students were exposed to movies that depicted sexual aggression and then given a situation to discuss concerning their potential to take sexual advantage of a young woman. Interestingly, the more aggression associated with the sex in the movie, the greater the "rape proclivity" found in their responses. Although the researchers did not collect data on the exposure of the males to violence in their childhood home or their current sexual behavior if they were dating, our results would predict that these attitudes would result in more use of violence in their homes. However, Donnerstein (1982) and Malamuth (1982) found that debriefing the subjects carefully in a discussion group that talked about the feelings that were aroused right after the movies lowered the "rape proclivity" to even lower levels than the baseline levels collected prior to exposure to the sex and aggression movies. This is important information for prevention programs for those children who are at high risk for developing such attitudes and behavior pairing sex and aggression when they become adolescents. Talking about their feelings like what occurs in psychotherapy may well be an important prevention tool.

CONCLUSIONS

The research project that we conducted found support for other research that links sexual abuse to other forms of violence in the relationship. Several points stand out and need further clarification. What role does early sexualization of a relationship play in later sexual violence that occurs? Obviously to answer this question, we would have to follow women over a long period of time to see what happens in their lives and once we appear as permanent or even semi-permanent parts of their lives, we will change the outcome. After all, we have learned that the less isolation and more supportive presence of others in the woman's life, the greater the chances of stopping the abuse or at least mitigating against serious effects! We also need more information about the interrelationship between child sexual abuse, specifically incest, and later sexual abuse in the relationship, and then, sexual abuse of the woman's children by the adult abuser. To collect the data in this area is more difficult given the interrelatedness of several legal systems (family, criminal and juvenile) and the involvement of child protective services. However, it is not impossible to do so as is discussed in the next chapter on children. Finally, it would be interesting to know more about the battered woman's perceptions of emotional and sexual intimacy and how that impacts on her during the time she is in the relationship. Comparing these data to women who are sexually abused as children but not as adults will help us gain more knowledge in this area.

Impact of Violence in the Home on Children

The impact of exposure to violence in the home on children has been found to have a most detrimental effect on them, even more significant than being raised in a single parent home. It would be a rare person who would argue that children would not be better off raised in a home with two loving and nonviolent parents. However, the data are clear; children who are exposed to violence have a significant risk for using violence themselves, becoming delinquent, demonstrating school and behavior problems, and having serious and life-long mental health problems including depression, anxiety and PTSD symptomology. In fact, some have suggested that an exposure to both domestic violence and violence in their community may be the most toxic combination for negative outcomes for both children and their parents (Holden, Geffner, & Jouriles, 1998; Jaffe, Wolfe, & Wilson, 1990).

The probability that spouse abuse has a profound influence on children who are exposed to it during their early years was found to be consistent with most psychological theories popular at the time of our research. Social learning theory would predict its significance for future violence as typified by Bandura's (1973) and Berkowitz's (1962) writings on the learned aspects of aggressive behavior. Eron and colleagues have detailed the role of parenting in the learning of aggression (Eron, Huesman, & Zilli, 1991). Gelles and Straus (1988) have theorized about the connection between wife abuse and child abuse using data from the Family Violence Research Center at the University of New Hampshire.

More recently, Cummings (1998) reviewed the data on conceptual and theoretical directions and discussed the interaction factors that occur from the different ways conflict and violence are expressed together with constructive parenting behaviors in a particular family. He found that children respond emotionally to adults' disputes by a variety of behaviors and those responses may be aggravated by some factors such as comorbidity of alcoholism in one or more parents, parental depression, and the meaning given to marital conflict by the children. On the other hand, Cummings also found that constructive conflict resolution may mediate the effects of children's exposure to destructive conflict and prepare them to develop better coping strategies for future exposure. Graham-Bermann (1998) found that although only 13% of the children from families where there was domestic violence that she studied met all the criteria for a PTSD diagnosis, more than half of the children were reexperiencing the battering incidents that they had been exposed to, 42% experienced arousal symptoms and fewer children experienced avoidance symptoms that are part of the criteria for the PTSD diagnosis. Others have also found PTSD in children who have been exposed to domestic violence in their homes (Goodwin, 1988; Hughes, 1997; Pynoos, 1994; Rossman, 1998; Rossman & Rosenberg, 1998; Terr, 1990).

Rosenberg and Rossman (1990) suggest the impact of exposure to domestic violence on children has ranged from minimal to placing severe limitations on personality development and cognition. Further, most child abuse experts agree that the next generation of abusers will come from those who have been abused themselves (Garbarino, Gutterman, & Seeley, 1986; Garbarino, Kostelny, & Dubrow, 1991; Gil, 1970; Helfer & Kempe, 1974; Holden, Geffner, & Jouriles, 1998; Peled, Jaffe, & Edleson, 1995; Jaffe, Wolfe, & Wilson, 1990; Rossman & Rosenberg, 1998).

Patterson's (1982) studies of aggressive boys, based on learning theory, assume that all social interactions are learned from that which is directly or indirectly modeled by other persons. Given the high rate of aggressive behaviors to which all children are exposed, and therefore learn, the question becomes why some perform aggressive acts at higher rates and in different patterns than others. The coercion theory developed to answer this question came from methodical observations of the interaction of behaviors emitted by family members studied in a variety of environmental conditions. The implication of coercion theory is that if modeling takes place in interactive, conditioning relationships, then children raised in violent homes are at high risk to develop those same violent patterns whether or not they are themselves deliberately abused.

EMPIRICAL EVIDENCE

Empirical evidence about the exact nature of the impact of witnessing or experiencing family violence on children has expanded during the past 20 years. Our data has added a little more to the small knowledge base. While we asked some direct questions concerning child development, most of our data is inferred from open-ended responses and thus, must be cautiously interpreted. We deliberately sacrificed the ability to question our subjects directly about present or potential child abuse because of the difficulty posed by Colorado's mandatory child abuse reporting law.

As a licensed psychologist in this state and principal investigator of the research grant, I was in the category of professionals who must report any *suspicion* of harm to a child. In some states the law requires some actual *knowledge* or *belief* of harm, a different standard. *Willful nonreport* of suspected abuse would have been grounds for removal of my license to practice psychology and criminal prosecution. As the principal investigator, all project staff were under my supervision, which made me liable for reporting any evidence they *suspected* or *uncovered* during the interviews. The widespread community publicity announcing our project caused several juvenile court judges to assure us that we were going to be held responsible to report any disclosures relevant to *potential, suspected* or *current* child abuse. Failure to report, we were told, would result in immediate prosecution despite our protests that accuracy of our data could be compromised if we were forced to report suspicions of child abuse. Nor would the Department of Justice's Certificate of Confidentiality, which was intended to protect our data from being subpoenaed in a court action, suffice.

This unexpected difficulty caused us to revise our original intent to collect data on perceived child abuse in homes where women were being battered. Instead, we compromised by asking about past child abuse and discipline procedures. We also agreed we would make a formal report if we inadvertently uncovered any current instances of child abuse. Since our research was designed to measure women's perceptions of events, there was no way to verify the accuracy of their self-report data. Therefore, potential risk for child abuse could not be directly ascertained from the questions we asked, and thus, could not be considered "willful nonreport" as the statute demanded. The resolution satisfied the Colorado legal community, NIMH, and did not compromise the project goals.

As a result of our dilemma, NIMH and the Department of Justice have negotiated a new agreement that extends the Certificate of Confidentiality to protect research projects needing to collect such sensitive child abuse data without being subject to the numerous states' mandatory report laws. There are also newer statistical techniques that allow for systematic sampling that can overcome this problem

(Berk, personal communication). We found that establishing personal contact with understanding caseworkers guarded against possible punitive responses toward those few women for whom we did file a report, with their knowledge and cooperation.

CHILD ABUSE CORRELATES

Despite these difficulties and subsequent compromises, our results— shown in Table 25—are consistent with other researchers in this area. It is interesting to note that 87% of the women reported that the children were aware of the violence in their homes. Most field workers now believe that it is closer to 100% of children who live in domestic violence homes even if they do not discuss their perceptions with their mothers. The APA Task Force on Violence and the Family (1996a) labeled exposing children to domestic violence as a form of nonphysical child abuse or maltreatment because of the similarity of the psychological effects that also occur with other forms of child abuse.

These results also point to the inadequacy of understanding this form of child abuse and neglect in previous, more medically oriented child abuse literature such as is represented by Helfer and Kempe (1974) that stress can physically injure children. Often, their condemnation of the mother for not protecting her child overlooked the possibility that she might have been without the ability to control the man's violent behavior against herself or her children. Perhaps the most visible case where this was graphically seen was with Hedda Nussbaum and her daughter, Lisa Steinberg. Hedda Nussbaum was an author and editor for a major New York publishing firm while her common-law husband, Joel Steinberg was a successful lawyer. However, he battered her and the children, sometimes while under the influence of cocaine, and eventually killed 6-year old Lisa. Steinberg was found guilty of manslaughter and sentenced to prison. Hedda Nussbaum was condemned by the public for failure to protect Lisa and the younger boy (Brownmiller, 1988). I suggest that perhaps any other intervention she might have done could have made things worse, perhaps even getting them all killed (Walker, 1989a).

The research here found a high overlap between partner and child abuse. While living together in a battering relationship, over one-half (53%) of the men who abused their partners also reportedly abused their children. This result compares favorably with other research that suggests as high as a 60% overlap between child and woman abuse. Further, one-third of the batterers also threatened to physically harm the children whether they did it or not. This compares with about one-quarter of the women (28%) who said they abused their children when living in a violent home, and 6% who threatened to abuse the children. Clearly, in our sample, children are at greater risk of being hurt by the batterers although not out of harm with one-quarter of their mothers who were being abused themselves.

One of the more popular myths about child abuse and family violence is that the man beats the woman, the woman beats the child, and the child beats the dog. It is so common that even nursery rhymes tell of such a hierarchy. Given its popularity, we tried to measure whether or not the woman abused her children when angry with the batterer. We found that 5% of the women said they did use physical violence against the children when angry with the batterer. But, only 0.6% of the women said they did so when living in a nonviolent relationship. This supports the notion that anger begets more anger. Violence begets more violence. Some newer research is suggesting that it is not just abuse that creates the psychological harm to children, but also the environment within which abuse takes place (Gold, 1997).

Our mothers said they were eight times more likely to hurt their children while they were being battered than when they felt safe from violence. Only 0.6% said they occasionally used physical force against the children to get something from the batterer. Thus, from our data, it can be concluded that the level of reported child abuse by the women was low enough to disprove the pecking order myth. The alternate possibility that men who beat their wives also beat their children has much more support from these data.

PROTECTION OF CHILDREN

In analyzing why mothers seem to get so much of child protective services caseworkers' and child abuse experts' wrath, the most plausible explanation seems to be the prevailing view that women are expected to take care of their children and prevent them from harm no matter what the cost to themselves. As in high-risk incest families, the presence of a strong mother reportedly does prevent serious child abuse (APA, 1996a, 1996b). Positive parenting by mothers can mitigate against damages from exposure to abuse. Thus, the focus of some child abuse treatment programs has been to help women become better wives and mothers, often without realization that these women were also victims of terrible abuse. Others, such as children's programs in battered women shelters focus on cognitively restructuring the family to define it as a mother-child bond without the inclusion of the father. Unfortunately, the divorce courts do not accept this model and often perpetuate the abusive environment by failing to protect either the mother or the child from the abuser.

Those who have studied the impact of exposure to domestic violence on children find that like other forms of conflict and abuse, there are certain experiences that children may have to build their resiliency to emotional damage. Johnston and Campbell (1993) have found that the stronger and more supportive the mother can be, the healthier the child. Obviously this calls for a new way to encourage judges to act—if they use the jurisdiction of the court to give the mother support and power, they will also be protecting the child. This clearly fits into the "best interests of the child" doctrine and should replace the common thinking dominating family law such as Hodges (1986) describes in his recommendations for equal parental access to children. Zorza (1995), Cahn (1991), Hart (1988), Hiltone (1993), Holden et al. (1998), Hughes (1997), Liss and Stahly (1993), and Peled et al. (1995), among others, present data to assist in making cogent arguments to the court for a new model to better protect these children.

Although the long term consequences of redefining the family unit on the child's mental health have not yet been scientifically or legally established, the critics have attacked this model as being evidence of women's vindictiveness and labeled it as *parental alienation syndrome* using old models of the two-parent home as needing to be extended to the child's equal contact with two parents. Gardner (1987, 1992) who is one of the loudest critics, does state that he exempts domestic violence cases from his model, but then he goes about redefining domestic violence in his own idiosyncratic way often excluding even cases that have police evidence of physical abuse if they don't meet his idiosyncratic criteria. There are data to support empowering the victim when one of the parents, usually the father, demonstrates the willingness to use violence to gain power and control over the other parent. Obviously, mediation does not work in these cases as to be successful, both parents must feel equal in the negotiations.

Washburne (1983) examined how typical child welfare programs reinforce traditional female role patterns rather than help women develop skills to strengthen their ability to be independent and strong. She cites examples of how cleaning up her home and improving her appearance are often required of a woman who wants her children returned from foster care placement. One of our subjects was in serious jeopardy of losing her children in a custody fight because when the assigned caseworker made an unannounced home visit she was feeding the children dinner from MacDonald's restaurants! It would be more beneficial to parents and children to teach them nonsexist parenting skills in treatment programs than perpetuating stereotyped roles that are no longer valid in our lives.

MODELING NONVIOLENT BEHAVIOR

Modeling learned behavior of parents is probably the most powerful way that violence as a strategy gets passed down to the next generation. In a 25-year longitudinal study, Miller and Challas (1981) found that men who were abused as children were almost two times more likely to become abusive parents than were women. While they do not look at the natural reinforcement of male aggression in a sexist society, their conclusions certainly support such a concept. We attempted to measure the differences between men and women on their attitudes toward the role of women. Our results indicated that there were widespread differences, probably due to sex role conditioning. These results are reported in Chapter 8.

Reports from battered women shelters support the learning theory of aggression. Male and female children, some as young as 2 years old, model "daddy hitting mommy" to get what they want from her (Hughes & Marshall, 1995). Shelters, in order to give mothers and children an opportunity to learn new ways of communicating with each other, have almost universally adopted "no-hitting rules." Washburne (1983) found that mothers are more likely to abuse their children when they are the major caretaker. This is consistent with our finding that mothers are more likely to abuse children when they are living in a violent situation. Some women report using more controlling parenting techniques out of fear that the batterer will use even more harsh discipline should the child continue to misbehave. Despite some of the difficulties in shelter living, including crowded conditions, even abusive mothers are able to learn and use new nonabusive, nonphysical discipline techniques (Hughes, 1997; Hughes & Marshall, 1995).

For the families surveyed in the Straus, Gelles, and Steinmetz (1980) study, the rate of marital violence increased in direct proportion to the amount of physical punishment experienced as children. Thus, the frequency and type of physical punishment of children need to be carefully evaluated. Early learning history of whether frustration and other negative emotions are linked with aggression can be of importance. Social factors can mediate the learned responses, both inhibiting and facilitating the display of aggressive behavior when experiencing frustration or other such emotions.

The battered women in our study reported that two-thirds of batterer's fathers battered their mothers, while almost one-half of their fathers and one-quarter of the nonbatterer's fathers battered their mothers. Three times as many fathers of batterers than nonbatterers battered sisters and brothers when they were growing up. A smaller number of mothers of batterer's were reported to batter their children but, again, it was more than the mothers of battered women or nonviolent men. These results can be found in Table 5 and discussed more fully in Chapter 2.

DISCIPLINE, PUNISHMENT AND POSITIVE COMPLIMENTS

In addition to inquiring about the perception of being battered as a child, we also directly asked about discipline methods used by their parents. We found that almost all of our subjects (89%) had been spanked as a young child age 6 or younger, while 83% had continued to be spanked when older. Even more surprising was the report that over three-quarters of the women (78%) had been hit by an object. About one-half of the batterers were reported to have received "strict" discipline while the other half received "lenient" discipline from their mothers. "Lenient" and "strict" were subjectively rated by the responders. But, nonviolent men were reportedly divided into approximately thirds: one-third experiencing "strict" discipline, one-third "lenient," and the remainder "fair" discipline from their mothers.

While more fathers were rated as administering "strict" discipline than mothers (for batterers), one and one-half times as many more nonbatterers fathers were perceived as "strict." Four times as many nonbatterers were reported to have received fair discipline from fathers. Approximately one-quarter of batterer's and nonbatterer's fathers reportedly were "lenient," which could also have been the catch-all category for noninvolvement in their children's upbringing. The actual data can be found in Table 6.

PERSONALITY DEVELOPMENT

Another measure of childraising patterns, albeit indirect, is the perception of whether or not separation and individuation from parents has been completed. The observation of the extreme dependency abused children have on their mothers and fathers to the point of protecting them by refusal to cooperate with social service investigations has been well documented (Helfer & Kempe, 1974; Lystadt, 1975). Such dependency is also seen in battering relationships (Dutton, 1980, 1995; Giles-Sims, 1983). Giles-Sims discusses the bonds that a closed system such as an abusive family can foster. Often, this pattern of intimacy gets carried over into children's marriages and families. In our questionnaire, we asked about dependency upon mothers and fathers and found that twice as many batterers as nonbatterers were said to still be dependent upon their mothers and fathers as adults. Over half of the violent men reportedly had unresolved dependency issues, which were seen as being perpetuated in their dependency upon their wives and children too. Direct measures of dependency in their children would be warranted.

Hughes attempted to measure the psychological functioning of children who came to an Arkansas battered woman's shelter using several standardized anxiety and self-esteem measures. She found the children displayed the characteristics of jumpiness, nervousness, withdrawal, fright, and impaired academic performance (Hughes & Marshall, 1995). Pizzey (1974) found fear, poor academic performance, confusion, reticence in discussing violence, and fantasizing about a different home life in the children seen at Chiswick Women's Aid refuge in London. Only one-fifth of Labell's (1979) sample of 521 battered women with 682 children reported emotional, behavioral, or physical problems. This is a much lower figure than would have been expected from a mental health professional's observations. Perhaps the abused women who were interviewed while in crisis and at a shelter couldn't identify their children's problems until they themselves were out of crisis.

The Hughes study actually measured the children's personality development. They found that preschool children were the most disrupted by violence in their homes and often showed signs of obvious developmental delay. Boys' self-concept tended to be more negative than girls', who had more anxiety, worry, and oversensitivity. As would be expected from all other reports, boys demonstrated more aggressive behavior than girls at every age. And, not surprisingly, mothers rated boys more negatively on conduct and personality problems than girls. Yet, all the children viewed physical punishment as the primary mode of parental discipline. Interestingly, a bimodal split occurred in mothers' discipline preferences. After a short stay in the shelter, one-half of the mothers reported preferring nonphysical discipline, while the other group continued to use physical punishment. Giles-Sims (1983) also found a drop in the number of previously violent families continuing to use physical punishment after a shelter experience. Considering the Straus et al. (1980) survey findings of widespread acceptance of physical punishment as a discipline technique, it is heartening that so many shelter mothers are adopting the no-hitting rule for their family.

Garbarino et al. (1986) has measured the impact of psychological abuse on children who are maltreated, and found that in many cases it has a more detrimental effect over a longer period of time. Children are able to communicate in their own way when they are distressed from the danger to which they are exposed (Garbarino et al., 1991). Cummings suggests that if parents resolve the conflict so that the child is aware of the peaceful resolution, it might mitigate some of the psychological impact (Cummings & Davies, 1994). Others have suggested intervention programs that remediate the damage (Peled, Jaffe, & Edleson, 1995). However, it is important to note that there are some studies that suggest that the very structure of the brain is altered by the biochemical changes from chronic post-traumatic stress reactions.

PHYSIOLOGICAL CHANGES FROM PTSD

Charney et al. (1993) have found changes in the levels of some neurotransmitters associated with PTSD. This includes elevations in adrenaline and noradrenaline that raise the heart rate and blood flow and prepare the body and muscles for quick action in the "fight or flight" reaction to danger that occurs in such traumatic situations. Focus is narrowed and agitation increased, which probably is associated with the difficulties in concentration and attention reported by victims. Greater levels of glucocorticoids help the body to deal with injury by reducing inflammation but also impact on the memory functions of the hippocampus. Memory may also be interfered with by the high levels of endogenous opiates that also reduce the perception of pain. High levels of dopamine in the frontal cortex stimulates thought processes but may also facilitate the intrusive memories and reexperiencing of the trauma. Serotonin levels have also been found to be lowered, which may interfere with regulating emotional arousal that is also associated with PTSD. Rossman (1998) describe these physiological changes and suggests that the prolonged threat to survival may leave the individual in a dysregulated state where perception, cognition and emotional systems are attempting to compensate for the changes being experienced. Children who experience prolonged traumatic stress may well experience permanent and irreversible physiological responses. Goleman (1996) suggests that the new field of psychoneuroimmunology (PNI) can help account for some of the cognitive, emotional and behavioral changes seen in children exposed to abuse in their homes. One of the most critical areas of emotion controlled by this mid-brain system is the social interaction between the child and peers including the lack of development of ability to experience empathy for others.

LEARNING THEORY MODELS OF STRESS AND AGGRESSION

Children tend to model and identify with powerful adults so that they, too, can feel safe and powerful. While children are young, many batterers are reported to be very nurturing fathers. They care for their sons and daughters and, when not angry, show genuine concern over their upbringing. Many battering incidents reportedly occurred over fights about who had a better method of taking care of the child. Yet, as children grow older and become more independent, these men are less able to tolerate the separation and individuation necessary for the child's healthy development. They often become as possessive and intrusive into their child's life as into their wife's. if they take too much control over the child's life, then self-esteem and feelings of self-worth are less likely to develop, and can result in learned helplessness when the child doesn't perceive personal power.

Children who grow up in violent homes show its effects in their overall socialization process as well as in mental health symptoms. The areas most likely to be affected are affectional relationships, anger, sexuality, stress coping techniques, and communication problems. They often develop with certain skill deficits including an inability to deal effectively with confrontation and aggression and have greater confusion about interpersonal relationships. Some children are developmentally delayed while others develop so rapidly they miss major parts of their childhood.

Learning to cope with angry confrontations and aggressive behavior is one of the critical areas for these children as reported in my clinical practice. Some adapt to the seemingly limitless anger expressed in their homes by withdrawing, both emotionally and physically. Unresponsiveness and failure to thrive is noted in some during infancy. Many learn to use television or the stereo as a way to shut out the loud yelling. This is one of the more popular tactics still visible when I visit battered women's shelters. As these children grow older, they are more likely to leave the house when the fights begin. Many continue this withdrawal pattern through the use of drugs and alcohol. Others react to anger in more aggressive ways themselves. Two- and 3-year-old boys and girls have been forced to join their fathers in actually beating their mothers. When their daddy is not present they become his surrogate and help keep their battered mommy in line. No doubt many of these children do commit parent abuse and granny-bashing as they become older. They also become aggressive with each other and perhaps repeat their violent behavior in their own adult homes. This finding gave way to the APA Task Force on Violence and the Family's admonition to always look for other forms of interpersonal violence when one form of violence is found in a family (APA, 1996a).

ANGER

Children who live in violence are exposed to more uncontrolled angry feelings than most. At the worst times, such anger can be displaced onto the children by parents who are too preoccupied with their own survival to adequately parent them. Other times, the parenting they receive is quite appropriate. Most of them learn how to control their parent's anger through manipulative tactics. They learn to expect unpredictable criticism, abuse, and neglect and cope as best they can, terrified of being abandoned. When they are young, they become confused that they are the cause of their parents' anger, and believe that if they behave better then the violence will cease. Thus, they become like other victims, accepting the responsibility for causing their own predicament, but feeling frustrated, depressed, angry, and so on when they cannot stop the aggression. When they are successful in getting the violence to stop, they develop feelings of omnipotence, which only encourage them to try harder for harmony at home. The association with unlimited violence causes them to fear anyone's expression of anger. As they grow older, they are more likely to give in on little things than take a chance of unleashing such rage. Yet, should the rage be unleashed, some become the aggressor in order to handle it by covering up their fear.

OVER-PARENTIFIED CHILDREN

Many of the children reportedly become so extra-sensitive to cues in their environment that they cease behaving like a child and become *over-parentified*, or begin to take care of their parents, so they can reduce the tension. They may try to stop the violence but fear making a mistake as their errors are measured in pain. As they grow older, many stop trying to please and drop out of productive society. Some continue to look toward peers for comfort and support, albeit with gangs and cults, or through sexual exploitation and other antisocial group norms.

PREMATURE SEXUALIZATION

Another area reportedly affected by the home environment is learning to use sexuality as a means of winning approval. Little toddlers can learn to smile cutely, and tell mommy or daddy, "I love you," as seductively as their parental models, to reduce tension and avert an acute battering incident. Sexual expressions can then be substituted for intimate love. The men take advantage of less powerful children by reinforcing and encouraging such behavior. The rate of incest between batterers and their children is much higher than ever suspected. These children—normally girls though in some cases, boys, too—have learned how to manipulate other men using their sexuality. For those who become prostitutes, the lifestyle can be more of a comfortable and familiar choice rather than a reflection of the rebellion professionals often assume it means. Unfortunately, many of these children are exploited and abused in this lifestyle.

ADOLESCENT DEVELOPMENTAL ISSUES

Teen-aged children are reported by others to become withdrawn and passive like their mother, or else, violent like their father. Davidson (1979) cites the tendency of teenage girls to identify with their fathers and also abuse their mothers. Pizzey (1974) describes her British teenagers in sex stereotyped terms; girls are seen as passive, clinging, anxious, with many psychosomatic complaints, while boys were seen as disruptive and aggressive. In many of those families, the girls, especially if they were older, had to do more than the usual child care functions. Hilberman and Munson (1978) report similar findings in their rural Appalachian sample. There is more likelihood of fathers abusing teen-aged children than of mothers committing such abuse (Martin, 1982), and some researchers have suggested that abuse during adolescence is a high-risk factor for later emotional and behavioral disturbance.

ADOLESCENTS AND THE JUVENILE CRIMINAL JUSTICE SYSTEM

Another way to look at the impact of a violent home life on children is to assess the childhood homes of those adolescents who have gotten into some kind of serious difficulty. I have been involved in evaluating several teenagers who have killed their parents. In each case, there was previous identifiable violence in the family. In two cases, incest was also suspected. In another instance, a father shot and killed his teenaged son after the boy previously had broken the father's arm. Upon closer examination, the obvious parent abuse was only the latest form of violent behavior that had occurred in this family. Steinmetz's (1978) analysis of parent abuse and Patterson's (1982) study of coercive family processes support the interrelatedness of these kinds of family violence. Interestingly, Kozu (1999) describes the Japanese family where the first type of abuse that brought public attention was filial abuse where children used violence toward their parents.

The U.S. Department of Justice Office on Juvenile Justice and Delinquency Programs (JJB, 1998) estimated that 2.8 million arrests of persons under the age of 18 were made in 1997 in the United States. This is an increase of 49% over the 1988 level of arrests of juveniles with a violent crime arrest rate of 19% greater than 10 years earlier. Juveniles accounted for one out of five (19%) of all arrests, one out of six (17%) of all violent crimes arrests, and one out of three (35%) of all property crimes arrests in 1997. They were involved in 14% of all murder and aggravated assault arrests, 37% of burglary arrests, 30% of robbery arrests, and 24% of weapons arrests in 1997. Juvenile murder arrests peaked in 1993 with 3,800 youth arrested. In 1997 the number decreased by 39% with 2,500 arrested for murder, which is 11% over the 1988 level. Interestingly, only 6% of those arrested for murder in 1997 were girls. Approximately 26% of the 2.8 million juveniles arrested for all crimes were girls with 16% violent crimes in 1997.

Girls are still more likely to be arrested for status crimes than other crimes in 1997 with 56% of the 1,400 arrested for prostitution, 58% of the 196,100 runaways and 31% of the curfew and loitering arrests. Only 9% of the 52,200 arrested for weapons violations were girls and they were only 9% of the 18,500 arrested for sex offenses other than prostitution. Girls were approximately 15% of the arrests for various crimes involving alcohol and other drugs except for liquor law violations where they made up 30% of those arrested. For most girls, this is the most serious crime that they were arrested for. Like adult women, girls are still being arrested for property crimes with 28% of the 700,000 arrests, forgery and counterfeiting with 39% of the 8,500 arrests, and embezzlement with 45% of the 1,400 arrests made in 1997.

When the statistics are broken down into age groups, it is clear that the younger juveniles, under the age of 15, were most likely to be arrested for arson (67%), sex offenses (51%), vandalism (45%), larceny-theft

(42%), other simple assaults (41%) and runaways (41%). Interestingly, 45% of the vandalism arrests were 14 or younger. Juveniles under the age of 15 made up 32% of the total number of juvenile arrests in 1997.

These data come from the Uniform Crime Reporting program of the F.B.I. who obtain the data from local law enforcement agencies. The major increases that are reported are reflective of greater numbers of juveniles committing crimes and are not due to a greater population increase in the number of juveniles. These arrest rates are not equivalent to number of persons arrested because the same person may be arrested for more than one crime during the year. However they do give us some idea of the contact juveniles are having with the juvenile justice system and for what types of crimes. While fewer juveniles have been arrested for major crimes in the last few years, the numbers are still extremely high. In fact, the number of these youth being sent to adult criminal court rather than being handled in juvenile court is increasing, reflecting a punishment rather than a rehabilitative atmosphere in the community. Unfortunately, there is no information to determine the relationship between exposure to family violence and subsequent arrest in these statistics although other studies of the juvenile system indicate a very high relationship as was discussed earlier. Certainly a prevention and rehabilitation rather than punishment model might be more useful in preventing future violence and crime with these youth.

The sex and violence scandals that are consistently being reported in various state juvenile detention and other facilities indicates that many of these youth simply go from one violent placement to another.

ALIENATED CHILD SYNDROME

A frightening subculture of these children is what I call the *Alienated Child Syndrome* that is seen mostly in teens whose relationships indicate that they are not well connected with other people. These youth can be easily persuaded to accompany others on a variety of missions ranging from a benign searching for companionship for an evening to "wilding" or going out and killing another person. These teens appear to have lost the capacity for empathy for another person and rather, appear to have no visible emotions or connections to societal norms. They are different from teens who join gangs and adopt the gang-norms rather than those of their culture. They seem to be alienated in a manner similar to those described in the popular book, *The Lord of the Flies* (Golding, 1959). I have worked with some of these teens after they are arrested for participating with others in heinous crimes, some of which appear to be senseless. Traumatized while very young, these teens do not subscribe to cultural norms. Nor do they have any connections with other people or groups to help give them guidance. Rather, they agree to go out with a spontaneously put together group of others, most of whom they do not know beyond acquaintanceship. Some of them might be homeless and drifting from one city to another while others might be from local homes, appearing quite normal from the outside, like Eric Harris and Dylan Klebold who gunned down and killed 13 others and themselves during the 1999 Columbine High School massacre in Colorado. There is usually one charismatic leader and one or more "enforcers" who are chosen by the leader to carry out the job of keeping control over the others. In the 1999 Columbine High School case, it appears that Eric Harris was the leader and managed to get help from several others besides Klebold despite his "weird" and "scary" fringe-type behavior.

There are several studies of the family backgrounds of teenagers who show up at drug treatment centers and drop-in centers around the country. Most report a history of abusive family behavior (Freudenberger, 1979). In an interesting study, King and Straus (1981) evaluate the retraining procedures in nonviolence for residents of Odyssey House, a New Hampshire residential drug treatment center. They found that the structured encounter groups along with a strictly enforced prohibition against violent behavior was quite successful in helping individuals use nonviolent and noncoercive problem-solving techniques. The typical home pattern reported for teenage girls who enter into the prostitution and pornography industry is one filled with physical, psychological, and sexual violence according to research from James (1978), Farley and Barkan (1998), and Farley et al. (1998). Barry (1979) describes the abuse that many of the prostitutes have experienced throughout their lives. All in all, adolescence is the time when children (and parents) need the most strength to cope with pressures. Those who have lived with violence at home seem to be more vulnerable to succumbing to those negative pressures. Yet, not all do. Examination of the mediating factors which can protect these vulnerable children is an important next step in research.

IMPLICATIONS FOR PARENTS RAISING CHILDREN

Perhaps, a most important first step is to reexamine our child raising practices, especially discipline methods. Straus et al. (1980) says the marriage license is a hitting license. We must also recognize that when we hit a child to teach that child a lesson, we also send the message that the person(s) who loves you the most has the right to physically hurt you in the name of discipline. When we teach children rigid sex role stereotypes delineating how women and men must perform in society, we also teach them to be insecure if their expectations are not met by the other person. Such sexism combined with violence training surely creates the atmosphere necessary to raise a batterer and a battered woman. To eradicate domestic violence and violence in the community, we must stop modeling both sexist and violent behavior.

CHAPTER SEVEN

Violence, Alcohol, and Drug Use

The association of alcohol and other drugs with domestic violence is well known by those who work with victims and perpetrators. However, the precise relationship has still not been empirically validated. It is commonly thought that alcohol and abuses of some drugs, particularly the amphetamines and cocaine derivatives are associated with violent behavior even though there is no clear cause and effect relationship nor is the strength of the relationship known (Coleman & Straus, 1983; Maiden, 1997; Van Hasselt, Morrison, & Bellak, 1985). Despite the knowledge of this high association, there are few programs that combine treatment for both domestic violence and substance abuse problems. Research has demonstrated that different treatment methods are necessary to change both behaviors (APA, 1996a; Maiden, 1997).

In most countries debate still occurs concerning the role of alcoholism in a variety of criminal offenses. In the United States, where domestic violence is a crime, some states differentiate between voluntary and involuntary substance abuse. This usually means that if it can be proven that the individual's reactions under the influence of alcohol and other drugs are not under his or her control, it could be considered an involuntary drug reaction and the person would have less responsibility under the law than if the drug response was controllable. This often creates a legal argument about whether or not the use of substances is under the person's control if an addiction is present (Collins & Messerschmidt, 1993). While it is generally known that alcohol abuse can increase physically violent behavior in the laboratory settings (Taylor & Gammon, 1975; Zeichner & Pihl, 1979), and other criminal behavior (Powers & Kutash, 1978), some of these effects can be due to expectation of other nonphysiological effects (Goldstein, 1975; Lang, Goeckner, Adesso, & Marlatt, 1975). Gondolf and Fisher (1988) and Jacobson and Gottman (1998) suggest that the high rate of alcoholism in the population of known batterers may play a role in their high arrest rate, also.

Linking alcohol abuse with batterers and battered women, then, is a natural association (Bard & Zacker, 1974; Frieze & Knoble, 1980; Gelles, 1972; Richardson & Campbell, 1980; Van Hasselt, Morrison, & Bellak, 1985). Some have found alcohol and other drug abuse to be a risk marker for more dangerous injuries and death (Browne, 1987; Hotaling & Sugarman, 1986; Walker, 1979). The association of violent behavior with drug abuse is less well documented although it has been appearing in recent reports of Post Traumatic Stress Disorder seen in Vietnam war veterans (Roberts et al., 1982). Given the high expectation of a relationship between alcohol, drug abuse, and violence, we carefully measured its reported use in our research.

ALCOHOL AND OTHER DRUG ABUSE
REPORTED IN STUDY

We measured alcohol and drug use by asking for general information about the batterer and nonbatterer using specific questions associated with each of the four reported battering incidents. The battered woman was also asked about her drug or alcohol use within the 30 days just prior to the interview. Few women reported use of either alcohol or drugs during that period, although more did report use during the acute battering incidents.

Table 26 indicates the women's report on the batterer's and nonbatterer's drug and alcohol use in general, during their relationship. These data support clinical reports that there is much more alcohol abuse, as compared to drug abuse, in those couples engaged in marital violence. In all areas except for marijuana use, the batterer abused more substances, when frequency was used as a measure of substance abuse. Our data are consistent with others' reports that battered women find the batterer's use of alcohol more of a problem than his drug use (Walker, 1979; Frieze & Knoble, 1980).

Our sample indicates a high frequency of alcohol use by both the batterers (67%) and nonbatterers (43%). For Frieze and Knoble's (1980) group, 61% of the batterers would fall in our "frequently" category, with 40% of their control-battered group (not self-reported, but admitting to battering once they were involved in the project), and 32% of the control reporting frequent use of alcohol. In Roy's (1978) study of 150 women who called the New York City hotline for help, she found the women reported that 85% of the men had alcohol or drug-related problems. Labell (1979) found that 72% of the batterers of the women seeking shelter were reported as having alcohol problems, and 28.9%

drug problems. Thus, while the number of frequent users of alcohol and drugs we found may seem high, our findings are consistent with those of other researchers.

Another important question in the field is the nature of the association between substance abuse and specific battering incidents. We asked the women detailed questions concerning the batterer's and her own use of drugs and alcohol at the time of each of the four reported acute battering incidents. The results are found in Table 27.

It is interesting to note that the batterers' use of alcohol and drugs stayed fairly constant over time, with a little more than half using alcohol during the four incidents. This does not tell us, however, if it is the same batterers using alcohol during each incident or if the individuals' patterns varied. It does confirm what others have reported, that alcohol is involved during over one-half of the battering incidents. The battered women reported using alcohol themselves, during about one-fifth of the battering incidents. This is within the normal population range found in other studies, including Calahan's (1970) national survey.

Drug use, again, is reported less frequently, with the batterers using drugs during about one-sixth of the battering incidents. Battered women's use of drugs was lower, about 8% for the first three incidents and 4% for the last one. One possible explanation for the apparent decrease toward the end is that they needed to be drug-free to perceive the alternatives involved in terminating the relationship.

The question of the relationship between alcohol use and the degree, severity, and number of battering incidents was explored in an analysis of the data done to meet part of the doctoral program requirements for one of the data analysts (Eberle, 1982). The discriminant results of the analysis she used are reported here. (Some of the numbers may be different from our other analysis, as these data were run using a smaller sample, N = 390.) A multivariate approach was used to discriminate differences between those batterers reported to abuse alcohol and those who did not use any alcohol at all. Our data permitted comparisons of multiple measures of violence, some of which were used to create composite measures.

This resulted in the creation of the following seven variables, which were used in the discriminant analysis: (1) the total number of battering incidents reported; (2) severity of injuries inflicted on the battered woman; (3) perceptions or actual violence toward the children in the family; (4) the batterer's criminal background; (5) the victim's use of alcohol; (6) the average age of the batterer for the four battering incidents reported; and (7) the batterer's socioeconomic status. The dependent variable used was a dummy variable created by computing the batterer's alcohol use-rate over the four battering incidents. Only those who either did not use alcohol at all or used it excessively through all four battering incidents were selected, decreasing the N to 131. There were 73 subjects whose batterers reportedly did not use any alcohol and 58 who used it excessively.

This procedure produced an interesting finding: The frequency distributions depict a bimodal distribution, with each battering incident having about 50% of the subjects using excessive alcohol, and the other half being sober. However, when looking at batterers' drinking patterns individually, they were not consistent in its use across the four battering incidents. For example, it was reported that the batterer could use "a lot" of alcohol during one incident, "some" during another incident, and "none" during the third. This inconsistent pattern of alcohol abuse across all the battering incidents had not been reported before, perhaps because multiple measures had not been available.

The women's reports of the batterer's overall drinking pattern, and her reports of his alcohol use during these incidents were correlated at .77. The mean differences between the two groups on the variables measured demonstrated that distinctions could be made using the variables themselves. The discriminant function coefficients show that two variables make statistically significant contributions to differences between no alcohol and excessive alcohol users. Battered women who use alcohol are more likely to be older than those who do not (.46). Three of the four violence measures contributed less significantly to the discriminant function, and the fourth, criminal behavior, was dropped from the analysis during the stepwise selection procedure. Adding other violence correlates to that variable might have given it more power. The variable which represented the degree and severity of the woman's injuries was approaching significance (.26), lending some empirical support to the clinical observation that batterers who abuse alcohol inflict more serious injuries on the women. More research is still suggested in this area.

This analysis shows some support for the discriminant function of the other variables used, as they are in the predicted direction, but they still do not make a major contribution. The .25 coefficient for the variable measuring social status indicates that violent men from a low socioeconomic status may be more likely to be alcohol abusers. This finding is supported by the literature which indicates that, in general, there are more drinking problems in the lower socioeconomic class (Calahan, 1970). Thus, batterers may not be different from the rest of the population when it comes to drinking problems. This is an important finding to consider, as Calahan's (1970) data indicated a 15% alcohol abuse rate for men and a 7 to 14% alcohol abuse rate for women. Our sample of batterers and battered women also falls into that range, when the consistent pattern over more than one battering incident is used as the measure.

ROLE OF ALCOHOL AND OTHER DRUGS IN BATTERERS

Understanding the role of substance abuse in batterers is complex and not completely answered by this study. The literature continues to report a high association between violence in the home and alcohol abuse. Graham (1980), for example, reviewed four models that help explain the association between alcohol use and aggression that included (1) a direct-cause model where alcohol abuse and aggression are connected by lowering inhibitions; (2) an indirect-cause model in which aggression is mediated by psychophysiological changes in the way messages are received and processed; (3) an indirect-cause model that suggests that the batterer's power is maintained when anxiety and tension are reduced by alcohol; and (4) a model that suggests alcohol and aggression are related to other factors such as an abuse-prone personality or learned behavior where the two factors co-exist together.

Maiden (1997) cites Graham's work but adds a developmental perspective. He proposes that alcoholism, in particular, "is the result of the excessive use of alcohol as a means of coping with situations where other coping mechanisms have either eroded or have not been learned in the first place. The disinhibition, dulling of emotions, and initial euphoria experienced when drinking heavily provides direct reinforcement for alcohol use and can subsequently provide reinforcement for abuse as a coping mechanism." (Maiden, pp. 37–38). In this model, the use of alcohol covaries together with the escalation of the domestic violence. Although this model would suggest that if the alcohol abuse were to be stopped, the domestic violence would also cease, in fact, Maiden's study of batterers who attended various drug treatment programs did not find that the violent behavior stopped even when the substance abuse was significantly reduced or eliminated.

ROLE OF ALCOHOL AND OTHER DRUG ABUSE IN BATTERED WOMEN

Alcohol and drug abuse has been found to be used as a form of self-medication to block the intense emotions that are often experienced by abuse victims, particularly physical and sexual assault victims. Kilpatrick found that the highest risk factor for alcoholism in women is exposure to prior abuse. Goldberg (1995) reviewed the literature on substance abusing women and found that although they were a diverse group, the major risk factors were not poverty or exposure to substance abusing parents but rather childhood physical or sexual abuse, adult victimization by domestic violence, and a partner who abuses substances. It is interesting that in this study, too, the women who reported to being alcohol-dependent were also living with alcohol-dependent partners. Some of those women said that they avoided further abuse by going out and drinking with their partner. It is not uncommon for women to become addicted to drugs that are supplied by their batterer who then has greater power and control over the woman as he dispensed their drugs based on how they behaved.

In the 1980s the government began to arrest and prosecute pregnant women who potentially were harming their children through the ingestion of alcohol and other drugs. However, when a closer look was taken at these women, it became clear that over 90% of them were battered women (Walker, 1991). Research by others found that there were no treatment programs for substance abusing, pregnant battered women. Battered women shelters would not take them nor would drug treatment centers. Putting them in jail was not a solution, especially since detoxification needed special techniques to protect both the mother and the baby. Removing the baby from the mother at birth exacerbated the child's potential developmental problems which appeared to have a direct relationship with the degree of bonding that could occur between the mother and the child. The best solution, of course, was to provide assistance to the woman to stop her substance use, get out of the violent relationship and bond with her baby. Given the fact that many battered women temporarily get more depressed when they leave an abusive relationship and are in greater danger especially if the batterer stalks and finds her, this is a problem without satisfactory resolution much of the time.

INTERVENTIONS

Although our data leave no question but that batterers are reported to drink and use drugs more frequently than does the battered woman, further study of these variables in abusive relationships is needed to provide more specific information. For example, in an analysis of the 50 homicide and attempted homicide cases in which the abused victim becomes aggressive toward the abuser, there is almost always report of alcohol abuse in one or both parties. The level of severity of injuries from the assaultive combat while intoxicated appears to be more serious in many of those cases. This finding held during an analysis of 100 additional homicide cases (Walker, 1989a).

The use of alcohol may start out to calm one's nerves or be a pleasant relaxant, but it quickly takes on menacing properties. So too for drug use which also reportedly starts out as a pleasant way to overcome tensions and anxieties, but soon takes over as a way of life. In one of our cases, the woman described how her entire days were spent trying to find ways to obtain sufficient prescription drugs to keep her batterer calm so he'd be less likely to beat her up. She, too, quickly became addicted but soon allowed herself to be caught by the police for passing forged prescriptions, perhaps as a way of finding safety in jail. In other cases that escalate to homicidal or suicidal levels, it has been found that cocaine and its derivatives, particularly crack and crank and amphetamines and methamphetamines are the drugs most likely to be used in addition to alcohol (Walker, 1989a, 1994).

It is important for drug and alcohol treatment programs to recognize that violent behavior cannot be stopped through alcohol/drug counseling. Neither will a substance-abusing battered woman gain the assistance she needs to become independent and remain violence-free. Programs which appropriately deal separately with the violence and the substance abuse are crucial. Communities that have special domestic violence courts often have a drug court that is associated with it. Thus, even if an alcoholic batterer becomes sober, he will not become a nonbatterer until he goes through a process designed to teach or help batterers become nonviolent. And women who abuse substances to self-medicate from the symptoms of PTSD need specialized treatment for the abuse they have experienced in addition to treatment for alcohol and other drugs.

Two Theoretical Perspectives

Personality Characteristics and the Battered Woman Syndrome

The limited psychological literature that existed prior to this research study attempted to measure the intrapsychic personality characteristics of battered women, looking for signs of mental illness. Women who remained in violent relationships were thought to have serious pathology that included a masochistic need to be hurt and punished. The Snell, Rosenwald and Robey (1964) study is typical of the reports that were in the psychology literature. Based on their interviews, Snell and his colleagues concluded that wifebeater's wives were frigid and had other personality characteristics that made them undesirable as wives. The implication that these authors give is that "good" wives don't get beaten and those who are abused must have flaws in their personalities—in other words, "they deserve it"! This attitude of mental health professionals still exists today amongst those who are uneducated about the problems that face battered women. Although we were the first empirical study to demonstrate that the cluster of symptoms seen in battered women was a syndrome that came from the abuse rather than a cause of it, most subsequent research have supported our findings.

DO BATTERED WOMEN HAVE A PERSONALITY DISORDER?

The search for personality characteristics that identify battered women continued until this research was originally published and then, it began to wane. Starr (1978) looked for a cluster of symptoms using popular personality test measures with battered women. Shainess (1979, 1985) attempted to apply a feminist perspective to a psychoanalytic interpretation of personality dynamics in battered women. She was unable to do so without contradiction, which left her needing to defend the psychoanalytic concept of *masochism,* a totally unacceptable concept in feminist theory. At one point she tried to equate *masochism* with *learned helplessness,* which is not accurate. Others have used psychoanalytic frameworks together with a family therapy approach. Even more interesting are those who make equally unsuccessful attempts to use the behavioral construct of learned helplessness as a bridge between other theoretical perspectives. Usually this is because they define learned helplessness literally, without any relationship to the meanings ascribed by the theoretical underpinnings.

THE *DSM-III-R* BATTLE WITH THE PSYCHIATRISTS

Interestingly, the construct of *masochism* did not go away during these past 15 years despite the lack of data to support it. Rather, the psychiatrists who create the categories for the *Diagnostic and Statistical Manual of Mental Disorders (DSM)* attempted to bring it back as a new category to be called, *masochistic personality disorder* at first and then in response to criticism, changed it to *self-defeating personality disorder.* It was to be listed under the section of Personality Disorders in the *DSM-III-R,* an unscheduled revision of the DSM system that was published in 1986. Until 1985, the DSM was published every 12 years to correspond to the publication of the *International Classification of Diseases (ICD).* The next edition, to be a companion volume to the *ICD-10* was due to be published in the early 1990s. The *DSM-III* was a new system of categorization that attempted to make diagnosis more reliable although it added about 400 pages of diagnoses and their criteria from the older, *DSM-II.* Many mental health professionals from a variety of disciplines were asked to participate in the development of the *DSM-III* so it came as a great surprise when the same group were not asked to collaborate with this revision. Fortunately, the psychiatrists' Committee for Women in Psychiatry found out about the plan and contacted the psychologists' Committee for Women in Psychology that was meeting in Washington, D.C. at the same time, and strong protests were made resulting in the proposed *masochistic personality disorder* category being included in the Appendix as a category requiring further study with the name-change to *self-defeating personality disorder.* The subsequent research did not support that such a distinct personality disorder existed so in 1994, the controversial category was dropped from the *DSM-IV.* None-the-less, the arguments among women psychiatrists and men and women psychologists exposed the lack of validity criteria for many of the newer diagnoses contained within the *DSM* nosology system even though there was reliability for some categories and calls for reforms were sounded. As Caplan (1995), Kutchins and Kirk (1997), and Lerman (1996) make clear, these reforms have not yet occurred and the entire diagnostic system has been held up to ridicule in the popular press.

PSYCHOLOGICAL ASSESSMENT OF PERSONALITY

Rosewater's (1982, 1985a, 1985b) research on Minnesota Multiphasic Personality Inventory (MMPI) profiles for over 100 battered women was a turning-point that helped measure and explain some of the initial misdiagnoses. Rosewater found that her sample appeared to have profiles that were similar to other emotionally disturbed women, particularly those with schizophrenia and borderline diagnoses. But when using a subscale analysis, inconsistencies were found that could differentiate battered women from the others. Rosewater concluded that it would be quite easy to misdiagnose battered women as having a serious mental illness if cautions weren't taken to account for the influence of having to cope with battering. For example, it is reasonable for a battered woman to believe she has been betrayed and that someone is out to get her without it being indicative of paranoid ideation. And, it is common for battered women to become cognitively confused without having psychotic ideation.

The analysis of personality from the Rorschach test using the Exner scoring and interpretation helps describe how the battered woman sees her personal world. The test draws upon the unique and common perceptions that individuals give to very ambiguous stimuli, inkblots. Using statistical frequencies together with personality theory, the Exner system makes some predictions of an individual's ability to organize their world while under stress or in less demanding situations. It is particularly useful in helping to understand those battered women who are unable to deal directly with their abusive environment.

Millon (1991) developed a test that specifically assesses for personality disorders based on the theoretical perspectives that suggest that they are infrequently found in the population, usually under 7%, pervasive across all areas of the person's functioning, and very stable and resistant to treatment. Obviously, the difference between a psychological symptom that could also be observed as a coping strategy when living in terror of further abuse and that is easily ameliorated by changing the situation and helping the woman find safety, does not meet this definition of personality disorder. Furthermore, the lack of either reliability or validity in differentiating all categories of personality disorders and the sexist bias that underlies the criteria used, all contribute to the admonition for psychologists not to give a battered woman a personality disorder diagnosis until after the person has been in therapy for a minimum of 6 months (Walker, 1994).

Herman's (1992) formulation of a complex post traumatic stress disorder diagnosis that occurs in many female trauma victims further explains the inherent problems in looking for a personality theory to explain battered women's psychological functioning. She found that many trauma victims, particularly those who have experienced multiple forms of trauma beginning in childhood, develop a complex form of PTSD that is directly related to the experiences and not personality. When their situation becomes safe, many of the so-called personality traits drop out spontaneously or respond to therapy unlike personality disorders. Barnett and LaViolette (1993) use behavioral constructs that also are more consistent with the clinical and research data on battered women while Hansen and Harway (1993) add a feminist family therapy approach.

MEASURING BATTERED WOMEN'S PERSONALITIES IN THE STUDY

The Battered Woman Syndrome Study approached the notion of personality characteristics from two perspectives. First, we wanted to measure those characteristics commonly associated with mental illness to look at the frequency with which they appear in currently and previously battered women. While we understood that cause and effect could not be gleaned from these data, some information could be gained concerning the role of personality characteristics for the battered women studied. Second, using a social learning theory analysis, it was expected that environmental forces would impact on an individual's personality, which would create certain predictable behavioral, cognitive, and emotional responses. Measuring personality variables from these perspectives lent clarity to what it is like for a woman to experience repeated violence.

Although at the beginning of the research it seemed obvious that all battered women couldn't be the same personality types, it seemed important to look at each woman's history for commonalties. It was suggested that both modeling of previously learned aggressive behavior and responses (Bandura, 1973), as well as rigid traditional sex role stereotypes (Walker, 1979), would create a greater potential or vulnerability for a man or woman to remain in a battering relationship. Actually entering into such a relationship was thought to be accidental, especially since the Straus et al. (1980) epidemiological study found such abuse to be tolerated by most people and actually present at least once during the year for 28% of their sample. Whether or not living with violence irreversibly changes a person's personality has not been measured, since we would need a large-scale epidemiological study to follow women across a life cycle to do so. However, different patterns emerge when women are measured across the life span, each occupying a different place in relation to the time of their battering.

ATTITUDES TOWARD WOMEN SCALE (AWS)

To measure the level of traditionality of the woman's own attitudes toward the role of women as well as her perception of the attitudes of significant other people in her environment, the Attitudes Toward Women Scale (AWS) was administered at four different times during the interview. The results of the battered woman's own attitudes and her perceptions of her mother's, father's, batterer's, and nonbatterer's attitudes toward the rights and roles of women are reported in Table 27. The woman's AWS score is reported twice. She was administered the original 55-item (Spence & Helmreich, 1972) which was first scored, and then rescored for the 25 items in the shortened version (Spence, Helmreich & Stapp, 1973). This permitted ease of comparison, with the scores on the shortened version representing her perception of her mother, father, batterer and nonbatterer's sex role attitudes. The sample size varies, as some of the subjects did not complete all of the scales.

The 25 items selected for the shortened version of the original Likert-type scale are highly correlated with the full test (Spence et al., 1973). The scores presumably reflect the degree to which an individual holds traditional or liberal views about women's roles. The higher the score, the more liberal the views. The normative sample consisted of college men, women, their fathers and their mothers. The norms for each group are also reported in Table 28.

It is interesting to note that, in our sample, the reported mothers' mean of 40.16 is about the same as college students' mothers' reported means of 41.86. The reported father's AWS score of 27.06 is considerably more traditional than the college students' fathers' reported mean score of 39.22. Thus, the attitudes toward the role of women were either different in the battered women's childhood homes than in those where the normative sample grew up, or they learned to think about gender roles differently (Caplan & Caplan, 1994).

As our sample of batterers and nonbatterers have a greater age span than either college males or their fathers, their AWS scores are more difficult to compare. Nonetheless, the nonbatterer's mean of 42.88 is about midway between the college student's 44.80 and father's 39.22, which could logically reflect the age differences. The batterer's score of 25.67 is sharply below the others. Both the batterer and the woman's father are perceived as being much more traditional toward women's roles than the woman's mother, the nonbatterer, or herself. Significance tests were not computed due to the difficulty in comparing the normative sample with our sample's heterogeneous age and educational level and the fact that these are the battered woman's perceptions, not the actual scores from each person.

The battered woman's mean score of 58.48 is higher than college females' mean score of 50.26 or mothers' mean score of 41.86. We originally predicted that these women would score at a more traditional level given their often subservient behavior toward their abusive partners. Also, given our sample's age range, it would be expected that they would score somewhere midway between those two groups. Instead, the battered women view themselves as more liberal in their sex role views than the other groups. Using the original 55-item norms, our subjects' mean score of 118.24 is more liberal than 81% of the normative group. This is a surprising finding, as it was predicted that battered women would perceive themselves as having more traditional attitudes toward women's roles. The prediction that she would view the batterer and her father as holding traditional views, however, was supported.

LOCUS OF CONTROL

Attribution style is a concept from social psychology where people are believed to have consistent ways to view what happened to them. These beliefs can be categorized into "internal" and "external" types. Those who are more "internal" believe that they have control over their lives—it is their abilities and competence or lack of it that results in what happens in their lives. Those who are more "external" believe that other people and situations are more likely to control what happens in their lives. Attribution theory suggests that whatever style the person has, it is pretty stable over time and across situations.

As a part of the standardized tests administered at the end of the interview, each subject was asked to complete Levenson's (1972) locus of control scale to measure her attribution style. This scale was preferred over the more common Rotter's (1966) I-E scale. Levenson's items are written to apply personally to each subject (i.e., whereas Rotter says "most people's lives," Levenson says "my life"), and this scale measures three distinct types of control: internal, powerful others, and chance (IPC), rather than the broader categories of internal and external control. The Levenson test gives a score for each of the three areas of attribution while the other tests put internal-external on a continuum.

Based upon clinical observations that a battered woman's life is usually controlled by the batterer, it was predicted that battered women would score significantly higher than the norm on the powerful others and chance scales, significantly lower than the norm on the internal scale. It was also hypothesized that women who were out of the battering relationship would be more internally controlled than women still in the battering relationship. As shown in Table 29 there were several unexpected findings.

Internal Scale

We predicted that battered women in general, and especially those women still in battering relationships, would score lower than the norm on the internal scale. What we found was that each of our subgroups, shown in Table 29, scored significantly higher than the norm. In other words, battered women, both in and out of the relationship, saw themselves as having a great deal of control over what happens to them.

It may be that battered women do believe they control their own lives. Battered women often manipulate the environment in order to minimize the opportunity for the batterer to find a reason to be angry. Most of our sample indicated that to avoid getting the batterer angry they would, on a day-to-day basis, keep the kids quiet so as not to disturb him (84%); make sure the house was clean when he came home (84%); cook something they knew he would like (87%); avoid subjects they knew he did not like to discuss (91%); and avoid starting conversations with him, waiting instead until he began talking to them (70%). In addition, 40% of the women thought that they could sometimes control the batterer's behavior. It may be this sense of internal control that is the hope that allows the battered woman to believe she will be able to change the batterer or the environment in such a way that things will get better.

Powerful Others Scale

We predicted that battered women, especially those women still in the battering relationship, would score significantly higher than the norm on the powerful others scale. Once again, our results were surprising. While significance tests between Levenson's norms and our sample, as shown in Table 29, confirm our prediction for the total sample and those women out of the relationship, battered women still in the relationship did not score significantly higher than the norm on this scale. Perhaps, for those women still in a battering relationship to acknowledge that their lives are chiefly controlled by powerful others (the batterer), the women would also have to accept the fact that they will not be able to change him or the environment to prevent further beatings. While in a violent relationship, the battered woman is so involved in doing whatever it takes to keep her batterer happy that she perceives this as being in control. The reality is that he does have control—by keeping her in fear of receiving another beating if she doesn't prevent him from getting angry.

Chance Scale

As predicted, battered women, both in and out of the relationship, scored significantly higher than the norm on the chance score. This is shown in Table 29. These findings are consistent with other data about abusive relationships.

A battered woman's life is often unpredictable. The meal she cooked last week, which conformed exactly to what he requested, may be dumped on the floor this week because now he says that he doesn't like it. There will be times, when no matter how carefully she plans things to keep him from getting angry, someone at work or a stranger on the street will make him mad and he takes it out on her. When this happens she resolves to try harder next time. Even the cycle of violence appears to make him unpredictable. He can be violent and abusive one minute and very loving the next. One battering may be followed by a great deal of loving contrition, while another time he may show little or no loving behavior. Given these uncertainties, battered women's attributional style may indeed be more complex than is measured by a single dimension locus of control scale.

In conclusion, contrary to expectations, most battered women in our sample perceived three different levels of control over their lives. While this finding is probably peculiar to the Levenson scale we chose to use, others are cautioned in interpreting other locus of control measures that do not report all three scale norms. These findings suggest that the internal-external locus of control dichotomy does not explain battered women's attributions. Those women still in a violent relationship did not report powerful others as being in total control of their lives. Perhaps one factor necessary for a woman to be able to leave the violent relationship is the realization that her batterer is, in fact, exercising his control of her everyday activities and of her life.

SELF-ESTEEM

The women's self-esteem was measured by use of a typical Likert-style semantic differential scale. She completed this scale for herself, for women in general, and for men in general. These results are shown in Table 30 and Figure 8.1.

It was predicted that battered women's self-esteem would be quite low and our results, surprisingly, show the opposite. The women reported that they saw themselves in a more positive way than they perceived either other women or men in general. Surprisingly, they perceived themselves as stronger, more independent, and more sensitive than other women or men. This finding of a positive self-image is unusual and inconsistent with current theories about battered women. It was not surprising that they saw themselves as having more positive characteristics than they viewed for men, but it would have been more likely to have found both with low self-esteem. It is possible that there is a bias toward needing to gain approval that influences battered women's cognitive responses. The desire to please the interviewer, like the need to please their batterers, may override their ability to accurately know and label their feelings.

An alternative and more likely explanation is that battered women develop a positive sense of self from having survived in a violent relationship and that causes them to believe they are equal to or better than others, at least in the ability to manage a complex and difficult partnered relationship. However, there is incompatibility between these high self-esteem findings and the reports of depression as reported in the CES-D results and the low self-esteem and K scores reported on other samples of battered women's MMPI's (Rosewater, 1985). Given these confusing results, more careful study into what goes into the measure of the self-concept of battered women is recommended.

DEPRESSION

Each woman was administered the CES-D scale (Radloff, 1977) to measure current depression. It was hypothesized that battered women are at high risk for a depressive disorder. Recent research has demonstrated that depression is a frequent mental health problem for women

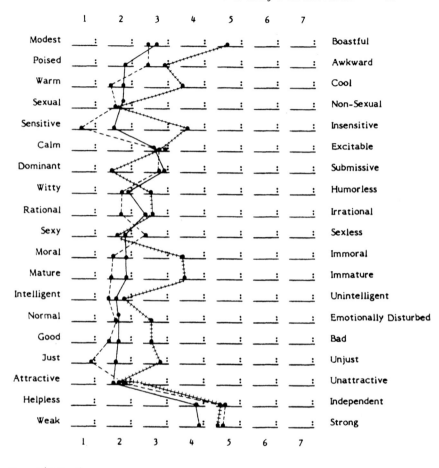

--- Woman (Subject)
— Women (In General)
⁺⁺⁺ Men (In General)

FIGURE 8.1 Perception of self-esteem for battered women, women in general, and men in general, as reported by battered women.

(Radloff & Cox, 1981; Weissman & Klerman, 1977). Women who are married, separated, or divorced are found to be more vulnerable than women who remain single. Those women who are also unemployed, and have young children at home, are at the highest risk to become depressed. The literature also suggests that the learned helplessness theory, field tested in this study, is synonymous with exogeneous depression, due to the perceived powerlessness over life events (Costello, 1978; Rizley, 1978; Seligman, 1975; Abramson, Seligman & Teasdale, 1978). Thus, we expected our sample of battered women to be in a high-risk group and for this to be reflected in high score on the depression inventory. These results can be found in Table 31.

Our sample received an average mean score of 18.19, which is well above the high-risk cut-off score of 16 and twice as large as the epidemiological study samples' means of 9.92 and 9.13. Thus, as predicted, the battered women in our study were highly depressed as measured by the CES-D. Further analysis revealed that the women in our sample who were young (18–24) were also more depressed than the older women. Although our sample's mean score was higher than Radloff's, it supports her data that indicate that younger women are more likely to become depressed than older ones. The battered women who were unemployed also showed considerably more depression on the CES-D than those who were employed outside the home, again consistent with the Radloff epidemiological study.

Surprisingly, for our sample the married women's mean depression score was 16.86, while those not currently married scored 18.67. When we looked at just those who were still married to the batterer at the time of the interview, we found that their mean score was 16.50. This finding is inconsistent with our predictions that women living with violence would be more depressed than those who have escaped the battering relationship. Women out of the battering relationship had a mean score of 18.74. This suggests that depression can be a consequence of terminating a battering relationship as it is for terminating any other kind of relationship. However, it wasn't until a number of years later that we began to realize that terminating a battering relationship did not stop the violence. Large numbers of batterers stalk, harass and use the legal system to continue their abusive control over the women long after the relationship has been terminated. In fact, some battered women are actually more safe when they live with the batterer than when apart (Walker, 1994). Thus, his continued abuse and the no-win situation they found themselves in may well exacerbate their depression.

Other measures of depression were also included in the interview. Most of these women did not appear to be clinically depressed to the interviewers. When comparing subjects' high CES-D scores with these other indices on which the battered women performed inconsistently, it would still be expected that the depression scores would be associated with lower scores on the self-esteem measure. As reported, however, our subjects scored high on the self-esteem measure, presenting a puzzling contradiction particularly since semantic differential measures usually tap into the affective domain. The learned helplessness and other depression theories would predict disturbance in the affective domain for battered women who score as high as our sample on the CES-D. One possible explanation is that the battered women modify their feelings about themselves in a positive way as a coping style to continue to function despite chronic depression. This explanation would fit with Seligman's theories of optimism as an antidote to depression (Seligman, 1991, 1994).

We also expected to find a pessimistic view of the world to be a concomitant cognitive perception for battered women. Such negative cognitions would be predicted by Beck's (1976) theories on depression. Again, our sample of battered women showed inconsistent thought patterns on questions designed to measure cognition. For example, one-half of the subjects agreed with the following statements:

I sometimes can't help wondering if anything is worthwhile. (48% agree)

Nowadays, a person has to live pretty much for today and let tomorrow take care of itself. (58% agree)

However, only one-third agree with these similar statements:

In spite of what some people say, the lot of the average person is getting worse, not better. (34% agree)

It's hardly fair to bring a child into the world with the way things look for the future. (31% agree)

On a question measuring cognitive perception of other people's motives toward the subject, 59% of the battered women felt people would generally try to be fair. Thus, our sample of battered women was not consistent in demonstrating the negative cognitions and moods we would have expected.

Lewinsohn's behavioral reinforcement theory of depression might help to explain some of our findings on depression (Lewinsohn, 1975; Lewinsohn, Steinmetz, Larson, & Franklin, 1981). It postulates that depression occurs when there is a sharp reduction in the amount of positive reinforcement people receive. A lower rate of rewards would result in a lower response rate, or passivity, which then spirals downward into a depressed state. Cognitive and affective disturbances occur simultaneously with the downward spiral or are a consequence of the lowered reinforcement rate. This is similar to the learned helplessness theory that postulates the lowered behavioral response rate or passivity, as a learned response to uncontrollable trauma. It also postulates distorted perceptions in the cognitive and affective domain. While the original learned helplessness theory did not specify when these cognitive and affective perceptions occurred, the reformulations suggest an attributional style which serves as a cognitive set for a depressive state to develop.

The analysis of lower reinforcement rates presented with the results of the Walker Cycle Theory of Violence, discussed in Chapter 10, demonstrates that women who were out of the battering relationship left after the ratio between the tension-building and loving-contrition phases sharply diverged. Women who were still in the battering relationship seemed to report more positive reinforcement (loving-contrition) following the last battering incident they discussed. According to the Lewinsohn behavioral reinforcement model of depression, these battered women might have been scoring lower on the CES-D scale because they were still receiving some rewards from the relationship, despite the negative factor of the violence. Once the cost benefit ratio changes, however, and the rate of reinforcement decreases, then the women may be more inclined to leave the relationship, but may subsequently become depressed as a result of the separation.

Since we did not match those women who scored low on the CES-D with those who had high phase three loving-contrition rates, this explanation cannot be directly corroborated. But clinical reports consistently refer to battered women who return to their abuse because they were too lonely, too frightened, too overwhelmed, and too depressed to continue on their own.

To ascertain the relationship between the CES-D and other personality indices, we correlated the seven summary scores and added the current health scale scores, since depression is often related to poor physical health. These results can be found in Table 32.

The correlation matrix shows a strong relationship between anomie, the measure of helplessness we've included, and the CES-D, with an r of .40. The CES-D is also correlated with the Powerful Others ($r = .35$) and Chance ($r = .36$) dimension scores on the Levenson IPC. This suggests that there may be a cognitive component to their depression that isn't measured very well by affective measures. The high correlation of the CES-D with the Health Scale (.46) and with the self-esteem measure (.36) would also support that our subjects were really clinically depressed. The correlation matrix strengthens the faith we have in the robust nature of the CES-D as a measure of this depression.

Radloff and Rae (1979) presented another model of depression, which may be the most helpful in interpreting our results. This model suggested that there is a causal sequence in which affective, cognitive, behavioral, and somatic realms of symptoms are logically linked. It looks at susceptibility or vulnerability, and exposure to those factors that precipitate or trigger these vulnerabilities. Radloff and Cox (1981) suggest that:

> The cognitive dimension of depression (the expectation that goals cannot be reached by any responses available to the person) is a basic factor in learned susceptibility to depression. Depression itself will not occur unless a goal situation occurs. In other words, the precipitating factors that activate this kind of susceptibility are goals (rewards desired or punishments to be escaped or avoided). Given a goal situation and the expectation that nothing the person can do will influence the outcome, then the person is unlikely to try to do anything. This lack of activity is like the motivational/ behavioral dimension of depression. Depending on the environment and the generality of helpless cognitions, such as a person would be faced with more and more inescapable punishments and fewer and fewer rewards. This would be expected to result in pain, anxiety, sadness and lack of enjoyment (the affective dimension of depression). (p. 339)

Radloff's work has identified a sex difference in susceptibility and in exposure to precipitating factors of depression. Being a woman and having been raised with sex role stereotyped behavior has conditioned learned patterns which make women who must deal with violent relationships more susceptible to developing depression. It is probable that the cognitive attributions associated with developing learned helplessness are different from the more generalized sense of hopelessness that Lewinsohn predicts develops at the same time or following a lowered reinforcement rate period. Our results, then, support the prediction that battered women will be at high risk for depression. We did not anticipate, however, that it would still be present in women who have long been out of the violent relationship. This finding is puzzling in a manner similar to those who have used the MMPI to assess battered women and find significant elevations on the depression indices.

Another possible explanation for the varied stages of depression measured by the CES-D and inconsistencies with other measures we used has emerged during the intervening years. Seligman has moved from the concept of learned helplessness that he created in the laboratory (see Chapter 9 for further discussion) to the prevention of depression by changing people's outlook to an optimistic rather than pessimistic style. We know that the impact of a particular trauma is different depending on the mental health status of the individual at the time of trauma, the prior resilience of coping strategies, the person's stress response, and the level of support received from the community. Perhaps the healing process is also individualized and the measures used here picked up the stage of healing in victims that was not otherwise recorded. Since depression is one of the areas that is significantly impacted upon in most trauma victims, often measured as an avoidance symptom, we may have found major differences had we had the ability to use one of the newer impact from trauma measures such as the Trauma Symptom Inventory (TSI) that gives several different depression indices (Briere & Elliott, 1998). In any case, this issue still needs further study.

Learned Helplessness
and Battered Women

When I first proposed using the theoretical construct of *learned helplessness* to help explain why women found it difficult to escape a battering relationship (Walker, 1978, 1979) I received support from scientists (Barnett & LaViolette, 1993) and criticism from the feminist battered women's community (Bowker, 1993; Gondolf & Fisher, 1988). Learned helplessness was confused with being helpless, and not its original intended meaning of *having lost the ability to predict that what you do will make a particular outcome occur*. At first I was puzzled about why a theoretical concept that accounted for the how the aversive stimulation of the battering incidents themselves became paired in an identifiable pattern with reinforcements such as the positive parts of the relationship would be so harshly criticized. A learning theory explanation of the effects that are so easily observed in battered women's coping behavior meant that what was learned could be unlearned, an important finding for developing future intervention strategies. The theory provided a coherent and reasonable counter-explanation to the prevailing theory of the times—masochism or more permanent personality traits in battered women that caused them to provoke their abuse and to stay in violent relationships (Shainess, 1979, 1985). Learned helplessness is a research-based theory, it is simple and elegant, and furthermore gives direction for prevention as well as intervention.

The criticism then, was a good lesson in battered women's feminist politics, the subject of which could fill another book! I must say I was disappointed that there could not be a good scientific data-based debate with its critics, primarily because they did not understand the theory. Rather they were reacting to the name that contained the word "helplessness," a concept that advocates were working very hard to deconstruct from the image of a battered woman. Eventually even those colleagues who understood the concept of learned helplessness began to reject it in favor of post traumatic stress theory, which was first introduced in the late 1970s and appeared for the first time in the 1980 version of the *Diagnostic and Statistical Manual of Mental Disorders, Third Edition (DSM-III)*. Interestingly, even the PTSD theory now has been rejected by some of its original supporters in favor of no coherent mental health explanation that might be misused against battered women to mistakenly pathologize them (Dutton, 1992; Dutton & Goodman, 1994).

Today, the debate over the misinterpretation of the term, "learned helplessness" is less important, particularly since the originator of the theory, Martin Seligman, has looked at the less controversial flip side, *learned optimism* (Seligman, 1991, 1994). Instead of concentrating on the negative, Seligman has used the same concepts, but by renaming them in a more positive direction, it makes them more politically correct. And while Battered Woman Syndrome has been similarly criticized for making it easier to continue to pathologize battered women, it is my opinion that as a subcategory of PTSD, it is the most useful diagnostic category to use for battered women when it is necessary to use a diagnostic formulation. In any case, the discussion about the theory of learned helplessness and learned optimism is relevant to finding a theory that helps to explain the phenomenon of domestic violence that many can embrace.

HISTORY OF LEARNED HELPLESSNESS RESEARCH

The theoretical concept of learned helplessness was adapted in this research to help explain why women who could develop such intricate and life-saving coping strategies, found it so difficult to escape a battering relationship (Walker, 1978, 1979). Seligman and his colleagues discovered that when laboratory animals (usually dogs, in their early experiments) were repeatedly and noncontingently shocked, they became unable to escape from a painful situation, even when escape was quite possible and readily apparent to animals that had not undergone helplessness training. Seligman (1975) likened what he labeled— *learned helplessness*—to a kind of human depression, and showed that it had cognitive, motivational, and behavioral components. The inability to predict the success of one's actions was considered responsible for the resulting perceptual distortions. Although not tested in this study, Seligman's theory was further refined and reformulated, based on later laboratory trials with human subjects (Abramson, Seligman, & Teasdale, 1978). For example, depressed humans were found to have negative, pessimistic beliefs about the efficacy of their actions and the likelihood of obtaining future rewards; helpless animals acted as if they held similar beliefs. Both depressed humans and helpless animals exhibited motivational deficits in the laboratory. Both showed signs of emotional upset with illness, phobias, sleep disturbances, and other such symptoms similar to those described as part of the battered woman syndrome as a subcategory of a post traumatic stress disorder.

LEARNED HELPLESSNESS HYPOTHESIS IN THIS RESEARCH

On the basis of clinical work with battered women, it was hypothesized that the women's experiences of the noncontingent nature of their attempts to control the violence would, over time, produce learned helplessness and depression as the "repeated batterings, like electrical shocks, diminish the woman's motivation to respond" (Walker, 1979). If a woman is to escape such a relationship, she must overcome the tendency to learned helplessness survival techniques—by, for example, becoming angry rather than depressed and self-blaming; active rather than passive; and more realistic about the likelihood of the relationship continuing on its aversive course rather than improving. She must learn to use escape skills compatible to the survival behaviors already adopted.

In order to test the hypothesis that women in a battering relationship would show more signs of learned helplessness than women who had managed to escape such a relationship, each woman in our sample was asked a series of questions about her reactions to the four specific battering incidents: the first, second, last, and "one of the worst." With the exception of the "worst" incident, these provided a sketch of the battering relationship as it developed over time. If learned helplessness occurs in battering relationships and must be overcome if a battered woman is to escape, women whose "last" battering incident marked the end of a relationship should have become, over time, more angry, disgusted, and willing to seek intervention; less fearful, anxious, and depressed. Also, these women's reactions to the "last" battering incident should indicate less learned helplessness than the reactions of women who are still in the battering relationship, for whom the "last" incident was the most recent but not necessarily the last in the relationship. Of course, since it took some initiative to come to our interview, the women in our sample who were still in battering relationships may not have been as "helpless" as women who heard about the study but took no action to participate. This factor may decrease the size of the differences between women we are referring to as "in" or "out" of battering relationships.

Figure 9.1 displays results relevant to this first hypothesis about learned helplessness. In the top panel of Figure 9.1 are displayed averages of the women's reports of fear, anxiety, and depression across the three battering incidents. The solid curve shows results for women still in a battering relationship ("ins"), the dotted curve, results for women no longer in the relationship they are describing ("outs"). The "ins" reached a higher level of these unpleasant emotions than the "outs," especially at the second time point.

In the bottom panel of the figure are average curves for anger, disgust, and hostility. The curves increase for both "ins" and "outs," but the level for outs is higher, especially at the "last" time point. For both groups, a measure of "resigned acceptance" was also administered. Both show a rise at the second time point.

Combining these results, it appears that "outs" reached a high point of fear/anxiety/depression and then became less fearful and depressed as they approached a peak of anger/disgust/hostility. At the same time, their resigned acceptance decreased. Perhaps the "ins" had not yet reached the peak of fear and depression, and their level of anger, while rising, hadn't reached the level of the "outs" anger when the "outs" decided to leave the relationship. Coming to our interview might have been a small step toward leaving, since anger was increasing and resigned acceptance was declining.

These results are compatible with learned helplessness theory. However, they do not indicate why some women become disgusted and angry enough to leave a relationship and others do not. Analysis of the cost benefit ratio, or specifically the relationship between positive and negative reinforcement, which is discussed in the next chapter on the Walker Cycle Theory of Violence, may prove more illuminating. Also possible is the reaction of their abusive partners to the woman's attempts to leave the relationship. As was later found, many men stalk women and increase the danger when she starts to leave (DeBecker, 1997; Sonkin, 1995; Walker & Meloy, 1998) while others are so cunning and controlling that the women are too fearful and paralyzed to leave (Jacobson & Gottman, 1998). No matter how good are a woman's coping strategies, she needs a different set of skills to be able to terminate her relationship with these types of batterers despite what Bowker (1993) suggests.

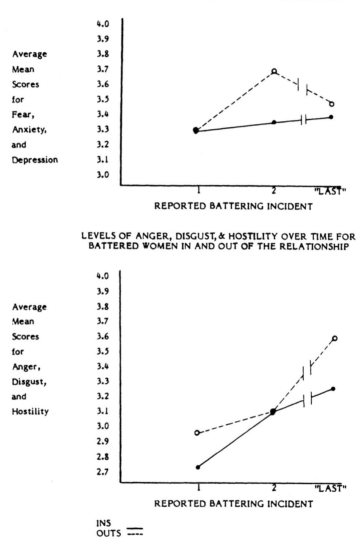

LEVELS OF FEAR, ANXIETY, & DEPRESSION OVER TIME FOR
BATTERED WOMEN IN AND OUT OF THE RELATIONSHIP

REPORTED BATTERING INCIDENT

LEVELS OF ANGER, DISGUST, & HOSTILITY OVER TIME FOR
BATTERED WOMEN IN AND OUT OF THE RELATIONSHIP

REPORTED BATTERING INCIDENT

INS ——
OUTS ----

FIGURE 9.1   Women's emotional responses to battering incidents over time.

It has also been suggested that "being a woman, more specifically a married woman, automatically creates a situation of powerlessness" (Walker, 1979, p. 51), and that women are taught sex role stereotyping, which encourages passivity and dependency even as little girls (Radloff & Rae, 1979, 1981; Dweck, Goetz, & Strauss, 1980). While most women do not perceive themselves as powerless in all situations, it is more likely that a battered woman who has not gotten community or family support will understand that the man holds more power in domestic violence situations even if only by his greater physical strength. Seligman's research indicated that the experience of noncontingency between response and outcome early in an animal's development increased that animal's vulnerability to learned helplessness later in life. He hypothesized that the same principles apply in human child raising practices (Seligman, 1975, 1997). To the extent that animal and human helplessness are similar, childhood experiences of noncontingency between response and outcome, including socialization practices that encourage passivity and dependency, should increase a woman's vulnerability to developing learned helplessness in a battering relationship.

In order to explore this possibility, many questions were asked in our interview concerning childhood experiences, parental attitudes, and family dynamics. Answers to these questions were combined into scales (e.g., childhood health, mothers' and fathers' attitudes toward women's roles, sexual abuse during childhood) and the scales were intercorrelated to see whether they could be combined to form a single measure of childhood contributors to learned helplessness. See Table 33 for description of items. For short, we call the resulting measure Child LH. The following scales were standardized and summed to form the Child LH measure (which has an internal consistency reliability alpha = .57).

1. The number of critical life events which occurred before age 18. "Critical events" included such things as divorce, death of a family member, sexual assault, moving—events that might make life seem relatively uncontrollable.
2. Mother's Attitude Toward Women Score, based on Spence and Helmreich's (1973) short form, as completed by the woman being interviewed when instructed to recall what her mother's attitudes were like "when you were growing up." (Coefficient alpha for this 25-item scale was .91).
3. Father's Attitude Toward Women Score (alpha = .93).
4. Number of battering relationships in the woman's childhood

home (e.g., father battering mother, mother or father battering the subject or siblings).
5. Subject's relationship with mother during childhood and adolescence. This measure was based on 17 items concerning discipline, communication, affection shown, and parental expectations and values. Coefficient alpha for this 17-item measure was .83.
6. Subject's relationship with father during childhood and adolescence. Also a 17-item measure, using the same items as above; coefficient alpha = .84.
7. Childhood health scale, based on 11 items covering such things as migraine headaches, eating problems, hospitalization, allergies, and serious injuries. Alpha = .73.
8. A measure of childhood sex acts, based on questions about forced fondling, oral sex, or intercourse. These acts were weighted equally in determining a total score because recent literature (see Chapter 5) suggests that impact is determined less by the act itself than by degree of force, perpetrator, and so on.

Although alpha for the combined Child LH measure is not as high as we would have liked (Alpha = .57), its components are generally reliable, and the SPSS program we used to compute reliabilities indicated that alpha would not have been higher if any component scale had been dropped. Further, it seemed wise to use a broad measure of possible childhood antecedents of learned helplessness in this initial exploration.

A similar procedure was followed to develop a tentative measure of learned helplessness within the battering relationship. Theoretically plausible indicators were intercorrelated and only those with Pearson product moment coefficients significant at the .05 level of significance were retained. Fifteen indices, described in Table 34, met this criterion. When standardized and summed, they yielded a scale with a reliability coefficient of .67. The components of this scale are as follows:

1. The frequency of battering incidents.
2. The number of abusive acts within a typical battering incident.
3–8. The number of injuries within each of six injury categories, averaged across four batterings described in detail during the interview.
9. The frequency with which the woman was forced by her batterer to have sex.
10. Whether or not the woman thought the batterer might kill her.
11. The extent to which the woman thought she could control the batterer or influence his actions.

12. The extent to which the woman adopted a placating stance toward the batterer in everyday life.
13. The woman's emotional reaction to the typical battering incident, summing across "fear," "depression," and so on. Coefficient alpha = .90.
14. The interviewer's rating of the woman's activity-passivity after each of the four reported incidents, averaged across incidents.

The combination of these variables was called Rel LH, or learned helplessness during the battering relationship. While a better measure of this construct could be designed for future studies, analyses indicated that reliability would not have been increased by dropping any of the components, and we wished to retain as broad a concept as possible for our initial investigations of learned helplessness.

In addition to measures of Child LH and Rel LH, we wanted to assess each woman's current state on the same indices that might be related to learned helplessness. The following current state measures were considered: depression (Radloff's CES-D scale), attributional style (Levenson's internality, chance, and powerful others scales), anomie (a 4-item version of Srole's [1956] scale), self-esteem (a 20-item scale created for this study), current health (an 11-item scale, parallel to the one designed to measure childhood health), and the subject's current attitudes toward women's roles (Spence and Helmreich's full-length scale, 55 items). Reliabilities for these measures ranged from .49 to .94; only Levenson's internal scale (.49) was below .70. Each correlated with every other beyond the .05 significance level. Table 35 lists these variables. It seemed reasonable, for preliminary analyses at least, to combine them into a single Current State measure by standardizing and summing the components. Current State yielded an alpha of .76.

In order to see whether Child LH is a determinant of Rel LH, and whether either of these is a determinant of Current State, a series of path analyses was conducted. In the first one, shown in Figure 9.2, the entire sample was included. Results indicate that both Child LH and Rel LH influence current state, and that the childhood measure is actually a bit more influential than the relationship measure. (For the final multiple regression analysis upon which the path diagram is based, $F(2,400) = 22.56$, p c .001.) Contrary to the hypothesis that childhood experiences cause a woman to be more or less vulnerable to helplessness in a battering relationship, there is essentially no relationship between Child LH and Rel LH. Thus, learned helplessness has equal potential to develop at either time in the battered woman's life.

Current State of Woman at Time of Interview
With Childhood and Relationship Variables

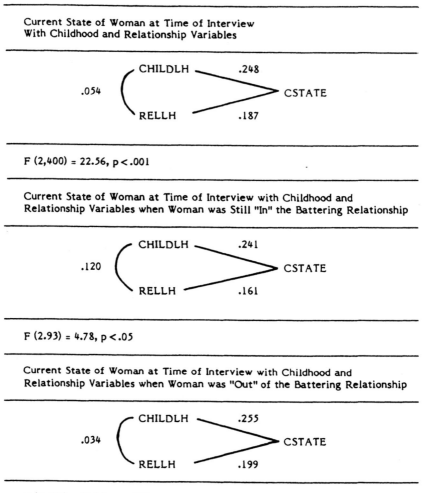

F (2,400) = 22.56, p < .001

Current State of Woman at Time of Interview with Childhood and
Relationship Variables when Woman was Still "In" the Battering Relationship

F (2.93) = 4.78, p < .05

Current State of Woman at Time of Interview with Childhood and
Relationship Variables when Woman was "Out" of the Battering Relationship

F (2,304) = 18.49, p < .001

FIGURE 9.2   Learned helplessness predictors of women's current state.

Because the path diagram might differ for women still in an abusive
relationship compared with women who have left such a relationship,
we recomputed the path analysis for each of these groups separately.
The two sets of results are also shown in Figure 3. Surprisingly, there
is not much difference, despite the fact that the current state of women
who are no longer in a battering relationship might be expected to be
less influenced by Child LH or, especially, by Rel LH. Even when we

look only at women who have been out of the battering relationship for more than a year (an analysis not shown in Figure 9.2), the path coefficients remain the same. This suggests either that the influence of Child LH and Rel LH persists, almost regardless of later experiences, or that subjects who selected themselves for our interviews at various distances from battering experiences were still troubled by them.

In order to explore this matter further, we performed an analysis of variance on each of the "learned helplessness" scores (Child LH, Rel LH, and Current State) with the independent variable being whether the woman was, at the time of the interview, (1) still in the battering relationship, (2) out less than one year, or (3) out more than one year. If large differences were discovered, it might mean that these three groups differ in ways that render the path analyses invalid or misleading. In fact, none of the tested differences were significant. The means, shown in Table 36, reveal some interesting trends, however. Women who are still in the relationship report worse (more "helpless") childhoods and fewer current problems with learned helplessness. If this is true, it might help explain why they are still in a battering relationship. Perhaps they did have somewhat more "training" for learned helplessness during childhood than women who have left a battering relationship, and either their battering experiences are not as severe or they do not yet see them as so severe. In the discussion of results related to the cycle theory that follows, the point is made that women still in a battering relationship did not report as great a level of tension-building before the last reported incident of violence. Since the differences in Table 36 are nonsignificant, we cannot be sure they are meaningful. Nevertheless, the pattern shown would be worth following up in future studies, using more refined measures.

Walker Cycle Theory of Violence

A second major theory that was tested in this research project was the Walker Cycle Theory of Violence (Walker, 1979). This is a tension-reduction theory that states that there are three distinct phases associated with a recurring battering cycle: (1) tension-building, (2) the acute battering incident, and (3) loving-contrition. During the first phase, there is a gradual escalation of tension displayed by discrete acts causing increased friction such as name-calling, other mean intentional behaviors, and/or physical abuse. The batterer expresses dissatisfaction and hostility, but not in an extreme or maximally explosive form. The woman attempts to placate the batterer, doing what she thinks might please him, calm him down, or at least, what will not further aggravate him. She tries not to respond to his hostile actions and uses general anger reduction techniques. Often she succeeds for a little, while which reinforces her unrealistic belief that she can control this man. It also becomes part of the unpredictable noncontingency response/outcome pattern that creates the *learned helplessness.*

The tension continues to escalate, the woman becomes more fearful of impending danger, and eventually she is unable to continue controlling his angry response pattern. "Exhausted from the constant stress, she usually withdraws from the batterer, fearing she will inadvertently set off an explosion. He begins to move more oppressively toward her as he observes her withdrawal. . . . Tension between the two becomes unbearable" (Walker, 1979, p. 59). The second phase, the acute battering incident, becomes inevitable without intervention. Sometimes, she precipitates the inevitable explosion so as to control where and when it occurs, allowing her to take better precautions to minimize her injuries and pain. Over time she may learn to predict the point in the cycle where there is a period of inevitability—after that point is reached, there is no escape for the woman unless the man permits it.

"Phase two is characterized by the uncontrollable discharge of the tensions that have built up during phase one" (Walker, p. 59). The batterer typically unleashes a barrage of verbal and physical aggression that can leave the woman severely shaken and injured. The woman does her best to protect herself often covering parts of her face and body to block some of the blows. In fact, when injuries do occur they usually happen during this second phase. It is also the time police become involved, if they are called at all. The acute battering phase is concluded when the batterer stops, usually bringing with its cessation a sharp physiological reduction in tension. This in itself is naturally reinforcing. Violence often succeeds because it does work.

In phase three that follows, the batterer may apologize profusely, try to assist his victim, show kindness and remorse, and shower her with gifts and/or promises. The batterer himself may believe at this point that he will never allow himself to be violent again. The woman wants to believe the batterer and, early in the relationship at least, may renew her hope in his ability to change. This third phase provides the positive reinforcement for remaining in the relationship, for the woman. Many of the acts that he did when she fell in love with him during the courtship period occur again here. Our research results demonstrated that phase three could also be characterized by an absence of tension or violence, with no observable loving-contrition behavior, and still be reinforcing for the woman. Sometimes the perception of tension and danger remains very high and does not return to the baseline or loving-contrition level. This is a sign that the risk of a lethal incident is very high.

ASSESSMENT OF THE CYCLE OF VIOLENCE

In our interviews with battered women, we asked for detailed descriptions of four battering incidents: the first, the second, one of the worst, and the last (or last prior to the interview). The first two and the last incident, taken together, reflect the temporal course of a stream of acute battering incidents. Each of these is an example of "phase two" in the cycle theory. After the description of each incident, basing her judgment on both the open-ended description and a series of closed-ended questions concerning the batterer's behavior before the event ("Would you call it . . . irritable, provocative, aggressive, hostile, threatening"—each on a 1–5 scale) and after the event ("nice, loving, contrite"), the interviewer recorded whether or not there was "evidence of tension building and/or loving contrition." Comparisons between interviewers' responses indicated a high level of agreement.

In 65% of all cases (including three battering incidents for each woman who reported three) there was evidence of a tension-building phase prior to the battering. In 58% of all cases there was evidence of loving contrition afterward. In general, then, there is support for the cycle theory of violence in a majority of the battering incidents described by our sample.

When the results are broken down chronologically, the pattern graphed in Figure 10.1 emerges.

For first incidents, the proportion showing evidence of a tension-building phase is 56%; the proportion showing evidence of loving contrition is 69%. Over time, these proportions changed drastically. By the last incident, tension building preceded 71% of battering incidents, but loving contrition followed only 42%. In other words, over time in a battering relationship, tension building becomes more common (or more evident) and loving contrite behavior declines.

Since our sample included 24% of women who were still in the battering relationship, it is possible that Figure 10.1 marks a difference in pattern between those who were in the relationship and those who had left the relationship by the time of the interview. The former group may not yet have experienced the truly final battering incident as they were asked about the last incident prior to their coming to the research study.

Figure 10.2 compares the pattern of these two groups. When we separate them, both show the same decline of loving contrition, but the patterns of tension building are different. Women still in a battering relationship report less evidence of tension building preceding the last incident before our interview. This may be a valid indication of a difference between battering incidents that cause a woman to leave the relationship and battering incidents other than the final one. Or it may indicate a defensive bias on the part of women who choose to remain in the relationship. Our data don't allow us to distinguish between these two possibilities.

It is clear, however, that our data support the existence of the Walker Cycle Theory of Violence. Further, over the course of a battering relationship, tension building before battering becomes more common (or evident) and loving contrition declines. Thus, results strongly suggest further investigation into the psychological costs and rewards in these relationships.

THEORETICAL IMPLICATIONS

Most battered women in our sample perceived three different levels of control over their lives. They scored significantly higher than the

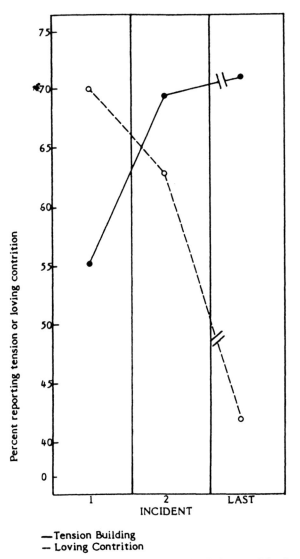

FIGURE 10.1 **Changes over time in tension building and loving contrition phases of the battering cycle for the total sample (N = 403).**

norms on the Levenson IPC Locus of Control Subscales of Internal, Powerful Others, and Chance. These findings suggest that the internal-external locus of control dichotomy does not fully explain battered women's attributions. Those women still in a violent relationship did not report powerful others as being in any more control of their lives

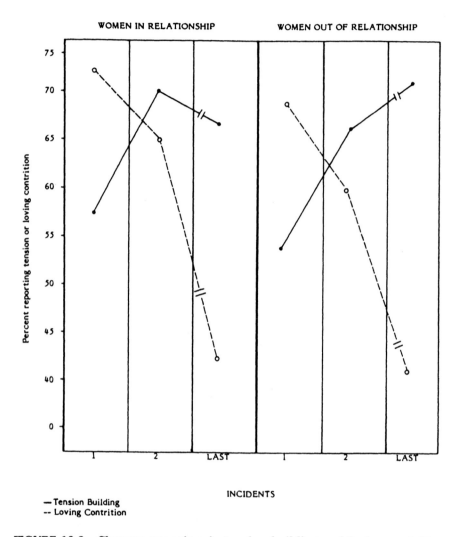

FIGURE 10.2   Changes over time in tension building and loving contrition phases of the battering cycle for women "in" and "out" of the battering relationship.

than themselves. Perhaps a battered woman cannot begin to terminate her marriage while there is this lack of realization that her batterer really is in control of her everyday activities and of her life.

Seligman's (1978) reformulation of learned helplessness theory would suggest an attributional style of assigning causality for successful experiences to external and specific factors and failures to internal and global ones. Thus, someone with an external attribution might think that their success was due to luck and a particular combination of things that day whereas their getting a beating was because they failed to keep their mouth shut and didn't pay enough attention to him. Our measurement of attributional style was not designed to test this reformulation as our study was designed prior to its publication. Therefore, our sample's perception of both internal and external causation may not be unusual in light of this reformulation of learned helplessness theory.

SELF-ESTEEM

The woman's self-esteem was measured by use of a typical Likert-style semantic differential scale. It was predicted that battered women's self-esteem would be quite low and our results, surprisingly, show the opposite. They perceived themselves as stronger, more independent, and more sensitive than other women or men. It is possible that battered women develop a positive sense of self from having survived in a violent relationship, which causes them to believe they are equal to or better than others. However, there is incompatibility between these high self-esteem findings and the reports of depression and other learned helplessness measures. Given these conflicting results, more careful study into the mental health of battered women is recommended. Depression was measured by the CES-D scale (Radloff, 1977). Our subjects scored higher than the high risk for depression cut-off score. Younger women in the sample were more likely to be depressed than older ones, as were those who were unemployed. An interesting but surprising finding was that women out of the relationship were more likely to be more depressed than those still in it. They were also not consistent in demonstrating the negative cognition and moods we would have expected in other indices within the questionnaire.

DEPRESSION

Lewinsohn's behavioral reinforcement theory of depression might explain some of our findings on depression (Lewinsohn, 1975; Lewinsohn et al., 1981). It postulates that depression occurs when there is a sharp reduction in the amount of positive reinforcement received by people. A lower rate of rewards would result in a lower response rate or passivity, which then spirals downward into a depressed state. Cognitive or affective disturbances occur simultaneous to the downward spiral or are a consequence of the lowered reinforcement rate.

This is similar to the learned helplessness theory, which postulates the lowered behavioral response rate or passivity as learned response to uncontrollable trauma. It also postulates distorted perceptions in the cognitive and affective domain. While the learned helplessness theory did not specify when these cognitive and affective perceptions occurred, the reformulations suggest an attributional style, which serves as a cognitive set for a depressive state to develop.

LEARNED HELPLESSNESS

The finding of a set of factors that could result in childhood learned helplessness, and another, responsible for development of learned helplessness in the relationship, supports the application of this theory to battered women. Unfortunately, actual learned helplessness is usually directly measured in a laboratory setting under experimentally controlled conditions. Our research attempted to identify its presence from variables that cause it to develop as predicted by the literature. Although our results are positive, it is strongly recommended that a controlled laboratory setting be constructed to test if learned helplessness can be easily induced in a sample of battered women comparable to this one. Such direct measurement is necessary to confirm the theoretical application to battered women.

WALKER CYCLE THEORY OF VIOLENCE IN THE RESEARCH

The Walker Cycle Theory of Violence (Walker, 1979) was also confirmed by our data. Sufficient evidence was found that there are three phases in battering relationships that occur in a cycle. Over time, the first phase of tension building becomes more common, and loving contrition, or the third phase, declines. Our results also show that phase three could be characterized by an absence of tension or violence and no observable loving-contrition behavior and still be reinforcing for the woman. In those cases, it is the relationship interactions themselves that propel the cycle and not just the three distinct phases with their corresponding behaviors.

   Lewis (1981) has tested the cycle theory in the laboratory to match its compatibility with the anxiety arousal model of the delay of punishment paradigm. This paradigm has been found to have three phases of anxiety arousal: increase during the anticipatory period; asymptote at the moment of stimulus delivery; and then, relief with a return to baseline levels. People have been found to prefer the immediate delivery of a negative stimulus in order to avoid a prolonged anticipatory period. Thus, the experimental model parallels the cycle theory derived from battered women's descriptions of the battering incidents. Lewis (1980) attempted to measure the differences between battered and nonbattered women's responses on a classic delay of punishment paradigm and compared these results to the cycle theory. The description of the cycle theory used came from her independent reading of published work (Walker, 1978, 1979) and not through direct contact with this project. Nevertheless, the results are interesting in that it extends the descriptive work to experimental laboratory analogues.

Lewis (1980) hypothesized that battered women have learned the probability of receiving a beating by recognizing specific predictive cues emitted by the batterer in phase one of the cycle. These predictive cues result in a high level of anxiety arousal, which the battered women may attempt to reduce through several different means, one of which is to avoid delaying the beating any longer. She hypothesized that battered women would be more likely to avoid delay of punishment in the experimental analogue she constructed. Using the Conflicts Tactics Scale (CTS) developed by Straus et al. (1980), she measured battering behavior and found that it was not useful in identifying an adequate sample of battered women. However, she did generate a sample with a variety of marital conflicts and found that the cycle theory held for couples' less violent disputes, also.

Thus, her results support her hypothesis that women may elect to receive a brief aversive stimulus immediately and yet also prefer to delay a somewhat longer aversive event. This research offers promising insights into why battered women chose various tactics to respond to the batterer's behavior, particularly during phase one of the cycle. For example, a woman may choose a delay tactic, such as withdrawing or doing something to calm the batterer, or she may choose to get the beating over with immediately, depending upon her perception of the intensity and probability of the predicted battering incident. The commonalties between the anxiety arousal model of marital dispute cycles demonstrated in the laboratory and the cycle theory of violence, which developed from battered women's descriptions, were supported in this analogue study.

COST-BENEFIT MODELS

The analysis of lower reinforcement rates presented with the results of the Walker Cycle Theory of Violence demonstrates that women who were out of the battering relationship left after the ratio between the tension-building and loving-contrition phases sharply diverged. Women still in the battering relationship reported more positive reinforcement (loving contrition) following the last battering incident they discussed. Thus, women who were less depressed while still in the relationship may have still been receiving some rewards from it despite the violence. Once the cost-benefit ratio changes, however, and the rate of reinforcement decreases, then the women may be more inclined to leave the relationship, but subsequently become depressed as a result of the separation. Further investigation into the psychological cost and benefits in these relationships is still necessary.

It is interesting that other family violence researchers are also examining the costs and benefits of battering relationships. Gelles (1983) recently presented an exchange/social control theory of intrafamily violence in which he attempts to construct a multidimensional causal model to account for all forms of family abuse, including child abuse, spouse abuse, and sexual abuse. Although Gelles does not use a social learning theory paradigm, he suggests that human behavior follows the pursuits of rewards and avoidance of punishment (Gelles, 1983, p. 11). As a sociologist, it is understandable that he utilizes traditional exchange theory (Blau, 1964) rather than the reciprocal contingency contracting models developed by behavioral psychologists (Barnett & LaViolette, 1993; Patterson, 1982; Weiss, Hops, & Patterson, 1973). If the discipline vocabulary can be set aside, it is apparent that there are similarities between this approach and the one suggested by our data.

Gelles (1983, 1993a) suggests that a multidimensional causal model needs to be explored—a concept these data certainly support. Inequality between men and women is one area that we both agree must be a part of that model. Our results indicate that sex role stereotyping is a primary cause for men battering women. Gelles also suggests that such unequal gender socialization patterns are causal in other forms of family violence, specifically sexual assault and child abuse. He states that the privacy of the family reduces accessibility to outside agencies of social control. Our results support this concept, as the social isolation measures were the highest for women living with their batterers. New research continues to support the multicausal model (APA, 1996a; Barnett, Miller-Perrin, & Perrin, 1997).

Once the cost of living in a violent relationship begins to escalate, paralleling the escalation of the seriousness of the abusiveness and injuries, women's help-seeking behavior breaks through the privacy of the home, if they perceive actual help is available. Gelles also includes the cost of loss of status because the label wife or child beater is less a factor in subcultures where aggressive behavior is held in high esteem (Brooks, 1998). Perceived status of the men was not measured in this study. However, our data suggest that this factor is probably significant so long as it does not approach the risk of the man losing his wife and family, which would then result in a loss of status in such subcultures. This analysis is consistent with the behavior seen by the man's mother toward his wife. The mother-in-law is often the most supportive to help the woman heal from an acute battering incident until the time comes when the woman is ready to leave the relationship. Women described being shocked at the immediate change in their mother-in-law's behavior toward them should they decide to leave the family.

While he goes on to describe other factors in his model, Gelles' primary thesis is that men abuse women because they can, and suggests changing the contingencies so that the costs become too high. While none of our results would be incompatible with this view, it is seen as not being comprehensive enough. For example, our data suggest behavior patterns in men and women that are associated with violence. We argue that these are temporary-state like characteristics related to the situation of being battered, for the women, and, perhaps more stable personality traits seen in the men. Battered women seem more likely to respond to the batterer's behavior than he does to hers.

Although the concept of mutual reciprocity cannot be disproved, the striking differences we found between the woman's perceptions of her behavior with the batterer and a nonbatterer lend strong support to this belief in her reactive behavior. Measurement of the tactics used by couples that do not take such inequality into account, such as the CTS, may well obscure the field rather than add to the knowledge base. It emphasizes the violent nature of all of society, while our results would place the greatest emphasis on the position of women in a society where they are the predominant victims of such violence.

CYCLE THEORY AND INTERVENTIONS

When I first began collecting data from individuals and using the information to plot their individual cycle graphs, it became clear that once the code for the individual's own personal cycle is broken, it becomes necessary for the woman to begin to protect herself and her children more vigorously. Although battered women are quite sensitive to the rise of tension and perception of danger, they often shut off their intuitive feelings while trying to calm down the batterer. Rarely do they connect the quiet during the aftermath of the violent incident with a constant repetitive cycle. Nor are they consciously aware of how similar the behavior the batterer displays is to the behavior they saw during their courtship period. Rather, they associate the phase three behavior with who they believed their batter really is. They reason that they were able to smooth the world for the batterer and so the *real man* emerged once again. This become a powerful message for the woman, fitting right into the sex role socialization that teaches women to believe that they are responsible for the health, well-being, and psychological stability of their husbands! Thus, it becomes important to teach battered women their cycle of violence so they can choose to stop being held captive by their belief that the person they see during the third phase is the real man and somehow, if the behavior he displays during phases one and two disappears, then they will be left with the person they fell in love with. Only when they see the inevitability of the recurring cycle and understand that their partner has both the ability to be both loving and cruel will they be able to better protect themselves and their children.

In battered woman shelters, support groups, and psychotherapy sessions, battered women are being encouraged to graph their own cycle of violence. It is important to gather data on at least four battering cycles. Usually, the woman is encouraged to remember the first time she was hurt by the batterer. Sometimes this includes a physically abusive act during phase one or two, other times it is some act that humiliated the woman and hurt her feelings. Most women remember the incident that made them first realize that this man was able to hurt them in ways they never dreamed of. By asking her to remember and recount the details of what happened before and led up to it, what happened during the acute battering incident part, and what happened afterwards, it is possible to get an idea of how to rate the seriousness of the incident, what level of tension the woman felt, and how much danger she perceived herself to be in at the time.

I suggest using a graph rather than the circle that many other battered woman center facilitators suggest because it is possible to demonstrate the escalation and repetitiveness of the cycle easier. I try to get materials to her from the actual project. On the vertical axis of the graph put the measurement of tension and perception of danger. Use the scale from 0 to 10 with anything over an 8 considered life-threatening violence. On the horizontal axis place the three phases of the cycle over time. By drawing the incidents on this graph, it makes a powerful statement that the abuse is escalating and that the woman is becoming more frightened of the dangerousness of her situation.

If I want to measure the rapidity of the escalation of violence in a relationship, I often ask for the details of the next (second) incident she can remember. This helps get data about how frequent and how serious are the acute battering incidents initially as compared later on in the relationship. I then draw that incident as continuous to the first on the graph. The next incident that I ask about is the last one before the woman has come in to see me. Sometimes this is quite recent but in other clients who don't come for treatment until after she has terminated the relationship, it might be quite some time ago. This becomes the anchor on the other side of the graph. Sometimes the loving-contrition in the third phase is still present, more often it has decreased or disappeared entirely. Then, I ask for a third (or fourth by now) incident that the woman describes as the worst one, unless the last one is the worst and then, it is one of the worst that she picks out to discuss. Although this incident frequently deals with humiliation and not necessarily physical injuries, it is important to diagram it attached to the others. The final incident that I request is a typical battering scene. Often more than one incident gets put together here but again, it is important to see how the woman perceives the abuse in general, on a day-to-day basis rather than just when there are more dramatic incidents occurring. In long-term relationships, there might be more than one typical incident. When there is sexual abuse in the relationship and the woman is willing to talk about it, those incidents are often reported in this section.

It is interesting to see how quickly most battered women catch on to the graphing of these battering incidents. In a film that I made about therapy with abused women, I demonstrate this technique in connection with the development of a safety plan (Walker, 1996b). Most battered women cannot leave the house when an acute battering incident is beginning because they wait too long and the batterer is in too much of an angry, controlling state to let her go. However, if women can be taught to recognize the signals that the tension is building and an acute battering incident is approaching threshold before exploding, then it may be possible for her to get out then. During the development of a crisis plan, battered women are often taught when to leave and they can decide if they want to tell the batterer that they intend to leave if they get scared his violence will escalate, but they will come back to discuss it later when he calms down.

Just knowing that there is a cycle to the violence and that it is repetitive helps the woman to better assess her situation. It also helps the man understand that he no longer will be able to manipulate the woman by his behavior during the third phase. Sometimes what seemed to be so loving in one context actually seemed a continuation of the controlling and over possessive behavior of the batterer. For example, in the film, Sara tells the therapist that after one battering incident her husband filled the dining room with lilac bushes so when she came downstairs that was all she saw. Then they spent the entire day planting those bushes. Sara liked that sequence, especially the attention that Dan, her husband gave her as they planted the bushes that day. However, he gave her no choice but to be with him planting bushes even though she might have made other plans that didn't include him. Not until the therapist pointed it out did Sara realize that her husband's supposedly nice gesture was an example of the third phase of their cycle that also had secondary benefits for his needs to keep her as close to him as possible.

PART THREE

Implications for a Violence-Free Future

Future Directions for Research

A discussion of future directions for research into the nature, causes, and prevention of family violence gained from this particular research project is very much in order here. The Battered Woman Research Center was founded as a way of calling attention to the obvious bias existing in research programs about high prevalency conditions detrimental to women. That bias came from accepting male-defined research assumptions and questions rather than collecting a systematic, empirical, objective account of the woman victim's perspective. To do so, it became necessary to compensate for years of oppressor/victim effects that biased women's own view of what was happening to them. Removal of the shame and stigma of having been battered contributed to victims' shedding the self-blame that comes from a position of oppression.

Neutrality is insufficient to create the researcher's objective field laboratory. Our feminist attitude created the safe place for objective scientific data to be collected. While the feminist perspective guided the choice of questions that were asked, previous research suggested that only such a perspective could gather objective data about this problem. The now classic Broverman et al. (1970) study indicated that the general public as well as the scientific community believed that there were two standards of behavior: one for healthy women and one for healthy men. The behaviors seen as necessary to be a healthy person were the same as those held standard for men. Obviously, a woman whose behavior met the standards could not also be a healthy person. Other empirical data collected by social scientists interested in how such sex role biases affected society indicated that most scientific research ignored such gender-based assumptions and thus probably was not very objective at all (see Unger, 1979).

Collecting unbiased but women-oriented data was a major task of this research program. Although it was not an easy task to accomplish, there is little doubt that it has been done. Hopefully, it sets a new standard for future research. Projects should not be undertaken unless outdated sexist assumptions are challenged. Particularly, data collected by and about men cannot be used to generically explain women's experiences. Women's worlds have both differences and similarities with men's. In the study of their relationship together, both perspectives must be utilized to overcome an objective gender stratification bias.

HISTORICAL ORIGINS OF SPOUSE ABUSE

The origins of spouse abuse have been traced back to the times when history was first recorded. Biblical references to wife-beating are commonly cited (Davidson, 1979) as are similar religious exhortations to treat wives with respect and tenderness (Hendricks, 1985). Patriarchy is often blamed for the introduction of sexism in society through its subordination of women concept (Stone, 1976), and the Dobashes (1981) carefully trace its linkages to spouse abuse. Familiarity with this historical analysis is critical for potential researchers so as not to get caught up in hypothesizing causation theories, which do not take its long history into account. History also forces researchers to look at linkages of woman-battering to other violent acts committed by men against those weaker and less powerful than themselves, usually women and children. Most agree that men continue to use violence as a method of getting what they want because it is successful and no one stops them (Martin, 1976; Straus et al., 1980; Walker, 1979; Berk et al., 1983; Koss et al., 1994). Feminists assert that all men benefit from the violence against women committed by a few (Leidig, 1981). Brownmiller (1975), in an historical review of rape, claims that rapists are the "shock troops" who serve to convince women to mate and marry with one man to provide her with protection against the other men's potential violence. Jones (1980) adds to this analogy by claiming that batterers are the "home guard" who serve to convince women to behave as men wish in order to escape further violence. The tenacity with which assaults against women continue provides the empirical evidence that violence is seen as a useful tactic to keep a male-dominant, patriarchal social order in place. Commonalities seen in strategies by men to exploit and abuse women also are seen in the psychological consequences for women (Koss et al., 1994; Walker, 1994).

Much discussion takes place concerning the breakdown of the family unit and its consequences for the future generation. Yet, the research reported here as well as almost all of the other empirical data available to date indicate that it is the very same nuclear family that is passing down the undesirable values of our culture, including violence and sexism. Left to its own ultimate conclusion—without interference from state, religious, or economic influences—the nuclear family has been rapidly dissolving in this country. Some claim it is a reaction to the withdrawal of extended family and community supports in our mobile society. Others say the long life span now possible through medical advances places too much stress on marriages. This is the first generation of people truly capable of living for 50 and 60 years together.

Still others, particularly those holding strong religious values, view the family breakdown as evidence of immorality and lessening of traditional values that bond people together, especially in large urban areas. While all these reasons may be valid, it may also be that without use of violence as the ultimate weapon, the family unit as traditionally designed could not stay together, as it simply does not meet people's needs. In fact, both historical as well as empirical data indicate it probably never met most people's needs very well.

The United States 1980 census data found that the average length of a marriage in this country was 6 years. The data in this research found that the average length of a battering marriage was also 6 years. Thus, it appears that violence may not be as useful a strategy for keeping relationships together in our society as it once was. This could be especially true during a period when women move forward to obtain their equal rights in society, no longer intimidated by the threat of the "shock troops" and "home guard." The legal system, called upon to mete out punishment for those who break society's rules, has only recently begun to punish wife beaters. This is another example of the widespread historical acceptance of such violent behavior. Pleck (1979) details the changes in social and legal attitudes in the nineteenth century, citing the variability between formal and informal means of punishment. She documents how community standards of justice, set by men to regulate the behavior of other men, were embedded in their own definitions of proper behavior for men and women. Jones (1980) provides a historical context of similar attitudes since the beginning of our country. Gelles (1972) found that individuals still reflect those notions of just discipline for infractions or perceived standards of behavior. Research must measure the impact of such norms of control for them, rather than ignore the social context in which violence takes place.

EMPIRICISM

The institution of ideas called science has grown out of the empirical philosophy of logical positivism. Inspired by the extraordinary advances in the realm of physics, its founders sought to develop a scientific methodology that was based on the experimentation and mathematics required in physics. This resulted in a separation between theory and observations, an inordinate emphasis on the experimental method, insistence upon careful clarity, but also simplification of concepts and emphasis on statistical analysis of observed relationships (Dobash & Dobash, 1981). While this criticism of empiricism is often seen as an impossible limitation for measurement of complex relationships, such as is found in woman-battering, newer advances in statistical concepts have broadened the empirical scientific tradition's usefulness in social science research. Carefully designed experiments, which pay attention to the inherent biases in institutionalized science, can contribute to our knowledge base.

One of the most prevalent biases in science is that of gender stratification. It permits an anti-woman stance to not be addressed but rather, be buried under the rubric of science being value-neutral or an objective, antiseptic tool for the discovery of pure facts. Wardell, Gillespie, and Leffler (1983) suggest that science is merely an institution based in the male domination of the social system in which it is located at this particular point in time. They refer to many of the sexist assumptions and victim-blaming focus even in the new domestic violence literature, acknowledging that the new researcher's honest commitment to ending sex role stereotypes and victimization of women is still evidence of the immovability of scientific bias.

The study of individual differences, so well-suited for the experimental method, is thought to be a root cause of perpetuating inaccurate assumptions about human behavior. What is needed, says a new generation of scientific researchers schooled in empiricism, is a focus on the situational and historical context, which then create both similarities and differences. Such complex interactional effects can be statistically analyzed (Berk et al., 1983), and integration of objective data collection with the "context specific approach" called for by Dobash and Dobash (1983) is indeed possible.

Changing research agendas calls for more than the skepticism properly addressed by Wardell et al. (1983), especially if research is to provide a knowledge base with which to understand violence against women, in and out of the home. And obviously, such research methodology also needs more than good intentions to move the institutionalized scientific system toward a new path. As is evident in descriptions of the research program undertaken here, feminist ideology was not enough to accomplish our goals. Technical competence that allows for constant monitoring, evaluating, and criticizing potential bias and flexibility to correct it once it is located is essential. This means identifying the potential areas where such bias could easily occur and devising strict antibias mechanisms to try to prevent it.

BATTERED WOMAN SYNDROME TESTIMONY IN COURTS

Scientists committed to the empirical tradition often do not look beyond their erroneous assumptions that a value-free research methodology actually exists. These scientists, usually male, criticize women scientists who attempt to control for the above stated biases inherent in the reigning popular methodology, by labeling their research as non-scientific or biased by feminist perspective. Gelles (1980) is guilty of such behavior to some extent with his academic criticisms of current research in the domestic violence field. But, to be fair, even he was surprised when others used his call for more empiricism as evidence to invalidate the already sizeable data base. Such a misinterpretation of scientific debate occurred during legal proceedings to determine whether the methodology used to study in the domestic violence field was sufficiently developed to support an expert opinion to aid the court in understanding why a battered woman might perceive the need to kill her batterer in self-defense (*Hawthorne v. State*, 408 So. 2nd 801 [Fla 1st DCA] 1982). Those interested in the application to forensic psychology can follow the legal debate in the appellate court by obtaining the Amicus Brief submitted by the American Psychological Association or contacting defense attorney, Leo Thomas, in Pensacola, Florida (or see Walker, 1989a).

In several battered woman self-defense cases, psychologists and sociologists have testified that any research that does not strictly conform to the experimental model, utilizing a control group and measuring a single variable, is unscientific. There is confusion about the need of a feminist perspective to correct already existing bias. Many scientists jump to the opinion that stating a particular perspective is the same as allowing it to render the scientific process of objectivity ineffective. For it is the process of conducting a scientific experiment that must be objective and value-free; the design of the experiment must have a theoretical premise, which by definition cannot be value free.

FEMINIST PERSPECTIVE AND RESEARCH

One of the important questions that feminist researchers must answer is whether or not their feminist perspective has injected bias in the other direction in their work. In conducting this research design, certain decisions were made that were appropriately influenced by the feminist perspective. For example, given the finite resources available, it was decided to sacrifice the traditional empirical experimental model, with a control group, for the quasiexperimental model using survey-type data collection. It was seen as more important to compare battered women to themselves than to a nonbattered control group. Comparing battered and nonbattered women implies looking for some deficit in the battered group, which can be interpreted as a perpetuation of the victim-blaming model. Our data indicate that the differences within the group of battered women studied ranged across the continuum expected for all women. From this, it is possible to hypothesize that whatever differences exist between groups are so minimal that they serve to confuse rather than gain additional knowledge about spouse abuse. Although an argument can be made to rule out such a hypothesis, the empirical method cannot do so. The null hypothesis would state that which we already have gathered evidence on "there are no significant differences between battered and nonbattered women!"

COMMUNITY LIAISONS WITH RESEARCHERS

As this project progressed, it gained community support. Numerous calls were received from the research subjects themselves, after interviews had been concluded, to report the positive experiences they had with our interviewers and the Battered Women Research Center in general. The battered women reported sensitivity to their life situation by our interviewers, careful advocacy for them (particularly with regard to legal and psychotherapy referrals in the Denver community) and, in general, high quality treatment. After the interview was completed, some research subjects made decisions to leave their batterers. Many of them kept in touch with their interviewers for some time regarding problems they had to face. For example, one woman called the Battered Women Research Center soon after her interview, to tell us her husband had just shot himself to death rather than appear in court to respond to assault charges she had filed. We provided some initial crisis intervention while we found her appropriate alternative services.

Some of the publicity came from obvious ventures like open houses and press conferences, resulting in radio and television coverage. The publicity that was most pleasing was the solid reputation of this project due to the work of the interviewers. As battered women subjects reported their experiences with the project to others they knew, particularly their therapists, family members, and friends, we not only gained a community reputation as a solid research project, but it also encouraged more battered women self-referrals. Our close contact with the Colorado Association for Aid to Battered Women, the Technical Assistance Center for non-profit agencies in the region, and the national battered woman's network provided national visibility and community linkages. We gained such a good reputation among the local mental health centers and private practitioners as a place where the battered woman client was well cared for, that referrals still came in several years after we stopped interviewing.

The role of a research program within the community is a controversial issue. Some academicians believe that an activist role creates a bias in the data. On the contrary, in this field, community activism assured us of a more diversified sample than is usually obtained when investigating an emotionally charged subject.

RESEARCH AND THE O.J. SIMPSON CASE

Interestingly, all the good will and reputation for good feminist research in this area was immediately ignored by some members of the feminist battered woman community in early 1995, when it was announced that I would be testifying on behalf of the defense in the criminal case of O.J. Simpson, who was accused of murdering his former wife, Nicole Brown and her friend, Ron Goldman. Various motives were ascribed to my willingness to work with Johnnie Cochran and the defense attorneys, including financial need/greed and desire for publicity and status. In fact, outright lies were printed in the books written by both prosecutors including the fees that I was supposedly paid for my work. None of the accusers appeared concerned about the possibility that the research data available did not support their belief that O.J. must have been the killer simply because he had previously battered Nicole. The scientific evidence didn't find him innocent, either. Rather, its inadequacy simply didn't permit a conclusion based on the known facts.

When I was contacted by Johnnie Cochran and asked to help the defense team better understand the reports of domestic violence in the Simpson marriage that were beginning to surface, I agreed to consult with them as it seemed like a legitimate use of my skills and experience. I asked that my work would be kept confidential unless we agreed otherwise. I also asked that I be given access to information that I needed, and that the defense team stop any possible trashing of Nicole Brown that they might have been doing—especially when I was told that O.J.'s defense was one of identification; he insisted he wasn't there. At no time did I think that I was trying to get O.J. off of a murder charge. Rather, I believed that I was simply applying my knowledge of the field to help the defense learn more about their case.

After poring through details of over 60 reported domestic violence incidents, it was clear that there weren't very many physically abusive incidents that were reported and of those that were, only a few seemed legitimate. There were some battering incidents that appeared to be phony, mostly because the people stating them had no known contact with the Simpsons and from their behavior, it appeared that they were trying to cash in on the publicity surrounding this case. Other reported incidents appeared to be legitimate psychological control and intimidation issues that did permeate this relationship. There were some physically abusive incidents such as the worst one reported, the acute battering incident on New Year's Eve 1989 when O.J. was arrested, prosecuted, and diverted into a treatment program, but these were early in the relationship and apparently had stopped with that 1989 incident.

Even during the 1993 battering incident, when O.J. smashed in the patio doors to enter Nicole's house during an argument, he didn't go up the stairs into her bedroom where she was talking to the police as was later recorded on the 911 tape. He didn't physically harm her although his voice made it clear just how angry and frightening he was at the time. Although we can never actually know whether or not there were other incidents of physical abuse—O.J. denies it and Nicole is dead—it is very possible that the 1989 incident was the last time he struck her. When they went back to live together at that time, O.J. signed a contract stating that if he ever hit Nicole again, their prenuptial agreement would be null and void. This represented a great deal of money to O.J. In fact, when they did divorce, in 1992, Nicole's attorney suggested the possibility of filing a personal injury lawsuit, either to give them more leverage for a better divorce settlement or for financial compensation for the abuse she had already experienced. This is why she went to see Dr. Susan Forward—at her attorney's recommendation—not for therapy. Nicole decided not to go forward with such a lawsuit. However, if O.J. had hit her again between 1989 and 1992, there would have been no need to explore such a lawsuit, as she could have obtained a much better divorce settlement by proving that the prenuptial agreement had been broken. Although there were many reports of intimidation, bullying behavior and verbal abuse during the last year of their relationship (from 1993 to 1994), there were no reports of physical abuse. Still, it doesn't mean that it didn't occur or that he didn't kill her. It simply means that there was no evidence of escalation of violence at the time of the murders.

However, just because O.J. was a batterer, it didn't make him a killer. If I had testified at the trial, I would have presented scientific data that are available about battering relationships. I did so during my deposition taken in the later civil trial. Over 2 million women are battered every year in the United States. Fortunately, fewer than 2,000 are killed each year by their batterers. This is much too small a number to use as a predictive factor. In general, the less frequent an event, the more difficult it is to predict. While it is known that approximately 50% of women (40% if white and suburban; 60% if black and urban) who are killed each year have a history of having been previously abused by their killer, that also means that 50% of the women who are killed each year do not have a history of having been previously abused by their killer. In the criminal courts it is necessary to have a higher percentage to rise to the "beyond a reasonable doubt" standard that is operative there. Retrospective data is not the same as predictive data. As we all know, hindsight gives us a much more accurate view of what we had just experienced. So, if I had testified in the criminal trial, it would have been to present the research data, which would probably have been useful for both sides.

Just as important as it is to make sure that the research is not biased, it is also important to make sure that the message advocates deliver to the public is not biased. A lack of credibility in either area can call into question everything else that is said. Although it would have been helpful for a public awareness campaign that was underscoring the dangerousness of battering relationships to believe that O.J. was the killer because of the prior abuse, in fact, most of the high risk factors that are often seen in lethal relationships were not present here. There was no continued fighting over the children, there was no escalation of frequency of severity of physical violence before the homicides, there was no current alcohol or drug abuse on the part of O.J.—although there was on the part of Nicole—and there was no reported sexual abuse. Of course, there also was the recent agreement that they would no longer be romantically involved with each other, there was time unaccounted for that evening, there was close proximity with each other, and there was the possibility that Paula Barbieri, the girlfriend with whom he reunited after the recent break-up with Nicole, had also meant to break up with him on that day. O.J. knew Paula was angry with him because he didn't permit her to accompany him to his daughter, Sydney's dance recital, but they had just given an interior decorator a check with instructions to redecorate O.J.'s Rockingham home to Paula's taste that same week demonstrating further intentions of permanency.

Whatever you or I might believe about these murders, it is clear to me that the scientific evidence both from a psychological as well as forensic point of view doesn't support any clear conclusions. Although I focused only on the domestic violence evidence, as an on-looker, I couldn't help but be impressed with the contamination of the blood evidence from the crime scene. That doesn't mean that people won't have their own emotional conclusions about "whodunit" here. However, it is important not to confuse empirical data with feelings, no matter how accurate they might be.

FUTURE RESEARCH

This research has given many answers as well as raised new questions. Although the data suggest numerous psychological effects of battering on women, more careful measurement is appropriate. Clarifying the nature of depression, anxiety, and other mental health indices is indicated to assist therapists and other community helpers design more responsive institutions. Although society must change its attitudes in order to stop spouse abuse, individuals make up the society. Therefore, a continuing search for analysis of the interactive effects on people that cause men to beat up women is still in order. The group that needs to be addressed is, of course, the violent men. When I wrote the first edition of this book, I called for the development of methods to bring the violent men into the laboratory as well as going out into the field. I suggested studying these men both in the situational context as recommended for women and in looking for individual differences, perhaps in the therapist's offices. Martin (1976) suggests that there has been bias in studying the men, which has been to pay too much attention to the situational context, that is, listening to his litany of complaints against the woman and accepting it as reason for the battering. Rather, a more psychological approach using a deficit model suggested by Ganley and Harris (1978) and Sonkin and Durphy (1982) needs to be used. Our data would support the existence of a violence-prone personality; current experimental methodology, with a well-drawn sample and some modifications as described earlier, could provide the knowledge we now lack. In fact, some of those gaps in knowledge have been filled in with the preliminary research of Jacobson and Gottman (1998), Dutton (1995, 1998), and O'Leary (1993) although we still have many unanswered questions.

Further research into the learned helplessness/learned optimism construct is also suggested. It is an intriguing concept to explain many of the psychological deficits thought to occur after the violence takes place and preventive methods for strengthening women, particularly those at high risk to become multiple abuse victims. Our data do not indicate that women who experience the most serious violence are the most helpless in coping with it. Such a finding would have supported the literature, which suggests the very terrorizing nature of the brutality alone keeps women locked in these relationships. In fact, we found that brutally beaten women, in general, do not stay that long in battering relationships as compared to nonbattering relationships. This is not to minimize the real impact of living with fear of bodily injury or death. But different women cope in different ways, and the learned helplessness/learned optimism construct provides one way to analyze the negative spiral effect of their psychological interactions.

Further research into the actual influence of sex roles on behavior is suggested by our data. Brooks (1998), Brown (1994), Caplan and Caplan (1994), Geffner et al. (1997), Kaslow (1997), and Levant and Pollack (1993) have begun this work. We need to understand why women who hold nonsexist attitudes toward the role of women are beaten into submitting to behavior that is the opposite of their attitudes. Do they label their own beliefs as deviant with standards that are impossible to meet should they choose a partner? Our sample gave some hint of such explanation. So many of the women choose not to enter a new intimate relationship with a man. Others expressed cynical resignation that all men were alike in their demands on women so they would have to "settle for less" if they wanted a relationship at all. Like many other feminist researchers, I have concern with the impact of rigid sex role socialization patterns on people's behavior. This research did not clarify its role for abused women, although it did suggest that they viewed the batterer's demands as oppressively rigid even though they tried to meet them. Although just how it works wasn't clarified, these data support the feminist logic that sex role rigidity is bad and sex-fair opportunities are good. More understanding of how this sex role differential works in male-female relationships is needed.

It is probably time to put aside the large-scale survey research programs, such as this one, which were necessary to identify and define the important variables we now know need to be studied. Now, we need large-scale longitudinal studies, which measure those individual and situational variables identified as being important to understand. Comparing samples across different cultures at different developmental times is an insufficient substitute because of the complex interrelationship of situational factors. A measure of frequency and severity of battering, such as suggested by the concept of a battering quotient, must be developed to replace the inadequate, unidimensional measures that merely count broken noses and black eyes. Despite our calls for this research 15 years ago, the inadequate Conflict Tactics Scale (CTS) is still the only measure being routinely used in research studies. Our data suggest that any measure excluding psychological abuse will miss the essence of the battering experience for the women. And, finally, longitudinal studies can measure the impact of experiencing violence on subsequent behavior of children.

Theories that continue to promote unidimensional causation of violence have been rendered outdated by this research and others, such as the Straus et al. (1980) epidemiological study and its replications throughout the intervening years. Multidimensional causation still needs to be clarified. The resource theory, expanded upon by Allen and Straus (1980), which suggests that violence is a resource invoked when people lack any other resources to gain power, is not supported by these data. If it were accurate, more women would utilize their resources or indeed, train themselves to become more violent. Historical analysis indicates that women have rejected offensive use of violence, though women will use violence in defense of self or children. The 1997 statistics reported in Chapter 6 on the rise of juvenile crime makes it clear that girls are still not committing a major proportion of violent crimes despite the fact that more of them appear to be exposed to violence and trauma in their homes and communities.

CONFLICT TACTICS SCALE

The Straus et al. (1980) Conflict Tactics Scale measure distorts women's use of violence by not differentiating between such offensive and defensive use. Gelles (1983) has attempted to enlarge this concept into a multidimensional theory of exchange social control. The exchange theory tenets are a behavioral approach to understanding social relationships in general (probably compatible with current social learning theory), while the social control aspects are said to relate to the explanation of different forms of social deviance. Subsumed under the social control theory would be the power issues raised by feminist sex role and violence analysis. Further, Gelles uses the social control approach as though it actually does have the potential to prevent intrafamilial violence, a concept that neither his own research, these data, nor others could support. Gelles suggests changing the social costs so that social control can indeed reach its potential. Giles-Sims' (1983) analysis from a systems perspective further draws a theoretical picture of how such a construct can be measured. Ideally, a society which is deliberately constructed from these tenets needs to be studied. Unfortunately, exchange theory would predict that the very nature of its being observed would create conditions that make serious physical abuse unlikely to occur.

COST-BENEFIT ANALYSIS OF BATTERING RELATIONSHIPS

A cost benefit analysis, suggested by these data particularly in understanding the repetitive nature of the cycle of violence in these relationships, is compatible with Gelles' (1983) approach. Karr, Long, and Witte (1981) apply economic analysis to the cost benefit factor and conclude that raising the cost of using violence in society will make the price too high to justify using it. Berk et al. (1983) develop a comprehensive analysis of how the criminal justice system can be utilized to raise its cost. Unfortunately, the criminal justice system is more of a punishment-based philosophy that has its problems in trying to provide rehabilitative as well as punishment simultaneously. It may be that a more comprehensive program that also includes loss of property and family contact including access to children is more of a threat than overnight in jail as is the current punishment in most jurisdictions.

The intervening years suggest that there will not be one program that will reach all those involved in domestic violence relationships due to their diversity. These data suggest that women are willing to pay a certain price for an intimate relationship but are willing terminate it when the cost exceeds the benefits received. Identifying what are the actual benefits and costs and how the ratio is formulated will be helpful in driving up the cost and, perhaps, reduce the violence. Research is needed to fill in the gaps of this still rudimentary, yet promising model.

CHAPTER TWELVE

Psychotherapeutic Responses to Changing Violent Relationships

When a battered woman seeks therapy while she is still in the abusive relationship, the most sought-after goal that she wants is for the therapist to somehow to fix the man by helping her to change her own behavior. She erroneously believes that the reality of their life together will resemble the potential that she and maybe he dreamt it could be during their courtship period. This is true for the clients I have seen for psychotherapy, the trainees who I have supervised, and those professionals who attend my workshops every where I travel. It was true 15 years ago, and it is still the answer that my audience wants to hear, today.

> "Make him stop his violence." *I just know that if I can make him stop beating me, everything will be fine!*

In North America, where psychotherapy is widely accepted as a means to change maladaptive behavior, the emphasis at first was to find an adequate approach to couples' therapy. It was thought that the woman needs to learn to stop whatever provocative behavior she was displaying in the relationship, and then, the abuse would stop. Today, the community standard for proper therapy has changed. Unless the man takes full responsibility for using violence, no matter what the woman does, the abuse does not stop. To help make it clear that it is his problem and not a system or family problem, it is widely accepted that both the man and the woman must be in treatment separately, at least initially. Then, once the man has taken responsibility for his violent behavior and has begun to change and the woman has regained her sense of self, learns to identify what she really wants and can make her own decisions, it may be possible for the couple to go into treatment together. Treatment models for a family unit rendered dysfunctional because of the man's violent behavior have had little success in effecting a permanent cessation of the violent behavior when they are the only form of therapy. Newer models that are used after successful completion of individual therapy have been developed by Geffner (Holden, Geffner, & Jouriles, 1998), Gauthier and Levendosky (1996), and Kaslow (1997) among others.

The development of offender-specific treatment approaches for batterers that include stabilization of feelings and changing cognition through psychoeducational and cognitive-behavioral approaches appear to have had the most success in stopping woman battering (Sonkin, 1995; Sonkin & Durphy, 1982; Sonkin et al., 1985) when therapy works. There are those who believe that there is an over-reliance on psychology today and that greater consequences for the abuser would make more sense. The research, however, supports common sense in suggesting that given the diversity among batterers, a variety of approaches used in different combinations would have the most success in stopping abuse. A new approach to helping battered women heal by using a combination of feminist, trauma and cognitive-behavioral theories appears to be the most helpful to move from victim to survivor. I have developed a comprehensive approach to working with battered women detailed in the book, *Abused Women and Survivor Therapy* (Walker, 1994) and illustrated in two video tapes (Walker, 1996b, 1998), and there are others who have developed a variety of approaches.

SOCIAL RESPONSIBILITY

In truth, the most effective response to changing violent relationships is to change the structure of society. If women had equal status with men in social, political, economic, educational, and family areas, then they would be less likely to live with spouse abuse. This is most clearly demonstrated when looking at other countries, particularly in underdeveloped areas. The January 1999 special edition of the *American Psychologist* (Walker, 1999) reporting on psychology and domestic violence in countries such as Chile (McWhirter, 1999), Greece (Antonopoulou, 1999), Israel (Steiner, 1999), Japan (Kozu, 1999), Mexico (Fawcett, Heise, Isita-Espejel, & Pick, 1999), Nicaragua (Ellsberg, Caldera, Herrera, Winkvist, & Kullgren, 1999), Russia (Horne, 1999), and other data gathered by Heise (1993, 1996, 1998). Many of the women interviewed in this research program blamed their need for some autonomy as instigation of the man's violent behavior. While they disliked his inability to tolerate their need to get a job or have a separate checking account, these women understand that most men have been raised to believe in separate and not equal gender roles. Few called themselves "women's libbers" or "feminists" and most would agree that such liberationists wore creating their own trouble. Yet, they agreed with the goals of the women's liberation movement. Contradictions like these abound in our society and are not just reflected in battered women's lives. But, until each of us feels free to pursue whatever goals we choose, without expressing our unhappiness through violence, we run the risk of being trapped in a destructive relationship. Experiments continuously are taking place in designing new relationships free from the restrictions of our sexist and violent past, but still filled with the warmth and joy of the intimacy we crave. Until we find those answers, our society will need to provide relief from the pain caused by its own failures.

BATTERED WOMAN'S SHELTERS

One of the most successful means of providing relief for battered women and their children has been the shelter or safe home concept. It began in England when Erin Pizzey opened the first refuge in 1972 (Pizzey, 1974) and rapidly spread to the United States and many other European countries (Martin, 1976; Roy, 1978; Davidson, 1979; Schechter, 1982; Walker, 1979; Berk, Newton, & Berk, 1986; Dobash & Dobash, 1981). Today, we find battered woman shelters in most countries. The presence of even just one battered woman shelter, though inadequate to meet everyone's needs, is critical to give the message to the entire community that abuse against women will be not be tolerated. This is particularly important when cultural and religious messages conflict, sometimes even facilitating further abuse by sending the woman right back into the violent home when she seeks help. Of course, there are limitations to the services that battered woman shelters can provide. Although there are few policies regulating who can use the shelter, the programs are usually designed to address women who are battered by men partners and not women partners. Male children over the age of 13 or 14 are rarely accepted into shelter, partly because many have already identified with their father's violent behavior and partly because it is a woman-oriented experience. Rarely can pets be accommodated, necessitating making other arrangements in the middle of the crisis that usually brings the woman to shelter. However, veterinarians in many communities have volunteered boarding these animals for the short time that women are in shelter.

While there have been a variety of shelter models provided, all of them meet the primary purpose of protecting women and children from a violent man's immediate abuse. Most shelters are located in their own home-like building whose address is not widely known within the community, but neither is it completely hidden so as not to encourage "hide and seek" type of game-playing for batterers. Usually 20 women and children can be accommodated at any time. During peak periods, overcrowding does occur. A typical shelter costs approximately U.S. $250,000 per year to operate. Some small communities cannot financially support a separate home and, instead, use a system of trained volunteers to provide safety in their own homes. Many places have both systems in operation. Rural areas train people to drive a battered woman to safety and, in some places, a relay system of drivers can get a woman to another state within a short time. An "underground railroad"—which can move women and children throughout the world, whenever it becomes necessary—exists. The presence in a community, then, makes a clear statement that spouse abuse won't be tolerated, and if it occurs, the community will provide a separate home for the victim.

While there has been lots of debate concerning the correct philosophy of a battered woman's shelter, few dispute its effectiveness in a crisis. Fifteen years ago, most shelters in North America were developed using a feminist model. Today, most shelters have evolved into a social service model, perhaps in order to obtain government financing to survive. Loeske and Berk (1981) evaluated what battered women in the Santa Barbara shelter deemed as helpful as an attempt to resolve the service provider/feminist organization issue. They found that stressing the immediate incident that brought about the woman's call to the crisis line was the usual entry into the shelter system itself. Almost one-half called for help within one day of an acute battering incident. However, over 20% of their callers reported the most recent incident had occurred a week or more prior to seeking help, indicating fear of the future might be more the woman's concern which finally brought her into the shelter. The diversity that was found in what battered women said they need and expect from a shelter indicates that no one philosophy could meet these needs. Loeske and Berk suggest that it might be helpful if the shelter worker and client both define their goals and the nature of available help within each situation.

Some shelter models suggest that staff roles be limited to woman advocacy and not provide direct services. In West Germany, for example, Hagemann-White (1981) describes the conflict surrounding professional training and pay for full-time work in the Berlin shelter and the other 85 shelters in the Federal Republic of Germany. She makes a compelling argument for promoting a microcosm of a woman-identified feminist society in the shelter to avoid being merely a band-aid and thus, encouraging women to return to abusive homes. Shelters are seen, then, as more than a crisis haven, but also a place to try out new social orders. In the past 20 years, battered women shelters have created a model of mothers and children developing a new family unit, free from violence. In most shelters, there are no-hitting rules forcing some mothers to learn new forms of discipline, particularly positive reinforcement strategies. This is important as one way to reverse the effects of being exposed to violence in childhood is for children to be exposed to many positive experiences. The typical visitation problems that occur when both parents are forced to share parental responsibilities in homes where there has been domestic violence often perpetuate the abuse and prevent children and their mothers from healing from the trauma. At least when in shelter, women have some time and psychological space to begin to think about their goals for the rest of their lives. Being together with other battered women often helps women to stop blaming themselves and emphasize their own strengths.

Rebecca and Russell Dobash (1981), American sociologists living in Scotland, argue that shelters must provide an alternative to the patriarchal structure fostered in a capitalistic society. Stark and Flitcraft (1983) agree with the need for such a political as well as social analysis. But, while their political analysis correctly predicts class oppression, there is no direct evidence that it makes a substantial difference in the rate of spouse abuse, which is found to occur across all social classes and in all political systems. Rather, it is the way in which women and men are socialized to relate to each other which seems to be most critical (Antonopoulou, 1998). Looking at women in Nicaragua has provided a good example of a country torn apart with political civil war that has been able to provide some services to women while rebuilding the political and economic infrastructure of the country. Not surprisingly, women who were never married during this period were found to be less depressed and suffer less from the trauma than those who also faced abuse within their marital homes (Ellsberg et al., 1999). The current oppressed status of women in Russia is demonstration that the promise of equality under a socialistic order, such as occurred under communism, didn't happen (Horne, 1999). Economic rather than political organization may well be a more important variable to women's safety.

Shelters organized around an alternative collective approach seem to have more difficulty staying funded than those more compatible with the social service philosophy within their own country. In the United States there has been much concern that fear of losing funds would be used as a way to scapegoat those feminist and lesbian women who work in shelters where the community political climate became more conservative. This has happened. The original feminist philosophy that prevailed in battered women shelters throughout the United States and Canada has been replaced in many communities by a more social services model. However, the politics of the battered woman movement has remained feminist, often causing conflicts that may impact on the quality of services delivered in some places. Since there are few training resources for shelter workers outside of the university or national organizations, these tensions remain a part of providing shelter. Further, the tensions between advocates and professionally trained service workers have not been resolved, again placing battered women and their children in the middle—facing hostile husbands on one side and hostile advocates on the other. When this type of situation occurs, no one gets her needs met. However, the political climate amongst lawmakers and policy makers is very supportive of finding better ways to provide safety for battered women and their children which does give strength to the important work of the advocates (Biden, 1993; Goodman et al., 1993).

In Finland, Peltoniemi (1982) and Peltoniemi and Aromaa (1982) describe four battered women shelters funded by the government for a 3-year pilot period. Over 500 women and an equal number of children used these shelters during the first year. Peltoniemi tells of the deliberate decision to choose a family-dynamic model instead of an alternative feminist ideology despite the Finnish socialist political system. The same occurred when Israel set up fifteen centers for domestic violence around the country where social services, not shelters, were offered. Even the funding source came from two different centers in the government—the women's programs and the family programs (Steiner, 1999). The arbitrary dichotomy of family versus feminist orientation is one that is unnecessary although understandable given the fear that women's demands for equality have engendered. Most shelters need to provide family support services and can still do this within a feminist ideology. The goal is to keep the women and children violence-free. If to do so means a separation between husband and wife, then it is necessary to isolate the violent man to protect the family.

The decision of whether or not to provide offender-specific treatment for the batterer has been more controversial in the shelter movement. Myers (1982) describes a program for working with the abusers run by the Houston battered woman's center because the women there have requested such a service be provided. Many battered women feel that they must get help for the men to try to get them to change their behavior before they are willing to give up the dream of making this relationship work. This is particularly true when using the criminal justice system, as described in the next chapter. Battered women are more likely to testify against the batterer if they believe he will get help to stop his violent behavior, whether or not they want to keep the relationship. The good psychoeducational programs are often supervised by or run by the battered woman groups in a community, as they are careful to include changing men's socialized attitudes toward women within their treatment programs. On the other hand, many shelters believe that any public or private funding received must go directly into programs for women and children victims. Obviously, in a system with finite resources, decisions must be made to prioritize services. Some shelters would disagree with the Houston approach, insisting as does Hagemann-White, that women must cease taking responsibility for the men's mental health. The need to make these kinds of political decisions has caused tensions that more often divide rather than unite those with different philosophies.

The feminist philosophy supports the power of each woman to make her own decisions. It suggests allowing a battered woman to have the option of trying everything she needs to do before giving up a relationship that has provided her with both pleasure and pain. Yet, there is also a responsibility to demonstrate viable alternatives to the current socialized concept of intimate relationships. The dignity and courage these women demonstrate, even at their greatest point of frustration, can be appreciated when they finally choose to be safe and free from violence. Shelters, whatever their philosophy, do manage to give them that choice. Most women in shelter need some support to move forward with their lives, whether they stay out of the relationship or try to fix it so that they and their children live violence-free. For some women, psychotherapy that empowers and validates them, can be a means to help carry it out. Thus, I have spent the past 15 years training psychotherapists and advocates in new ways to deliver psychotherapy services that empower women to help them go from being a victim to being a survivor.

EVALUATION FOR BATTERED WOMAN SYNDROME

Battered women seek psychological services for a variety of reasons— usually to provide some assistance in coping with a particularly difficult life situation. Sometimes a woman will come to a therapist because of the violence itself, while other times another reason gets her there. Problems with the courts, substance addiction, psycho-physiological pain complaints, and school problems of children are frequent indirect reasons for seeking out a clinician. Pleading by family, friends, lawyers, shelter staff, and her own determination to stop the abuse are the usual direct reasons. Whatever brings her to a therapist's office, it is predictable that her basic lack of trust will pull her out if certain measures aren't taken to convince her that the therapist will be helpful (Moore & Pepitone-Rockwell, 1979; Walker, 1994). Several assumptions work well to establish rapport and create the atmosphere she needs to be able to confide her story. The first one is to believe a woman when she claims to be battered. It is rare that a woman would make up such ghastly stories, and if it should happen, inconsistencies during the interview will alert the clinician's suspicions. Many of the new strategies for detecting malingering and deception have not been normed on a population of battered women, who may have self-interest in claiming to be battered when they are not, but also may be telling as much of the truth as they can given their long history of lying and manipulating to cover up for the abuser when they believed they could be hurt more if they exposed him and didn't follow his orders. In performing an evaluation, it is always necessary to remember that what appears to be pathology in a non-abused woman, may well be a coping or survival strategy for a battered woman. Whether or not she can drop that behavior when it is no longer necessary for her safety is the best test of how embedded it is in her personality structure. Obviously, this will necessitate a period of time, usually 6 months to 1 year, of her being free from violence and abuse.

HISTORY GATHERING

It is suggested that the therapist allow at least 2 hours for the initial interview with a potential client. More time may be necessary if the woman appears to be in crisis. The first hour is usually spent taking a brief history and building trust. If successful, then the battered woman will begin to detail the abuse in the second hour. When I do an evaluation with someone who has not yet taken any steps to terminate the relationship, she and I explore how she might do so safely, examining the trouble spots carefully. I offer to develop a safety plan with her and listen for information in her recitation that will be helpful to do so. Active listening without giving interpretations of behavior can help validate the woman's experiences and reassure that you will not label her "crazy" as both she and her partner have feared. I also label her as a battered woman at some point in the interview so that she has a name for the symptoms she is experiencing. In addition, I give her information about battered woman syndrome and Post Traumatic Stress Disorder helping her to understand that a normal person may be expected to respond with the PTSD and BWS symptoms in order to cope with the situation. While it may initially frighten some women to be labeled as battered, it also gives them a justification and explanation for the changes they know they have experienced in cognition, emotions, and behavior. It also gives them hope that they can be helped to feel like themselves again.

In evaluating the risk of further danger, it is most important to learn the frequency and severity of the violence both at present and in the past. There are various checklists that can be of assistance in gathering the information in a systematic way (DeBecker, 1997; Sonkin, 1995; Walker, 1994; Walker & Meloy, 1998). Estimating the rapidity of the violence escalation can be done by using data gathered about the first acute battering incident, a typical one, one of the worst, and the final incident, similar to what we did in this research study. This four-incident method was developed during the research project and has stood the test of time. Since many women minimize violent acts and injuries, it is important to ask specific questions about them. Inquiries are made into threats to kill, available weapons, choking and other life-threatening acts, violence potential toward others, and specific examples of psychological abuse. While physical abuse is easy to recognize, it is often difficult for therapists to ask for specific details. Figley (1995) and Perlman and Saakvitne (1995) describe the potential effects of trauma on those who provide assistance to trauma victims where it is not unusual to develop secondary post traumatic stress symptoms themselves. The APA (1996a) Presidential Task Force on Violence and the Family suggested that it is common for professionals who hear repeated stories of the violence to skip the details either because they felt that recounting them would be too difficult emotionally for the victim or they were unable to hear it again. Becoming too compassionate or too emotionally distant from the victim will impede the ability to be genuine and authentic in therapy and may suggest the need for a referral or consultation before proceeding. In fact, trauma theory makes it clear that it is important for victims to repeatedly talk about their experiences so that they can gain mastery over the emotions raised and learn new cognitive schemas that give the trauma different meaning (Foa, Rothbaum, Riggs, & Murdock, 1991; Kolodny, 1998) than the initial distortions that sometimes come from retrospective guilt and memory errors. Some treatment, such as EMDR (Shapiro & Forrest, 1997), is more oriented around preverbal memories and therefore, emotional responses are dealt with differently. If the woman currently is separated from her partner, it is important to learn how frequent their contact is and what kinds of conflicts occur when they do have contact. Escalation around access to the children is an important sign of increasing danger to both the women and the children (Sonkin, 1995; Walker & Meloy, 1998). The woman's perception of the level of the man's anger at any particular time is also important as she usually is the best judge (Walker, 1994).

It is crucial for the woman to understand that the purpose of therapy, should she decide to pursue it after the evaluation is completed, is to help her grow and regain her emotional strength and sense-of-self in a violence-free environment, not to terminate the relationship. At some point, she may decide that the only way for her to continue to grow is to leave the battering relationship. This is important because many batterers attempt to intrude on the therapy to make sure the treatment will not be antithetical to his interests in keeping the relationship the same. When he questions the woman, which most report that the man inevitably does if he knows she is in treatment, then she can honestly report that "my therapist is not interested in whether or not we stay together, just in my staying violence-free and safe." This also minimizes any power struggles that may result from the initial phase of therapy and permits the woman to begin to develop trust in the therapeutic relationship. This may change once the woman starts to feel stronger and more assertive in the relationship, and the woman must be prepared for the possibility that the batterer will react negatively to her growing strength. It is difficult for most batterers to accept any independent actions from the woman, particularly if he is dependent upon her and feels anxious that she will not be there for him. Such reactions often result in a greater amount of power and control through coercion and psychological means first, and then physical abuse should he perceive that he is losing control over her.

In highly lethal situations, the clinician has a responsibility to share perceptions of danger with the woman and others, where appropriate. It is important to be honest that good therapy will help her be safer, but not always out of the way of the batterer's harm. If the batterer is in treatment and the woman is willing to give permission, it may be helpful to have some communication with his treating therapist. However, this must be done carefully so that it does not interfere with her trust of the therapist's total allegiance to her. Battered women, like other trauma victims, do not have the ability to perceive neutrality or even objectivity. Either someone is totally on her side, or that person is perceived as being against her. Yet, at the same time, therapists cannot condemn the batterer, himself or it may be seen as another power struggle for the woman. Rather, it is important to inform the woman that the battering behavior is unacceptable without passing judgment on the man himself. Examples of how to do this can be seen in training video demonstrations (Walker, 1994, 1998).

SAFETY PLANS

During this first evaluation, I encourage a woman still living in the relationship to devise an escape plan for when the violence escalates. First, she identifies the cues she perceives as a signal for an impending battering. Most battered women can do this even though initially they may have difficulty verbalizing such cues. Sometimes the first cue is physiologically perceived anxiety, other times, it is a change in the man's facial expressions—particularly his eyes that are described as "getting darker," "no eye-contact," "looking like nobody is home," and other recognizable patterns being repeated. Then, we discuss a plan of escape including specifying strategies that must be preplanned to execute it. For example, locating the nearest telephone, either near a store or in a neighbor's home. Or, having an extra key to the car hidden, spare clothes left with a neighbor, a personal bank account or other access to cash, alerting children to a danger signal, and so on. Finally, we rehearse the plan of escape, step by step, estimating how much time it will take for various activities, such as dressing the baby in the wintertime. The goal is to make it an automatic and familiar response in crisis, in much the way of routine fire drills. It makes the therapist less anxious and frightened for the client's safety, and gives the woman some hope of really being able to escape. It is important to remember that most women who have developed learned helplessness as described in Chapter 9, have traded coping strategies for escape strategies and are unable to think that escape is even possible during a crisis. Even if this woman does not return to therapy, she has learned an important escape plan that may save her life.

FORMERLY BATTERED WOMEN

Evaluations may also be done with formerly battered women who are still experiencing the after-effects of living in violence. These women may seek therapy to help them through the transition period or perhaps because some other problem has caused the reawakening of the original trauma symptoms. It is common for battered women to experience multiple types of trauma including child abuse prior to the battering relationship or sexual harassment on the job either before or after the battering. In some cases, the presence of a new relationship with a man can trigger old psychological response patterns learned during the battering relationship. There appears to be a loss of resiliency each time a woman experiences a new trauma rather than being able to learn how to better cope with it. For example, after a serious earthquake in San Jose, Costa Rica many battered women experienced new PTSD symptoms reawakened by the new traumatic event even though it had little resemblance to interpersonal violence except in the feelings of fear and lack of power to control the event.

The same format for an initial evaluation is followed with the addition of a carefully detailed description of the couple's current contact. Since the separation period is reported as one of the most dangerous times, all precautions should be explored, encouraging her to have the least possible contact. Strong legal sanctions, should violence erupt, are important deterrents, both for the man and for the woman who is helped to feel safer and more likely to protect herself. The data indicate that there is no such thing as being over cautious during this period; all vigilance is appropriate. If child visitation is necessary, strict limits need to be imposed by the courts and followed by the woman. However, even if she continues to have contact with the man despite court orders, it is his responsibility not to violate the restraining order unless the court also formally restrains her. Mutual restraining orders are not as effective in stopping the batterer's violence and are becoming less popular with the courts, so it is a reasonable expectation that only he can experience legal consequences for not following court orders. On the other hand, it is important to help the woman realize that if she voluntarily initiates contact with the man, she is giving him a double message and therefore, may be prolonging the conflict. Having the children picked up and returned at a neutral place such as a friend's or relative's home, a busy shopping center, or even the nearest police station may avoid any additional harassment, especially if she can persuade others to accompany her. Supervised visitation may have to be arranged if the man's violence is out of control in front of the children. Negotiation sessions concerning property distribution are best left to a trusted and knowledgeable attorney with support from the therapist. Often, such an evaluation can be used to obtain a restraining order in cases where emotional and/or physical damage is significant.

TRADITIONAL PSYCHOLOGICAL DIAGNOSIS

An important part of a clinical evaluation is ruling out other emotional disorders. As this research study and others have found battered women in all strata of society, it can be generalized to expect that some will have serious mental health problems that will respond to survivor therapy (Walker, 1994). Some emotional problems can be directly attributed to an outcome of the battering relationship, while others may be more longstanding in nature. The standard clinical interview and the DSM-IV or ICD-10 diagnostic manual can provide the most efficient means of evaluation, especially since the various psychotherapy professions recognize this procedure. Furthermore, the client may then be entitled to medical insurance reimbursement for the therapist's fee for services although the managed health care plans carefully regulate mental health treatment, sometimes to the detriment of the client getting proper services. Private therapy is an alternative to managed health care or government-supported mental health centers. Therapists who are competent and well trained in domestic violence need to be selected.

In some cases, it is appropriate and necessary to use standardized psychological tests to augment the clinical evaluation. Measurement of cognitive, personality, and trauma-related symptom functioning can be done by using the traditional tests but supplementing the usual interpretations with knowledge about trauma victims performance (Dutton, 1992; Rosewater, 1985, 1987; Walker, 1994). Cognitive functioning is most often measured by using the Weschler Adult Intelligence Scale-Third Edition (WAIS-III) while personality can be measured by objective tests such as the Minnesota Multiphasic Personality Inventory-Second Edition (MMPI-2) and subjective tests such as the Rorschach and Thematic Personality Inventory. Figure drawings such as Draw-a-Person, House-Tree-Person, and Kinetic Family Drawings are also useful, as are Sentence Completion Tests. The new trauma inventories are very helpful for designing therapy treatment plans, particularly when needing to obtain an objective measure of trauma symptoms before and after therapy. The Modified Fear Survey originally developed by Wolpe and modified by Kilpatrick et al. (1989) and Kilpatrick and Resick (1993) is a good checklist for trauma-related fears, while the Trauma Symptom Inventory (TSI) developed by Briere and Elliott (1997) is a standardized measure of PTSD and BWS symptoms that can also be useful in litigation to demonstrate the emotional damages from abuse. Briere and Elliott (1997), Dutton (1992), and Walker (1994) provide more specific discussions for psychological interpretation of standardized tests when evaluating the impact of abuse on cognitive, affective, and behavioral domains.

The five-axis system of diagnosis using the DSM-IV (APA, 1994) allows for recognition of the Battered Woman Syndrome usually subsumed within the diagnostic criteria for Post Traumatic Stress Disorder, coded on Axis 1. There are provisions for coding a new crisis under the Acute Stress Reaction, if trauma symptoms have only been present for less than 1 month, while the PTSD category is used if the symptoms have been present for more than 1 month and have impacted on the woman's social, occupational or other functioning. The initial trauma must be experienced as something that is dangerous enough to cause bodily damage or death and creates the feelings of fear and helplessness. Surely, most domestic violence incidents will meet this definition, especially when the pattern escalates over time. This category is appropriate to use whether the violence is ongoing or it has stopped, but psychologically continues to have an impact on the woman's functioning usually through reexperiencing the trauma mentally. Nightmares, intrusive memories and persistent fear that the violence is recurring when exposed to similar situations are a feature of this reaction to extraordinary stress. So are other observable anxiety reactions including specific phobias and panic disorders, especially common in women who have also been sexually abused. Emotional lability with frequent crying spells is common as is a euphoric response to less tension followed by fear of punishment for feeling so good. Many women go back and forth in their feelings about the batterer, experiencing memories of both the good and bad times. Sometimes, these volatile emotions can be controlled through teaching the woman her own cycle of abuse as outlined in Chapter 10.

Battered Woman Syndrome (BWS) includes disruption in interpersonal relationships, usually from the isolation, overpossessiveness, intrusiveness and jealousy displayed by the batterer. Women need to relearn how to trust and develop good social relationships, differentiating friends from acquaintances and other interpersonal strategies usually learned by adolescence. Creating and maintaining good boundaries between themselves and others is another skill in interpersonal relationships that may have been damaged during the overly intrusive battering relationship. Those with BWS may also have a distorted body image having had so little control over how the batterers treat their bodies. Women who have also been sexually abused, particularly incest survivors and those who have been sexually harassed sometimes gain a lot of weight, almost as if they are creating a barrier to better control intrusive touching. Intimacy problems including sexual intimacy with another partner can be a lasting part of BWS that therapy can help resolve. Perhaps the longest lasting symptom from BWS is the hypervigilance to cues of further danger and exaggerated startle response. Women report being "jumpy," "nervous." "scared easily," "feeling anxious," "panicky," and other symptoms of high levels of anxiety for many years after they intellectually know that there is no more reason to fear being abused. Perhaps, like animals who have once experienced a forest fire and then scamper around trying to escape when someone just lights a match, BWS leaves the battered woman with a hypersensitive autonomic nervous system response that is designed to enhance her survival.

Long-standing depression and bipolar disorders may also be diagnosed in addition to the PTSD if it is apparent that the depression is more pervasive than reactive to the abuse. Given the confusion surrounding the measured depression of the women in the research sample, unless there is evidence of such a long-standing depressive disorder, such as a prior history especially of the bipolar type, I prefer to defer an additional diagnosis. If the depression does not abate with therapy specific to alleviating the trauma effects, then a separate diagnosis should be made. Even in cases where the woman has a family history of affective disorders, it is possible that she may never have developed a full-blown depressive disorder had she not have been subjected to the abuse. This may an important finding should she get involved in litigation that involves her mental health.

An Axis II diagnosis of a more longstanding personality disorder can be made simultaneously, if appropriate, although my recommendation is to wait while the woman is in treatment to see what symptoms drop out because they are no longer needed as coping strategies and which ones remain despite the woman having survived and feeling safe. I usually reserve any diagnoses in this category during an evaluation as so many battered women characteristics caused by the battering itself could be confused with other classifications including schizophrenic or borderline symptoms (Herman, 1992; Rosewater, 1984, 1985a; Walker, 1993b). In fact, the entire category of personality disorders have come under scrutiny as having the potential to misdiagnose women because of outdated sexist assumptions and unreliable and invalid criteria that underlie their development (see Chapter 8 and Brown, 1992; Caplan, 1997; Herman, 1992; Kutchins & Kirk, 1997; Lerman, 1996; Root, 1992; Walker, 1993b for further discussion of misdiagnosis with personality disorder labels.)

Axis III permits recording concomitant physical disorders that are often found present in battered women. The research findings on health problems indicate women do report them, often seeking medical attention and relief before coming to a therapist (Chalk & King, 1998; Koss, Ingram, & Pepper, 1997; Koss & Haslet, 1992; Russo, Denious, Keita, & Koss, 1997; Warsaw, 1989). Many injuries from "accidents" treated in hospital emergency rooms are from domestic violence (Bureau of Justice Statistics, 1997). So too for those who report chronic pain (Toomey, Hernandez, Gittleman, & Hulka, 1993) and other medical problems (Koss et al., 1997; Warsaw, 1992). Physicians today have better training to deal with their patients who are being abused (Burgess et al., 1997; Campbell, 1995; Hamberger, 1997; Hamberger & Ambuel, 1997; Saunders & Kindy, 1993). Many such health problems go into a spontaneous remission once the woman is out of the stressful environment of a violent home. This occurrence may support a differential diagnosis of Post Traumatic Stress Disorder, Battered Woman Syndrome or an additional Rape Trauma Syndrome if sexual assault effects are also present.

A rating of the impact of life stressors and other traumas is recorded on Axis IV. This permits the context of the woman's life that may impact her recovery to be attended to in addition to the symptoms observed. Victims who have experienced multiple episodes of different trauma or repeated physical, sexual, or psychological abuse usually have a more severe reaction to domestic violence. Yet, many with resiliency factors in their background have a less severe reaction to serious abuse while others with high risk factors in their history, may be more severely traumatized in a less serious abuse situation. Recognizing individual coping styles, the level of functioning for the previous year is also evaluated and recorded on Axis V using the rating scale provided. A rapid improvement in behavior measured in this axis is also an indication of a reactive state rather than a more serious intrapsychic or personality disorder.

Given the enormous amount of information needed to make a differential diagnosis, completing the evaluation in either one long or several shorter data gathering sessions is suggested. I find that a 2-day intensive period, sometimes working together with a trained associate, produces the most accurate details. During the interview a balance is maintained between gathering information and supporting the woman. The evaluation cannot become an unstructured therapy session or adequate information will be sacrificed. On the other hand, if the woman is not properly supported, she cannot report the necessary details. Thus, skill is required to know when a woman needs to stop responding to the direct questions in the interview and receive some emotional support in order to then continue relating painful details and when to move along without stopping to complete the questionnaire format.

In the Battered Woman Syndrome Questionnaire (BWSQ) currently used for the evaluation, structured questions adapted from the format used in this research project are asked about the relationship, how conflicts were handled, their sexual relationship, drug and alcohol use, as well as other areas. Then, the woman is encouraged to describe what it is like to live with this man in her own words. The combination of forced choice and open-ended questions seems to elicit the best data. Browne and Thyfault (1981) have written on further details of this interview procedure. Little has changed in the procedure over the years although many parts of the interview that did not yield sufficient additional information have been discarded.

THERAPY ISSUES WITH BATTERED WOMEN

Not all battered women need therapy to recover from the effects of repeated traumatic abuse. Many find that living in a violence-free atmosphere along with successful experiences in social, family and work relationships is sufficient for them to heal. Others receive enough love and support from a therapeutic program, such as a shelter or battered woman's counseling group. But, given our therapy-oriented culture, many battered women do seek out counseling. The tales of harm caused by inadequately trained and poorly informed therapists have been told elsewhere (Walker, 1979, 1980c, 1981a, 1984; Rosewater, 1985; Davidson, 1979; and Martin, 1976, among others). The women in this study said they wanted adequate counseling to help their batterers, who many said they still loved. Many also said they wanted counseling to help them get over the psychological effects from abuse more quickly. However, the typical battered woman is a difficult therapy client unless her special needs are met. Many of her characteristic ways of behaving, which help to keep her as safe as possible, can get in the way of therapy intervention.

BARRIERS TO THERAPY

The worst nightmare for most battered women who reach the point of wanting to leave the relationship is the threat of losing custody and control over protecting their children. Fear of such retribution, either more serious harm or taking away her children keep women trapped in these relationships and this fear also is a barrier to coming into treatment. It is realistic to be fearful of losing the ability to protect one's children, as is discussed in the next chapter, and therapists must be aware of the possibility of being subpoenaed into a legal battle despite professional guidelines that suggest separation of therapy from forensic roles. Many of the coping strategies that protect women from further harm, such as minimization of the abuse, denial that it was so bad, forgetting or repressing the acute battering incident, or even self-blame can become barriers to treatment. So too for the shame, guilt and lack of trust that surround the woman's feelings even when she starts to deal with the battering relationship more realistically. The cognitive confusion that may protect women from having to do something about better protecting themselves is a shield in therapy, too and is one reason why cognitive interventions need to be used early in the treatment plan. A fear of losing control is ever present in the battered woman because making a mistake could be fatal. Always sitting on her emotions, for expressing anger and pain may be too dangerous at some times, the battered woman fears she will explode when she finally lets them out. Helping her build a cognitive framework so she gives new meaning to these feelings is an important therapeutic strategy to overcome this barrier early in treatment.

Validating the woman's pain and her perception of her experience can help overcome the barriers that fear of being not believed, misunderstood, trivialized, and blamed can create. Many women say that they fear that the therapist will pressure them to do "something" before they are ready to take actions, so they do not even want to take that chance and enter treatment. Finally, there is the secret fear that maybe they really are "crazy," just like the batterer has been telling them and they will lose everything including the last shreds of self-esteem if the therapist finds out and labels them. It is important to understand these barriers so that therapists can avoid intervention strategies that may seem appropriate in other situations, but will exacerbate women's fears so that they cannot return or use the therapy as effectively had other strategies that help mitigate these fears been used first.

STAGES OF THERAPY

Different treatment models suggest different stages that occur during the therapy process with many acknowledging that treatment needs to deal with complex affective, cognitive, developmental, interpersonal, sociopolitical, and biological consequences of domestic violence. In the Survivor Therapy model (Walker, 1994, 1996) there are five basic stages of treatment including: (1) assessing and labeling the abuse; (2) developing and rehearsing the safety plan; (3) dealing with the psychological, and in some cases the physiological effects of trauma; (4) addressing other psychological effects of the abuse as well as childhood issues including any abuse that may have occurred then; and (5) preparing for termination. In a later revision of this model, Walker (1998), these steps were expanded as follows: (1) identifying, assessing and labeling the abuse and its effects; (2) helping the woman find safety and protection; (3) regaining cognitive clarity; (4) helping heal the PTSD and physiological effects; (5) addressing the psychological impact from prior experiences including childhood issues; (6) rebuilding interpersonal relationships; and (7) integrating the trauma into the life pattern and becoming a survivor.

Short-term treatment often covers the first two or three phases, while long-term therapy goes across all stages understanding some may be revisited and reworked at a later time. Goals of therapy often include the client's control over her memory, mastery over PTSD symptoms, greater regulation of emotions including expanding the range of affect tolerated, greater self-esteem, feeling more empowered with taking control over decisions impacting her life, an integration of memory with emotions, the ability to form interpersonal relationships based on trust, and a new sense of purpose in life. Resolution of trauma symptoms often comes about after there is control over recurring intrusive memories that cause the woman to feel like the abuse is ongoing and stimulates the coping symptoms so they cannot be mastered. Time is needed to gain some emotional distance from the experiences so that healing and reintegration is complete. Therapists need to share power with the client so that misperceptions do not occur that can keep the symptoms from receding. Thus, an authoritarian and directive approach is less effective than one that encourages an egalitarian relationship between therapist and client such as the feminist therapy model. The most reported reason for battered women to drop out of therapy before termination is reached is feeling too pressured by a well-intentioned therapist to do something that she wasn't ready to do, yet. Just listening to the woman and helping her clarify her choices and their consequences can be the most effective treatment.

GOALS OF THERAPY

The ten most important goals of therapy with a battered woman are: (1) helping to ensure the woman's safety; (2) helping the woman to see alternatives to the abuse and explore her options; (3) validating her thoughts, feelings, and choices; (4) helping her regain cognitive clarity and judgment; (5) helping the woman to make and trust her own decisions; (6) helping her to become less anxious, less avoidant and more emotionally responsive; (7) helping her to reestablish a sense of boundaries between herself and others; (8) helping her to reestablish supportive interpersonal relationships with women and men, family, friends, and intimates; (9) fostering her understanding of the broader sociocultural bases of her oppression; (10) modeling for her a more egalitarian relationship in which both parties contribute to the formulation of goals (Walker with Lurie, 1994).

Research demonstrates that stress-related symptoms from trauma normally result in high levels of anxiety, as well as high levels of avoidance and emotional numbing and that victims can adapt to this repeated stress over a period of time so that both cognitive and affective functioning is compromised. Cotton (1990) suggests that the biochemical changes may indeed inhibit the return to pretrauma levels of functioning depending on numerous factors that need to be assessed. Goleman's (1996) description of some of the new psycho-neuro-immunnological (PNI) studies are better able to measure the interaction between biochemical, structural and psychological functions. Various medications, especially the newer Selected Serotonin Reuptake Inhibitors (SSRIs) and other similar in this class, may need to be tried in order to get an individual woman's system reregulated although the psychological issues are critical for compliance.

TREATMENT TECHNIQUES

COGNITIVE-BEHAVIORAL

Cognitive-behavioral approaches to healing from trauma have been most promising during this past decade (Meichenbaum, 1996). Foa, Rothbaum, Riggs and Murdock (1991) have developed empirically validated strategies to work with rape victims that are also helpful for many battered women. Strategies to reduce anxiety and get better control of these feelings include techniques such as relaxation training, cognitive-restructuring, and guided imagery.

HYPNOSIS

While hypnosis has been found to be successful for reregulating both high levels of arousal and avoidance symptoms, in fact, it may preclude the woman exercising her legal rights because of the controversy over the suggestibility to implanting new memories that may not be accurate. Therefore, I do not recommend using hypnosis without full informed consent of the client and only in cases where it is critical to her survival to reduce symptomology. This is often seen in women who have developed extreme dissociative symptoms that can produce life-threatening alter egos or other dangerous tension-reducing behavior. If hypnosis is used, then auto-control techniques are an important feature of the method selected. Teaching someone control over what she is thinking in her mind can usually be accomplished with various thought-stopping techniques. This helps reduce the intrusive memories and the high levels of anxiety that come from the feelings of being out of control. Systematic desensitization to high arousal cues where it does not involve safety and ability to sense impending danger is another set of strategies that can be taught to the woman.

Aroma Therapy

Using adjuncts to therapy are also very helpful to women who often are motivated to do everything they can once they start to feel better. I have used "aroma therapy" as a adjunct because of its ability to stop some of the PTSD symptoms and reduce anxiety. I help the woman choose what aromas she finds pleasing and suggest she carry a small amount of them with her so that any time she feels herself getting aroused, she can first check out if there is a dangerous situation, and then can use the aroma to help calm herself so she can problem solve in a more careful and less anxious way. Commercial shops that have an array of various aromas are a good place for this woman to experiment with finding those that are pleasant aromas to her. An unintended but beneficial secondary effect is that she is getting support for learning how to find and make her own choices rather than simply pleasing someone else.

Eye Movement Desensitization Reprocessing (EMDR)

Another very useful therapy technique is Eye Movement Desensitization Reprocessing or EMDR. First developed by psychologist, Francine Shapiro (Shapiro & Forrest, 1997), the underlying philosophy of the technique is consistent with the latest research on trauma memory. Without necessarily using verbal cues, the woman is encouraged to remember an incident by replaying it in her mind and simultaneously, the therapist uses a physiological technique to try to wipe the memories from her memory by stimulating those areas of the brain through eye movement desensitization. If indeed trauma memories are stored in the mid-brain structures, then verbal cues needed for cognitive memory storage are unnecessary to either reach those memories, bring them into cognitive awareness so they can be decathected from their intense and uncontrolled emotions, and processed back into cognitive memory. The enormous sense of relief that women report from very few EMDR treatments make this an important method to try, especially for those who have multiple victimization experiences and are unable to separate out which memories come from which traumatic event. Although Shapiro is careful to warn that this method has not been tested in litigation, it could be seen as potentially destroying memories and therefore limit the woman's legal options. However, it does not involve the suggestibility factor that is seen in hypnosis studies; rather, it helps the victim process the memories which verbal psychotherapy does too, but takes a much longer time to get there.

RELATIONSHIP BETWEEN CLIENT AND THERAPIST

An important part of any psychotherapy is the relationship that is established between the woman and the therapist. This relationship should be a model for her in relearning how to socialize with others. It should be a safe place where she can try out new social skills that she may need to learn or reestablish those interpersonal relationship skills she had but couldn't use for fear of precipitating another battering incident. Many battered women have kept their sense of humor through all of the terror of living in the abusive relationship. For some it is a life-line; being able to laugh at themselves protected them from total emotional devastation. Using that sense of humor in therapy is often a way to build on the woman's strengths and important to the healing process. Even through the normal process of feeling and expressing their anger at the unjustness of their situation, that little spark of humor can come through and be a buffer from the powerful angry feelings. It seems to be more difficult for male therapists to permit the woman to hold onto her anger for a period of time, which may be different for each woman. Trying to shut off her anger too quickly may interfere with complete healing. It is important to help her find nondestructive ways of using that anger as a motivator, as well as reassure her that it will eventually dissipate and she won't feel such anger all the time. This reassurance that she will not feel like she is on a roller coaster all the time is critical in treatment. Sometimes reading materials on domestic violence can help the woman recognize that she will feel better. Like in all good therapy, timing to introduce any of these techniques is critical.

SPECIAL ISSUES FOR BATTERED WOMEN

MANIPULATION

Perhaps the most difficult characteristic with which to work is the need battered women have to manipulate everyone in their environment. This manipulative behavior is also seen in other victims who report that they believe that there is less likelihood of a being hurt again if the environment is kept as stress-free as possible. Such behavior is often reinforced by its very success for battered women, particularly in slowing the tension-building that occurs in phase one of the violence cycle. Victims of repeated abuse become frightened of any outsider's influence, even therapists' offers of help, fearing any change in the precarious balance of the system will trigger batterers' anger. This wariness is often labeled as paranoia rather than accepted as a coping strategy or natural consequence of constantly living under siege. Manipulating the environment successfully takes constant vigilance and quick preventive strategies that are sometimes interpreted as frantic hysteria, rather than appropriate goal-directed behavior. The distortion is in the women's thinking that maintaining a stress-free environment for the batterer for any length of time is indeed possible.

If the therapist recognizes the danger that any change really could set off another battering incident and takes the woman's fears seriously, a battered woman usually will relax and allows herself to consider less emotionally costly and burdensome means of keeping safe. Since many women experience both hypervigilance and denial of any potential for abuse, the therapist's task is to provide a less contradictory and more stable view of her reality. Repeatedly discussing previous battering incidents, including using the woman's own words to review the violent details, helps convince both the client and the therapist of the continued danger, even during periods of apparent calm in the third phase of the cycle.

HYPERVIGILANCE

Even when the woman is no longer in actual danger, she may react as though violence is still a possibility, until she learns new ways of responding. Using guided imagery to go back over the incidents and revise the endings, may give the woman more power to protect herself.

Many women learn how to do this on their own, often labeling it as daydreaming. Some use martial arts or self-defense classes as a way to feel more in control. Others find exercise at a health club or dance classes where they take back control of their bodies can all be helpful adjuncts to therapy. The important aspect is the new experience of feeling they can maintain their power in the future, in case the past starts to repeat itself. This is accomplished when they accurately remember what happened in the past and can visualize themselves doing something different. It helps reverse the learned helplessness by providing a new way of responding should such an experience recur.

Some therapists trained in relaxation or hypnosis techniques teach them as anxiety control measures. Many of the battered women in the research study described how they unknowingly put themselves in a state-of-mind that is similar to what is sometimes described as a hypnotic trance in order to get through the pain of the brutal attacks. For these women, it is useful to learn more about self-induced hypnotic procedures should they find themselves needing them again. Providing women with techniques they can readily master becomes another way of reducing some of the anxiety and hypersensitivity. EMDR, as described above, is an important new treatment that appears to have good success with PTSD symptoms especially difficulty in managing the reexperiencing of trauma events mentally. Desensitization hierarchies and cognitive behavioral techniques are also quite useful for specific phobic responses, probably conditioned during the violence. Cognitive therapy fits with most battered women's need to control their own minds. Body therapy techniques can also be slowly introduced. Support, understanding, and easy access to the therapist's reassurance at crisis times, also helps reduce the generalized level of anxiety especially when the full emotional impact of everything begins to be felt.

SELF-ESTEEM AND ATTITUDES TOWARDS WOMEN

While self-esteem issues need to be addressed during the therapy process, this research indicates they're more complicated than originally viewed (Walker, 1979, 1981a). Although the women do have low self-esteem, they also perceive their own strengths in surviving a horrible experience. In psychotherapy, supporting the woman's own strength by using specific incidents to remind her of those abilities, will help her reevaluate her own self-worth. Once she gets in touch with her own core of strength, she will be able to work on changing the other areas. Care should be taken not to unleash powerful feelings, especially anger, too quickly before she has experienced her own ability to be in control of them. As was mentioned earlier, the feminist-trauma model of survivor therapy holds that it may be best to start with the woman's strengths in a cognitive-behavioral approach to help protect her from being overwhelmed too quickly by the flood of confusing feelings that eventually will be part of the therapy. Cognitive restructuring procedures that broaden her choices are most compatible for long-term therapy.

This research started out with the premise that battered women needed to work on expanding their attitudes to encompass a more liberal view towards women's roles. However, the results of the AWS, reported in Chapter 8, indicate that they already hold liberal attitudes, so support for choosing nontraditional options is what is needed. Therapists who hold sexist attitudes themselves, or who use therapy techniques which have been found to restrict women's choice and behavior, such as psychoanalysis, cannot provide her with what she needs. For a more complete discussion of the benefits of feminist therapy techniques see Brown and Ballou (1992), Dutton and Walker (1987), Rosewater and Walker (1985), and Walker (1994).

REEMPOWERMENT

Allowing the woman to regain her own power in the therapy relationship is an important step to reexperiencing power in other areas of her life. This can be done in individual therapy or with a group of other battered women. Listening to other women's descriptions of both the violent and the loving parts of their relationship helps put it all in perspective. A second stage group for women to learn new ways of relating to men and women is a powerful adjunct or alternative to individual therapy. Intimacy skills as well as new ways to confront and express angry feelings are more easily acquired in a group setting. The ultimate goal of therapy is to become a survivor, putting the effects of victimization in the past and getting on with life. There is every confidence that battered women can do it, based on the information gained from this research project.

THERAPY ISSUES WITH BATTERERS

Treatment programs for batterers have become more commonplace in different parts of the world as well as in North America during the past 20 years. Often called "offender-specific," "anger management,"

"Duluth model," or simply "domestic violence" programs, most attempt to stop the batterer's violent behavior through psychoeducational techniques together with the threat of jail and other punitive consequences. A surprisingly large number of those arrested for domestic violence get court-ordered into these short-term programs and about three-quarters of the men who get there appear to stop their physical abuse while under such scrutiny (Harrell, 1991). Most advocates believe that an overnight in jail makes the threat of further consequences real for many men who have never faced the criminal justice system before. Obviously, it will not have the same deterrent effect for those who have spent time in jail or prison for other criminal offenses and in fact, the arrest and referral to court-ordered treatment may increase the violent behavior in a small number of men, most of whom do not have good ties to the community. Despite the success of these programs for the power and control batterer, the behavior change is not maintained by those batterers who have other mental disorders and need additional psychotherapy to help them deal with becoming stabilized.

The women in this research sample have suggested the existence of a violence-prone personality pattern in the men. Much of their information is consistent with direct clinical observations of the men who reach court-ordered programs by psychologists such as Dutton (1995), Hamberger et al. (1997), Jacobson and Gottman (1998), Ewing et al. (1984), Lindsay et al. (1992), Pence and Paymar (1993), Saunders (1982), and Sonkin (1995). This personality pattern is thought to be shaped by the individual man's interaction with his environment and its norms. It is considered to be learned behavior, usually learned in the context of a childhood home where violence was the prevalent way to deal with angry feelings. The notion that violence is an unfortunate but natural outcome of anger continues to be accepted as a way to resolve family disputes. Most people still support acceptance of a batterer's statement that he hit his wife because he was provoked or under tremendous stress, if he can cite her obnoxious behavior. In fact, our culture tells us often through the media that it is all right to use some violence at home, up to a point. The message is that it is okay to push or shove your wife and hit your children in the name of discipline, provided you do not really hurt them (Koss et al., 1994).

Given our need for privacy within the family, many abusers still do not recognize that slapping your wife to teach her a lesson is prohibited under the law. The long history of men being responsible for disciplining their wives has left the legacy of not understanding that all assaults are illegal and inappropriate. Thus, both inequality between men and women as well as a learned history of violence contributes to the individual's choice to use violent behavior within the family. If such ideas and behavior are learned, we can unlearn them. However, some traditionally trained therapists treat batterers as though they cannot be expected to stop their physical abuse until they understand what causes them to react in this inappropriate way. The guidelines for the treatment community makes it clear that the woman's safety comes before the man's need to fully understand his behavior. He must learn behavioral controls first—cognitive understanding and processing his feelings comes later.

Information for therapists treating batterers has become available in the literature. Saunders (1982) describes an approach to such therapy intervention detailing therapists' responses which emphasize, support, confront, and provide assistance in stopping the batterer's violent behavior. Saunders includes assertiveness training to teach men how to ask for what they want and how to accept a refusal without resorting to violent behavior. Also stressed is cognitive restructuring which teaches violent men how they talk themselves into becoming more angry, so they can learn to use new self-talk statements to cope with their angry feelings and avoid escalation into a violent incident.

Ganley (1981a, 1981b) has also provided training materials for therapists. Her behavioral approach also includes techniques for reducing learned anger arousal patterns in batterers. The research gained from this study suggests that behavioral and cognitive programs will provide more structure for men who have obvious deficits in control when experiencing their feelings. Psychodynamic and analytic therapy has not been demonstrated to be of value in treating the men. Either group or individual therapy modalities have had the most reported success (see Sonkin & Durphy, 1982).

Batterers who also have a substance abuse problem usually need both kinds of treatment (Sonkin, 1995). While it is not possible to conduct psychotherapy with someone who is high on alcohol and other drugs, once detoxification takes place, it is possible to be in both types of treatment at the same time. In Miami, for example, substance abusing batterers are often referred to both court-ordered, offender-specific treatment groups to stop their violence, and acupuncture treatment to control their drinking or other drug use. In other communities controlled drinking groups or other drug treatment programs are available, although sometimes there is not sufficient communication with the domestic violence programs.

One of the more difficult dilemmas has been for the courts to determine what therapists have been properly trained to offer these treatment programs. In some communities, such as in Colorado, the battered women's lobby has persuaded the legislature to mandate separate credentialing for those who have met training requirements without regard to their general psychological training. In other communities, like Florida, the legislature was persuaded to mandate one specific type of treatment, based on the Duluth model, for all batterers (Pence & Paymar, 1993). As might be expected in the United States, entrepreneurial groups have developed standardized short-term treatment programs and persuaded the courts to send batterers to them. In some cases these programs may be quite effective, but they are educational and not psychotherapy. Thus, they will not provide the required assistance for all batterers, especially those who have concomitant mental disorders that interact with their violent behavior.

CHARACTERISTICS OF BATTERERS

There has been general agreement within the literature that descriptions of batterers' characteristics or behaviors are more useful to service providers than broad categorizations or diagnosis. Batterers are known to come from all sociodemographic backgrounds without racial, ethnic, educational, economic, or social class differences (Straus et al., 1980). Most abusers are male, and the results of this study supports previous estimates that approximately 0.6% may be women. Among the most prevalent characteristics is the tendency to minimize or deny the seriousness of their violent behavior. Unreasonable sexual jealousy, intrusiveness, and an overwhelming need to control the women is another cluster of behaviors found uniformly. Batterers, like other con men, are often very manipulative and can appear both charming and seductive as well as mean and hostile, giving rise to descriptions that they are like the Dr. Jekyll and Mr. Hyde type of personality (Walker, 1979). Many abusers are also violent outside of their home. Some only direct their abuse towards their wives while others also abuse children. Sexual abuse is often a part of their violent behavior.

Characteristics of batterers identified by the Belmont conference participants and supported in the literature since then include:

1. Externalize problems
2. Demonstrate jealousy
3. Use aggressive words and behavior
4. Minimizes and/or denies and/or tells frequent lies
5. Is impulsive
6. Shows self-deprecation

7. Makes suicidal gestures
8. Diagnosed with depression, bipolar or other mood disorders
9. Inability to behave intimately with others on a consistent basis
10. Uses unusual amounts of controlling behavior
11. Tries to resolve problems physically
12. Cannot empathize with others
13. Makes unrealistic demands
14. Compulsive use of alcohol or other drugs
15. Demonstrates a lack of interpersonal and coping skills
16. Is manipulative
17. Demonstrates sociophobic behavior
18. Exhibits contempt for women
19. Shows compulsive reference to sexuality
20. Defies limits
21. Has past history of violence
22. Has low tolerance for stress (Mott-MacDonald, 1979)

These characteristics may be exhibited in different combinations at different times, but certain general themes appear. It is believed that these men's strong psychological dependency on the women with whom they are in a relationship is partly due to low self-esteem and to their learned response of projecting anger on external objects.

Some of the Belmont conference participants who worked with sex offenders provided some insight into differences between spouse abusers and other male offenders. Episodes of batterers' violent acts seem to increase in frequency and intensity over time, which is different than the typical violent offender who becomes less violent with age. Incest fathers were said to be generally nonviolent and nonphysically coercive although in homes where there is both spouse abuse and incest, such patterns were intermingled. Rapists were described as similar to batterers in their aggressive and violent response to anger and rage although rapists' acts of sexual violence were said to decline as they aged. Child molesters, like batterers, were said to continue to be sexually abusive regardless of increasing age.

DSM-IV diagnosis for male spouse-abuse offenders ranges across most diagnostic categories. Many have inadequate and borderline personalities, while others demonstrate symptoms indicative of the antisocial and explosive disorders. Some of the more dangerous men meet the criteria for a paranoid schizophrenic diagnosis. Given the wide range of concomitant problems, diagnoses legitimately fall across all categories. And, not surprisingly, many wife beaters do not demonstrate a sufficient number of behaviors to the therapist that would permit a diagnosis at all. To them, spouse abuse is their entitled right and they are reinforced by a society that doesn't tell them they can't beat her.

COURT-MANDATED TREATMENT PROGRAMS FOR BATTERERS

A recent upsurge in court-mandated treatment programs provides indication that a nonvoluntary, specialized treatment program can provide both the external motivation and the new skills some men need to change their violent behavior. Given the cyclical nature of the violence, and its tendency to increase in frequency and severity, a community treatment program for spouse abusers needs to have several components. At this time, three basic components have been identified: (1) for initial or early offenders, (2) for chronic spouse abusers who can benefit from nonresidential treatment, and (3) for offenders while incarcerated.

The most successful program providing an educational approach for first-time or early spouse abuse offenders is modeled after the Drunk Driving educational workshops. The first one known was developed in Spring Valley, New York by Dr. Steven Shapiro, Executive Director of the Volunteer Counseling Service of Rockland County. The most useful counseling treatment program for chronic spouse abusers for which we have information is the Learning to Live Without Violence component of the San Francisco District Attorney's Family Violence Project. It was developed by Dr. Daniel Sonkin who has written a workbook for men based on its success (Sonkin & Durphy, 1982) and more recently, a manual designed to assist counselors in implementing the program (Sonkin, 1995). The Duluth model of intervention began in Minnesota and uses a brief educational model that stresses learning new sex-role socialization patterns in addition to anger management (Pence & Paymar, 1993). A program to stabilize stalkers was developed by Sonkin and Walker (1995) for JurisMonitor, a company that also provided electronic home arrest and monitoring devices for those batterers who were restrained from going near their partners. An important feature of this program was the ability of the ankle bracelet to emit signals that went directly to a monitoring station if and when the batterer violated the restraining order and went within the forbidden territory. The court was then able to process violations of their restraining orders with evidence and not have to determine who was telling the truth when each party told a different story. This program is still available from BI, a Boulder, Colorado based company.

To implement these programs all criminal justice system components must cooperate. All offenders should be required to complete the educational workshop in nonviolence prior to beginning the counsel treatment group. Preadjudication diversion should only be permitted in certain misdemeanor cases. Abusers shall be ordered by court directly into the counseling treatment program or can be recommended by educational workshop counselors. Both programs should be conducted by the same staff so as to provide the continuity needed if and when abuse escalates instead of ceasing. It is critical to have well-trained staff, with adequate professional support, as the nature of the battering is known to rapidly escalate to lethal levels.

SPOUSE ABUSER EDUCATIONAL WORKSHOP— VIOLENCE AWARENESS TRAINING

Violence Awareness Training is a 6-week course on the recognition and consequences of spouse abuse designed for men who have assaulted their mates. It is modeled after the successful Rockland County, New York program described in a manual written by Phyllis Frank and Beverly Houghton (1981). It is educational rather than therapeutic in nature although, given the specific population, some group therapy is accomplished. The goal of the workshop is to Stop the abuse by teaching men that, "(1) violence is illegal; (2) violence is damaging; (3) violence is learned and can be unlearned; (4) alternatives to violence exist; (5) each individual is responsible for his own acts and his own violence; (6) the batterer deserves help and support in changing his behavior; and (7) help is available." These goals are met through small group discussion, co-led by two trained counselors, with media presentations and lectures by authorities in the field. Because of the initial hostility displayed by most men, leaders (usually male and female) need training in group dynamics as well as ability to present cognitive materials. A written program plan for each session can be found in the Frank and Houghton manual. These can be readily adapted to other population needs. Attendance records should be forwarded to the court and an evaluation component designed within this program should be conducted to measure effectiveness. If brief process records of sessions are made, they should remain confidential. Follow-up telephone calls after the 6-week sessions are terminated should be made on a periodic basis to the man and separately to his partner, to check on his progress and remind him of the other available services. If no further offenses reoccur within 3 years, the misdemeanor charge can be expunged from his record and a felony conviction can be reduced to a misdemeanor. Project records cannot be destroyed.

Spouse Abuser Therapy Program—Violence Counseling Program

The Violence Counseling Program should be an ongoing therapy service modeled after the program developed by Sonkin and Durphy (1982) for postadjudication diversion in the San Francisco Court System. It is a behaviorally oriented treatment program designed to assist the abuser in stopping his violence immediately, recognizing that maintenance of a nonviolent response to anger, frustration, and stress will come with the learning of and rewards for new conflict resolution behavior. Thus, the goal of counseling is to help the batterer learn new ways to respond to situations that could have called forth his assaultive behavior. Since these men are chronic abusers who have reacted with violence for a long time (even if this is their first offense), it is expected that the therapy program will take 1 to 2 years to complete.

While some offenders will need individual therapy, most will be treated in groups of eight to ten men with two trained therapists leading each group. Professional supervision is also necessary given the highly volatile nature of this population. Specific areas to be covered include anger recognition and control, stress management, assertiveness training, dealing with feelings, alcohol and drug abuse, conflict resolution, and communication skills. The Sonkin and Durphy (1982) workbook and anger log is required as part of their materials.

Men are usually referred to this program by the court. Attendance records are carefully kept and immediate feedback given to the referring court should the offender stop attending scheduled sessions. Disruptive or extremely violent men are referred back to the court should therapists decide this program is inappropriate for them. If another assault is committed while in this program, the offender is sent back to the court for noncompliance with the diversion program. If a Treatment Planning Team is established, then communication concerning progress will be established with them. Evaluation is usually built into this program so as to measure its effectiveness. Follow-up contact with those who complete this program is maintained on a periodic and regular basis as described in the education workshop programs. Records of individual sessions are brief, remain part of the project, and are confidential. Such records cannot be destroyed.

TREATMENT PLANNING TEAM

It is appropriate to establish a team of professional and community members to monitor the progress of this program and determine that offenders get to the right program(s) without falling through the cracks as can so easily happen in any nonresidential corrections program. In some cases, abusers will need additional concurrent treatment, such as alcohol detoxification. In other cases, more intensive mental health treatment is necessary and can be provided by the private as well as public sector. Thus, the Treatment Planning Team would have the responsibility of developing an appropriate community referral system by locating such resources.

A Treatment Planning Team needs to consist of representatives from the city and district attorney's offices, Legal Aid Society, public defender's office, domestic violence unit detective (or its equivalent), probation office, mental health and Social Services. In addition, representatives of self-help men's groups, battered women shelters, private practice psychotherapists, and community volunteers should be invited to serve on this team. The Treatment Planning Team should have a budget and regularly scheduled meetings that should be open to the press if names of cases are held confidential. The Treatment Planning Team should be responsible for evaluating initial continued appropriateness of assignment of offenders to the educational workshops and counseling programs. Possible programs to consider are:

1. Violence Awareness Training (Educational Workshops)
2. Violence Counseling Program
3. AMEND, EMERGE, or similar men's anti-violence group
4. Mental Health Center program for domestic violence offenders, if available
5. Private Practice professional psychotherapy
6. Hospitalization for serious psychiatric disorder
7. Incarceration
8. Other concurrent treatments such as alcohol and drug abuse programs, child abuse, and sex offender counseling, and so on.

The Treatment Planning Team, in conjunction with the Nonresidential Spouse Abuse Program staff, should develop a contact report format to facilitate communication on the attendance and progress for each offender assigned to the diversion program. Noncompliance with diversion should be reported by the Treatment Planning Team to the court immediately. Appropriate warning of potential danger must be given to the victims. All cases of repeat and extremely violent offenders must be returned to the court immediately for other disposition.

The Treatment Planning Team should work with the District Attorney's Victim Witness Office to provide support services for victims including a referral to shelter, attorneys, psychotherapy, and other resources as needed. Police training should include contact with the Treatment Planning Team.

In conclusion, a nonresidential treatment program for spouse abusers can be a viable alternative to other punishment. There are three components to the proposed program: (1) an educational approach for first-time or early-identified wife batterers, (2) a therapy approach for chronic spouse abusers, and (3) establishing a coordinating council to maintain adequate liaison with an already overloaded criminal justice system. It is anticipated that a residential component in the jails and prisons will be added once these three programs are well established.

There are few reports of successful treatment of batterers in the literature and those that do appear rarely go beyond a 6-month follow-up period (Margolin, 1979). Even where there has been reported success it is around 25% of the known batterers stop all their abuse of women. While this isn't a high number, it is still better than none. Approximately, another 50% of known batterers do stop their physical abuse while in a treatment program but not their psychological abuse. In fact, Harrell (1991) found that many treatment programs help make the batterers even more facile at using psychological intimidation, bullying behavior, and verbal and psychological abuse. And, clinical reports indicate that 25% of the known batterers continue to abuse women while in an offender-specific treatment program.

FAMILY THERAPY

Modifications in traditional family therapy—a family-oriented but flexible individual approach—have been recently suggested by family therapy leaders (Geffner, Barrett, & Rossman, 1995). They acknowledge the high risk of couples who go into crisis because of frequently occurring battering incidents. Systems theory that advocates that violence occurs as a result of the family interaction, is only correct after the violent behavior begins. Once the family interactions all become regulated by the violent behaviors, its potential for destructiveness becomes obvious.

In my clinical therapy and supervisory experience, the woman's fear of another battering incident often controls her responses so that she cannot gain as much understanding of her behavior as is possible in individual or group counseling. If the man can tolerate his behavior becoming the focus of treatment, then couples therapy can sometimes teach them both better skills to postpone the violent behavior or to avoid being in its path once unleashed. It has not been able to help the violence stop permanently. More often, however, the man has such difficulty taking responsibility for his own behavior that pressure is placed upon the woman to cease upsetting him. Since each person has different needs, one therapist is often inadequate. The woman needs to be believed, validated, and protected from the man's harmful acts. The man needs to be supported, confronted, and taught to stop his violence. Using cotherapists, each taking a supportive role for the battered woman or batterer, is the most beneficial way to proceed with couples' therapy, if it is used at all. I only recommend family or couples therapy when it is impossible to provide individual or group psychotherapy (Walker, 1980c, 1981a, 1984). Family therapy cannot succeed in changing values of a society that by its structure tolerates violence against women.

CONCLUSIONS

The psychotherapy techniques described are merely band-aids to help some people deal with the ravages of domestic violence in their lives. This is not to belittle the influence it has on those people. Therapy does make them feel better. But, it is not a panacea, by any means. Violent behavior, usually used by men against women or children, is produced and reinforced by a society that tolerates it. Thus, elimination of the systematic discrimination against women as well as changing our attitudes which foster violence will be the only way to stop men from battering the women they love.

Legal Responses to Changing Violent Behavior

The societal institution responsible for maintaining social order that exists in almost every country is the legal system. In the United States, advocates who began working with battered women in the 1980s believed that the most important step to end threats of violence was to punish the batterer and hold him accountable for his misconduct. To do this the legal system had to be encouraged to take action whenever domestic violence was raised. In 1983, following in the successful experience of the President Reagan's Task Force on Violence and Crime, the Attorney General initiated another task force on Violence in the Family. Lois Herrington, the Assistant Attorney General in charge of victim rights was appointed the head of this investigative body and they reviewed research, other documents and witness testimony from all over the United States concerning the problem of violence in the family. In their report they state their conclusions; the legal system and in particular, the criminal justice part of the legal system should deal forcefully with stopping family violence. This signaled a major change in the attitude of the country and resulted in the criminalization of what had previously been considered private matters. Someone committing any form of violence in the family, not just where the damage was so egregious that notice and intervention could not be avoided, would be subjected to arrest and prosecution to the fullest extent of the law!

Even though the criminal laws have become stricter and the prosecution of batterers is more common today, it is still the domestic area of the legal system that most couples in a battering relationship eventually come to use. Contrary to public opinion, most violent relationships end in divorce or dissolution of the marriage bonds with its concomitant property settlement, maintenance, child support, custody, and visitation arrangements. In the research project, we found that the average battering relationship lasted 6 years and, to our great surprise, we learned that the average marriage in the United States at that time lasted 6 years, too. However, we also found a bimodal distribution in domestic violence relationships with some ending within a 2-year period and other violent marriages lasting over 20 years.

Not surprisingly, divorce court proves to be the most difficult area of the law in which to obtain justice for battered women and protection for their children, particularly when the batterer fights for custody and visitation of their children and continues to place both the woman and the children in danger from his violent behavior. Although there are laws that direct judges to consider domestic violence in making their decisions about access to children, the prevailing belief still is that two parents are better than one, even if one of them is at high risk to inflict psychological or physical harm on the mother and the children. Even those abusive fathers, whose physical and sexual abuse of their children is known, are allowed to exercise their parental rights, although sometimes they are supervised for awhile. This is further discussed below.

Another area of the law that some violent families have contact with is the juvenile division where child abuse, dependency, neglect, or delinquency come under scrutiny and the job of protecting children reverts back to the state. Although we did not collect data to prove our theory that being raised in a home where children are exposed to domestic violence produced serious effects similar to other forms of child abuse, more recent studies certainly have gathered the empirical evidence to support it (see Chapter 6). Many of these cases find their way into the judicial system, especially when the family is poor and from a different culture. The marginalization of domestic violence families when they are recent immigrants is documented in almost every country including the United States (Walker, 1999). In fact, the United States Federal courts and the immigration authority (INS) have recently become more involved with domestic violence cases since 1994 when the Violence Against Women Act included a provision that permits a battered woman whose legal status is determined by her abusive husband to apply for citizenship on her own so she would no longer be dependent upon the abusive man to keep her in the United States. This civil rights law will be described further.

In most countries and states, there is provision in the legal system to assist victims who have been harmed by someone to be financially compensated for their damages. The civil tort area of the law in each state of the United States attempts to right injustices committed against individuals, not just society at large. Replacement of lost property and compensation for damages suffered can be awarded should a civil lawsuit be won. Sometimes punitive damages can be assessed as a punishment for harming people, making it important for the offender to stop his violence even if it is just to protect his property. It is interesting that the civil law requires a determination that the man intentionally committed the act (of assault or battery in this case) and not that the man intended to harm the woman in order to hold him legally liable for her damages. In one civil case in which there was expert witness testimony (see *Curtis v. Curtis*, 1988, Idaho) the formerly battered woman won and collected an award of over $1 million from her abusive partner.

In many countries, wives are not permitted to testify against their husbands, usually for fear that they will betray secrets that are believed necessary to hold the marital relationship together. However, that also puts battered wives in jeopardy if they cannot testify as to their husbands' abusive behavior should he invoke the immunity. Thus, before these laws could protect battered women in most countries, like in the United States, it is first necessary to remove what is legally called, *the interspousal tort immunity* that has existed. Today that has occurred in most states and now battered wives are legally entitled to sue their violent husbands in civil court in an attempt to recover costs for the physical and mental damages that their beatings caused. However, as might be expected in a paternalistic and patriarchal legal system, it is not used as a remedy as often as it might be. In some states, such as New Jersey, these so-called *Tevis* claims must be filed along with divorce or separation actions. Case law has now made it clear, however, that the plaintiff is entitled to a jury trial rather than just before a judge, should it be requested.

In all of these areas it was first necessary for experts to be able to testify on behalf of a battered woman or child. It is difficult to legally prove that domestic violence has occurred especially when property rights or access to children are involved. Documenting incidents, calling police for seemingly minor infractions, and following through on the appropriate recommendations are often necessary for the proof. Cases where the woman has tried to resolve the family problems herself leave her with little evidence to be used in a court of law. However, the presence of battered woman syndrome is an important marker in demonstrating that domestic violence did take place and adds to the woman's credibility.

CRIMINAL LAW

In most democratic countries, the criminal justice area of the law applies sanctions for breaking the rules that govern our behavior. Community standards in the United States guided lawmakers in both setting the rules and choosing the punishment meted out for infractions against the local, state, and federal statutes. Over the past 20 years, the criminal laws in most countries including North America, have been strengthened so that abusive partners can and are prosecuted to the fullest extent of the law. While punishment has been increased in most jurisdictions for all crimes, including domestic violence, many communities in the United States have adopted a treatment approach when dealing with domestic violence, permitting most first time offenders to enter and complete a special treatment program designed to help change batterer's attitudes toward women as well as stop their violent behavior. These programs are described in Chapter 12. If treatment does not help them stop the violence against women, then they are subject to more serious punishment depending on the seriousness of the acts and injuries inflicted on women. In addition to punishment for physical and sexual abuse in their own homes, violent offenders are subjected to stalking and harassment laws for causing apprehension in the victim by threatening violence.

The battered women in this research project told of calling police only to find that they did not take seriously their complaints. Even in those cases where the police did make an arrest, it was common for women to go down to the jail and make bail for their abusive partners. If a case did get to court, it was common for battered women to become fearful of their batterers' anger if they testified against them, and so they recanted their earlier testimony and denied the abuse. Everyone knew that nothing was going to be done anyhow. However, once the police began to make arrests consistently and the women were given the support of victim witness advocates who worked in the prosecutor's offices, women were more likely to follow through on their testimony, especially if there was a treatment program available to help the batterer stop his violent behavior. This changed the role of the criminal justice system and put it squarely in the middle of the lives of those who have lived with domestic violence. Special domestic violence courts were begun in various areas of the country including Denver, Miami, the Boston area, California and other places. Women could obtain restraining orders without needing an attorney and received referrals to counseling and advocacy services for themselves and their children. The power of the court began to empower battered women so that they were able to see for themselves whether or not their batterers were motivated to or capable of change. When it worked well, it gave them the opportunity to make decisions about their lives.

Under the new states' *Domestic Violence Protection Acts* that have been passed during the 1980s, those accused of domestic violence can be removed from their homes for a specified period of time if their partners apply for a criminal or civil protection order, even if they are not present to tell the court their side of the story. This is called an *exparte* court order and helps solve the problem that used to occur when the man fled the scene and couldn't be located to serve a court order that was necessary to validate it. Of course, those accused do get the opportunity for a full hearing before the judge usually within 3 to 30 days depending on the jurisdiction, but this gives both the woman and the man time to accept the seriousness of the violence in their homes. Sometimes temporary custody and financial arrangements can be ordered by this judge until the family court can intervene and apply the appropriate legal standards, especially when young children are involved.

Wife beating is a criminal offense in every legal jurisdiction of the United States and almost every other country that belongs to the United Nations, which has taken on as a priority the eradication of violence against women during the past 2 decades. Seriousness of the level of the crime is dependent upon the degree of force used, injuries suffered, and presence of weapons. Misdemeanor charges are generally resolved by fines paid to the local or state court, probation, and/or court-ordered counseling, although short jail sentences are an available alternative. In some places there are special domestic violence courts that provide better-coordinated services for victims and swift prosecutions for the offenders. Court-ordered counseling programs have been developed as a way to avoid a lengthy jail sentence and in many jurisdictions courts can now order 1 to 2 year jail sentences that get suspended, so that they can keep the man in long-term counseling (Walker & Corriere, 1991).

Felony charges are more serious, usually handled on a state court level, and punishable by longer jail terms. Sometimes restitution to the victim is ordered. More likely a local victim compensation fund is available for expenses, although many jurisdictions exclude benefits to domestic violence victims. The double standards for prosecutions of domestic assault, compared to a stranger assault; caused us to lose one of the most potentially effective systems our society has to help stop violence. In the United States, the Victim's Compensation Act of 1984 has helped many battered women get money to receive medical and psychological help if they cooperated with the state attorneys to prosecute their batterers. In other countries that have a government-sponsored medical system, this compensation is not as important. However, training physicians and mental health professionals to recognize, properly assess and treat the effects of domestic violence has taken place in the past 15 years. The American Medical Association has had major educational campaigns for doctors, while the American Psychological Association has created policies and published materials for psychologists. Other mental health groups have made similar efforts although some remain more paternalistic in their approach than many advocates would prefer. However, the climate for healthy debate over libertarian versus paternalistic interventions has not yet been established with continued fighting between the different professional and nonprofessional groups working with battered women and their children.

Psychological learning theory postulates that behavior is repeated when it is successful and terminated when it is not. The most difficult behavior to extinguish is that which has been reinforced on an unpredictable, intermittent, random, and variable schedule. Thus, swift punishment immediately following the undesirable behavior with continued external controls has potential for eliminating the undesirable behavior. The key to its success, however, is the immediate and consistent use of the negative reinforcement. The criminal justice system has the capacity to provide the required immediate and consistent response by activating its ability to arrest, prosecute, and punish men who batter women. Unfortunately, there is little ability to make quick responses nor is there much consistency in this system.

MEDIATION

The mediation and conflict resolution approach, so successful in other adversarial areas of the law, serves only to reinforce men's violent behavior. Yet, when there is little consequence for inappropriate and abusive behavior, it becomes important to try every available avenue to stop the violence so it is understandable that some argue as passionately for mediation as do the advocates against it. This has created laws that either mandate mediation or mandate that it does not take place, often restricting the efforts that might succeed with a particular family. This is also true for batterers treatment programs as is further described in Chapter 12. In fact, there appears to be some success reported with a type of "shuttle" mediation, where the attorneys get together and bring to their clients negotiated positions for their consideration while they are sitting in adjacent rooms.

POLICE RESPONSE TO ASSAULT

The results of this study supported a major change in police response, from mediation to arrest policy, in domestic disturbance calls. This has occurred and the attitudes of the police have for the most part now changed and a pro-arrest and prosecution policy guides their response today. This change was predicted to be more helpful to the victims based on their responses. Since it also sets into motion the prosecutorial process, such an arrest policy should ultimately benefit the men by providing immediate consequences to their violent acts. Those communities in which this arrest policy is already in effect report widespread acceptance by police, who have better training to follow such procedures than to act as counselors in an unreasonable situation. The pro-arrest policy was recommended by the Police Executive Research Forum after research demonstrated its effectiveness (Loving, 1981). A complete police investigation at the scene of the crime is required to allow prosecutors to move forward with creative prosecutions, especially when the battered woman becomes a reluctant complaining witness.

Berk (1993), one of the early proponents of the pro-arrest policies in place now and one of the main researchers in the Minneapolis arrest study in the early 1980s, reviewed the scientific evidence and states that "on average we can do no better than arrest." However, that assumes the policy is followed and the batterer is the person arrested. In many cases, law enforcement cannot or will not figure out who was the aggressor and arrests both parties (Meloy et al., 1997). If there are young children in the home, the woman quickly figures out (especially with a little help from the police or state attorney) that if she pleads guilty and agrees to go into an offender-specific treatment program, she will be released and permitted to go home to her children. If she exercises her rights, then the children may have to spend some time in the custody of child protective services (Zorza, 1995). Faced with this choice, many women agree to take the plea offer and go home. However, later, this conviction may come back to haunt them in unknown ways—especially if they are in the professions. Also problematic is the fact that many police officers are poorly trained in domestic violence and use their own personal biases to decide when to make an arrest. So, for example, if a woman is thought to have played a role in causing her abuse, the officer may decide that she is not a *good enough* battered woman and fail to make the arrest. Buzawa and Buzawa (1993) describe some of the problems that have arisen with the new arrest policies and caution not to consider them a panacea to the issue of domestic violence.

Adoption of the following procedures, presented in invited testimony to the President's Task Force on Victims of Crime, in Denver, Colorado on October 6, 1982, can upgrade a police department's effectiveness in stopping violence:

Sheriff and police officers need to adopt rules and regulations empowering them to treat a domestic disturbance call as the serious crime-in-progress call that it is. This means police must be trained in the best methods to protect themselves and the family members when they respond to the call. Mediation, conciliation, and reasonableness are not effective during an acute battering incident. "Why a burglary happened" is not usually asked when police respond to a call at the nearby 7-11 convenience store. Rather, police are trained to make an arrest, upon probable cause, of course, and to preserve the crime scene for answering those questions later. The same procedure must also apply to family crime calls. Police, victims', and offenders' lives may be saved.

An arrest should be made upon *probable cause,* which is defined as observation of injuries or other indicators that an assault did or still is occurring. Pictures should be taken to preserve the record of the injuries and property disturbance. Witness statements should be taken immediately, preferably taped. Officers' reports should be complete and state the condition of each party and the surrounding area. If the scene doesn't come up to probable cause levels, then the woman should be informed of her alternatives, including in many places the right to make a citizen's arrest. Medical attention should be obtained for any injuries, and she should have the option to be taken to the nearest battered woman's shelter. This gets the woman help and lets both parties understand how serious violence is. If the man has fled the scene, but there is evidence an assault did take place, the police must vigorously pursue him. Today the abuser can be charged with a crime and a warrant taken out for the abuser's arrest by the police officer's sworn statement whether or not the offender was at the scene of the crime when it occurred.

These recommendations represented a major change from the typical way a domestic disturbance complaint was handled 15 years ago and still today, in some places. Usually, one was not quite sure of the law enforcement officer's right to intervene in a family matter, mediation was typically unsuccessful, the woman's story was disbelieved, the police would leave as fast as possible hoping to prevent their own injury, and the battering would continue to escalate behind the closed doors. While pro-arrest policies are not popular initially, the communities where they have been instituted find they are successful (Berk et al., 1983; Berk, 1993).

Once an arrest is made it goes to whoever handles filing of complaints. Unless it seems like a nonbattering-related incident, police should bring it to the highest possible level and not file a simple municipal ordinance violation. Decisions on whether to charge a misdemeanor (minor level) or felony (a major crime), and at what level, need to be made by one consistent person. This process is often called *vertical prosecution.* At first advocates called for cases to have standards consistent with other assault crimes applied to domestic violence crimes. However, most jurisdictions have now adopted special domestic violence standards so that they can retain control over a batterer for a longer period of time than a simple assault or even an assault and battery charge would permit. If there is a special domestic violence or family crime division within the state attorney's office, it is less likely that questionable cases will fall through the cracks

STATE ATTORNEY'S RESPONSE TO ASSAULT

Prosecuting a spouse abuser is neither a popular or easy job for the county or state attorney. The sheer volume of cases that will have to be handled, should arrest policies become routine, can be overwhelming. For example, the cases estimated for the City and County of Denver went from approximately 3,000 to close to 10,000 during the first year the new policy was in effect, according to Project Safeguard's records. Project Safeguard is a community not-for-profit agency that oversees the domestic violence training, education, and court processes for the city of Denver. Founded in the mid-1980s, the purpose was to provide a centralized agency to work together with the city agencies to institute these new policies and serve as an oversight function to make sure they were working to the benefit of the women and children who they were designed to protect. In Dade County, Florida where Miami is the largest city, the arrests went from 3,000 to 12,000 the first year the new domestic violence court was in effect. Four county court judges sit daily in domestic violence court hearing cases and they work closely with drug court and child protective services providing referrals to interventions as unusual as acupuncture and as typical as offender-specific counseling and battered women shelters in several different languages. A routine procedure for effective prosecutions will streamline this process, but it is necessary to have the requisite personnel to run the program.

It is recommended that once the charge is filed, a prosecutor who will stay with the case is assigned. If the police or sheriff have done their job, the prosecutor's staff can more easily follow through on preparing for trial. Victim witness advocates are extremely helpful. It is important to be clear that the decision to drop charges rests solely with the prosecutor. The victim can threaten to be uncooperative, but if medical records, pictures, and good officer witness accounts are available, her cooperation is less vital to the successful outcome. Previous police contact calls and other records can establish a domestic violence pattern. Expert witness testimony can support the assertion that the battered woman syndrome and fear prevent her from being a better witness. It is important not to pressure or coerce the woman into cooperating with the legal system if she chooses not to do so.

Some have feared that the batterer will become more violent if arrested and charges are filed. Research shows that most abusers do leave the women alone, at least while charges are pending, once they know they have no power to influence the state attorney (Sherman & Berk, 1984). Restraining orders are protection for most women who get them (Meloy, Cowett, Parker, Hofland, & Friedland, 1997) although obviously those who engage in stalking behavior won't be deterred by court orders (Burgess et al., 1997; deBecker, 1997; Meloy et al., 1997; Walker & Meloy, 1998). In some research it was found that violent men with few ties to the community are the most likely to escalate their violence once a report is made (Dunford, Huizinga, & Elliott, 1989). Thus, it is important to provide some victim protection especially in these cases. Although there has been some controversy over using an arrest policy without referral to a treatment program for the offender (Buzawa & Buzawa, 1993) in fact, Berk (1993) makes a compelling argument that the programs in six sites that replicated the original Minneapolis study were not identical to the experiment and some of the different findings can be attributed to those differences. Obviously, this is an important argument—if you do not replicate an experiment exactly, it will be difficult to compare and generalize the results. However, it is clear that when carefully implemented an arrest and subsequent intervention protocol is the most likely to stop the domestic violence behavior. It is also apparent that prosecutions early in battering relationships really do work to stop or at a minimum, slow down violence in the home, according to all reports. However, if the family law courts do not support the criminal or civil remedies being sought, both the woman and children are placed at higher risk for further harm or even death when they try to use the legal system.

It is a real no-win situation for some battered women. They will continue to be battered if they do not get help and they will be hurt worse if they do! This is critical for those who work with battered women to understand!

DOMESTIC VIOLENCE COURTS

A separate domestic violence or family crime division is important to keep track of cases and follow through with whatever punishment might be ordered by the court. Once an arrest has been made, offenders tend to show up, repeatedly. Learning theory predicts that it will take time for offenders to catch on once the decision has been made to follow through with punishment for noncompliance. Many of the families involved in domestic violence arrests have multiple problems and have different needs beyond stopping the violence. They often need drug and alcohol abuse counseling programs, parenting programs, and other social services. For poor minority or immigrant families, contact with the criminal justice system usually earns the women contact with a social service agency looking for child neglect, abuse, or even sexual assault. It is not unusual for social service workers to misinterpret different cultural traditions as a form of maltreatment causing even more problems. Sometimes the arrest signals other departments, such as probation, where to find someone and make contact for unrelated crimes. Rarely has any agency been able to work on a sustained basis with the abuser, except perhaps in drunk driving programs that are more short term in nature.

To really deal with domestic violence, it is necessary to establish a community-wide task force to assist the domestic violence divisions in the state attorneys' offices and probation departments so they can begin to identify which offenders might benefit from postadjudication diversion programs, and which ones need to go directly to jail or prison. Postadjudication diversion is most successful, as offender programs need the leverage of the guilty plea. If the man doesn't attend or take it seriously, then he can be returned to jail or prison for the rest of his sentence. Communication needs to be maintained with the courts and the woman during the time he is in a counseling program to confirm that his violent behavior has stopped. Those who administer such treatment programs say the men are not able to report accurately (Dutton, 1995; Lindsay et al., 1992; Sonkin & Durphy, 1982). Some repeat offenders are too dangerous for community corrections programs and—to protect them and their victims, as well as society—they must be incarcerated. Despite the difficulties in developing successful rehabilitation programs in prison, our society must continue to experiment.

OTHER VIOLENT CRIMES

Perhaps one of the most surprising findings in this study was the report that 71% of the batterers had been arrested for other criminal acts and, of those, 44% had been convicted. This compared to a 34% arrest and 19% conviction rate for the men who do not beat women. In looking at the violence history for both violent and nonviolent men, it is clear that the batterers were three times as likely to have grown up living in a violent home. And they were also more likely to physically or sexually abuse their children. To complete the generational cycle of violence, those children are more likely to leave home at an early age, engage in crime on the streets, and repeat the violence in their own homes. Contrary to other studies of violent men, these abusers get more violent as they get older.

Perhaps the most important information learned from the battered women interviewed was their frustration with the inadequate response received from the criminal justice system. Bureaucratic delays, inadequate responses, and lack of knowledge and training prevented this institution from being responsive in life-threatening situations. Some of their inadequacy comes from lack of competence and societal reluctance to adjudicate in family matters. These research results provide the data that family violence spills over outside the home. It affects job performance, medical care costs, crime on the streets, drug and alcohol abuse, and begets more violent behavior in the next generation. At one conference, someone suggested that the family is a more successful training ground for violence than the military!

RESTRAINING ORDERS AND PEACE BONDS

Use of the criminal justice system to issue and enforce orders restraining violent men from contact with women they hurt is another remedy often rendered ineffective by sexist biases within the system. Attorneys fearing the orders will not be honored do not seek them. Women fearing further violence say they often do not report violations of the restraining order, even if they have been successful in obtaining it. The courts rarely use their limited power to enforce judges' restraining orders. In jurisdictions where peace bonds are available, the threat of loss of money in addition to contempt charges makes restraining orders obtained in criminal court more powerful than those in civil and domestic court jurisdictions.

Our data, as well as Berk et al. (1983) and Meloy et al. (1997) suggest that the restraining order can be quite an effective deterrent to further violence and harassment if the offender has reason to believe it will be enforced. The process obtaining it can help reverse the effects of learned helplessness as it gives victims a sense of power and belief that protection against further violence is possible. In many communities, obtaining a restraining order has now been simplified and there are little costs associated with it. For example, in Denver a special domestic violence court issues exparte civil restraining orders every afternoon at 1:30 P.M. First, the victims are invited to attend several group sessions facilitated by advocates that teach them how to fill out the restraining order forms and the types of offenses that are eligible for a restraining order request are described. Victim advocates also discuss the other resources available in the community for victims, offenders and their children so that the cycle of violence can be broken. These temporary orders can be made permanent at a later hearing where the alleged abuser is notified that he can attend and protest the order if he so desires. Often judges have the power to award temporary custody and support at these hearings, so they are important to attend if there is a chance that the marriage will later dissolve.

WOMEN AND CRIME

There is growing awareness that many women currently incarcerated in prisons across the country for a variety of offenses have been battered. A study for the Colorado legislature found that over two-thirds of the women in prison stated that they had been abuse victims (Walker, Stokes, Monroe-DeVita, in preparation). Estimates of up to one-half of them committed the crime for which they are being punished to avoid further beating. Forging checks to pay his bills, stealing food or other items that he denied the children, selling drugs to keep his supply filled, hurting someone else so he didn't hurt her were all acts committed under control of the batterer's threat of, or actual, violence. Some women struck back, most often with great force and usually in self-defense. Few of these women received an appropriate defense for their acts. Most listened to their attorneys' suggestions to avoid trial and plead guilty, often to a lesser negotiated plea rather than pursue a duress or diminished-capacity defense. Today psychologists who testify to the psychological impact of abuse on their mental health functioning and current state of mind at the time of the incident allow more women to present expert witness testimony at their trials.

Several women's prisons have begun to organize women's self-help groups spurred on by consultation from local battered women's task forces. Women in the Wyoming Women's prison in Evanston and Missouri's Women's Prison in Rentz have sponsored conferences to educate themselves so as to avoid becoming victims of violence upon their release. Women incarcerated in the Colorado prison system have begged for interventions, but the legislature has yet to appropriate the funding. Women wardens who understand the special needs of their prisoners have begun to design programs which provide new opportunities in job training, education, and counseling. A community corrections facility in Lakewood, Colorado, designed a model program for women, that allowed them to build upon their strengths and develop new skills and abilities. It is important for authorities to recognize that most women offenders are victims also.

WOMEN'S SELF-DEFENSE CASES

Occasionally (between 10% and than 15% of all homicides in the U.S.) a woman will kill her abuser while trying to defend herself or her children. Sometimes, she strikes back during a calm period, knowing that the tension is building towards another acute battering incident, where this time she may die. When examining the statistics, we find that more women than men are charged with first- or second-degree murder. There seems to be a sexist bias operating in which the courts find it more difficult to see justifiable or mitigating circumstances for women who kill (See Walker, 1989a for a more complete discussion of these cases). The now classic Broverman et al. (1970) studies demonstrated that the kinds of behaviors and emotions expressed when committing an aggressive act will be viewed as normal for men but not for women. On the other hand, women's violence is more likely to be found excusable, if her insanity under the law can be demonstrated. Any changes in the insanity laws will probably have the greatest impact on women and other assault victims who reach a breaking point and no longer know the difference between right and wrong and/or can no longer refrain from an irresistible impulse to survive.

In most states' criminal codes, the use of self defense is permissible if the woman can demonstrate that she had a *reasonable perception of imminent danger.* The definition of what is a reasonable perception has been the subject of debate amongst legal scholars—is the standard what a "reasonable person" or a "reasonable woman" or a "reasonable battered woman" perceives that counts? Is the perception an objective one that anyone might be expected to conclude, or is it a more subjective perception that is based on everything the battered woman knows and has experienced? In most states, this argument has been resolved in favor of a compromise—using both objective and subjective perceptions.

Another major area that has had to be defined is what does *imminent* mean. In some interpretations, imminent is seen as immediate but in most jurisdictions, it is believed to mean *about to happen* as if on the edge of a cliff and you are about to fall off. Obviously, this is important because many battered women kill in self-defense by using what otherwise might be viewed as a preemptory strike—like getting a gun and shooting him while he is coming toward her with outstretched arms and a look in his eyes that reminds her of the last brutal beating. It would be a reasonable perception for that woman to believe that serious bodily harm or death is imminent primarily because she has been threatened with death and previously suffered serious bodily harm when he acted in the same way.

In some jurisdictions, self-defense is defined as the justifiable commission of a criminal act by using the least amount of force necessary to prevent imminent bodily harm which needs only to be reasonably perceived as about to happen. The perception of how much force is necessary, then, must also be reasonable. Such a definition works against women because they are not socialized to use physical force, are rarely equal to a man in size, strength, or physical training, and may have learned to expect more injury with inadequate attempts to repel a man's attack. Thus, some courts, such as Washington State in 1977 in the Wanrow case, have ruled it would be reasonable for a woman to defend herself with a deadly weapon against a man armed only with the parts of his body he learned to use as a deadly weapon. Courts also have been allowing evidence to account for the cumulative effects of repeated violence in self-defense and diminished-capacity assertions. Expert witness testimony has been admitted in many states to help explain the reasonableness of such perceptions.

One of the major changes in the criminal law is to allow battered women to present evidence of the cumulative effects of abuse in courts through the testimony of a psychologist using what the court's refer to as battered woman syndrome. Although some advocates do not like the title for political reasons—fearing that labeling the symptoms as a syndrome will infantalize and pathologize battered women, in fact, the legal system has thoroughly embraced the concept and uses it mostly to assist battered women in criminal and civil cases. Here, the legal system uses the term "battered woman syndrome" different from psychologists. Rather, the courts combine the entire research project together under that title so that the cycle theory and learned helplessness are combined under the dynamics of battering relationships along with the psychological symptoms that are often seen as a result of the abuse.

While the use of battered woman syndrome is very useful in criminal and civil cases, it has not been useful in custody actions. Unfortunately, women are still losing custody and access to their children in family courts, and the tendency has been to blame the term, "battered woman syndrome," rather than the lack of understanding and sometimes, gender-bias and outright ignorance of judges who refuse to educate themselves as to the truth of the needs of these children exposed to domestic violence and continue to blame women for complaining about the abuse they receive. Recent exposes of the mislabeling of women even by powerful psychiatrists indicate that these fears are not unfounded (Caplan, 1995; Kutchins & Kirk, 1997; Lerman, 1997; Walker, 1993a). However, discarding the term instead of using educational methods will not better serve the purpose as is stated in other sections here.

CIVIL LAW

A number of the women interviewed told of filing civil lawsuits against their former husbands asking to be compensated for their physical and psychological injuries. Until fairly recently, state laws did not permit women to sue their husbands, but removal of *the interspousal tort immunity* has opened the way for filing of such legal claims. This legal remedy has potential to raise the actual dollar cost of violence so high that men will carefully consider the consequences prior to committing an assault. It also has benefits for individual women that go beyond their recovering the actual dollars expended to heal from their attack.

Being a plaintiff in a civil suit implies an offensive approach. Using such assertive and even aggressive behavior helps women express their anger at having been victimized in a socially acceptable manner. For many of our women, winning money was less important than the whole process of feeling as though the balance of power had changed and knowing they could control their tormentor. The civil law is a long and tedious process, and may be difficult in exposing the woman's entire life including embarrassing things, too, but many of the women stated they enjoyed learning the legal rules and watching the batterer have to conform to them. It wasn't seen as revenge, but rather retribution for all that the men had put them through. Winning on ideological points was sometimes as therapeutic as having their financial claims prevail.

Psychologists are now giving battered woman syndrome testimony in these civil courts to prove the psychological damages suffered by battered women. In New Jersey, for example, the *Giovine* and subsequent cases have ruled that domestic violence is a *continuing tort* and therefore, removed the time limit that bars some older incidents from being presented in a case. In many states, women are expected to file within 1 to 2 years of an assault. Thus, extending or removing the time limit is important because for many battered women it isn't until they are out of the relationship and beginning to heal that they can start to deal with the long-term effects of abuse and put them in perspective. In

New Jersey, however, the claim for damages must be filed in the same court that hears divorce actions although it is now possible to request a jury trial that previously had been barred. The 1994 Violence Against Women civil rights act also removes the need for a time limit so that women who are barred from taking civil actions in state court may choose to use the federal laws for justice.

FAMILY OR DOMESTIC LAW

The most often-asked question when domestic violence is discussed is why women remain in battering relationships. Judged as the adults who they are, and with the belief that they can exercise their free will, which is usually impossible because of the batterer's interference, it is commonly believed that if a woman terminates the marriage, she will no longer be battered. The information learned in this research indicates just how erroneous this view is, especially when children are involved. The violence doesn't cease should she pursue divorce or dissolution of the marriage, but rather, escalates to higher levels, even becoming potentially lethal. The men are at greater risk for emotional breakdowns, homicidal, and suicidal reactions. Media stories about despondent husbands who shoot and kill the whole family have become more commonly linked with spouse abuse, as reporters become more sophisticated in their understanding of domestic violence. Thus, while termination of domestic violence relationships is still the best way to stop the abuse over the long term, safety must be provided during the transition period that can last around 2 years.

In those states that have eliminated all grounds on which to grant dissolution, except for an irretrievably broken marriage, there are no accurate statistics on how many marriages terminate because of physical or mental cruelty. Knowledgeable divorce attorneys and judges usually can tell when spouse abuse is present, however. Negotiations around property settlements usually escalate into angry demands by the man for more than his fair share. His evasiveness and obvious refusal to cooperate with full financial disclosure create strife between the man and his attorney. The battered woman is usually recognizable by her willingness to settle for far less than her fair share just to get the divorce completed and keep the man as calm as possible. These women rarely fought to establish their long-term security needs, preferring to keep the peace, as would be consistent with their survival behavior in the relationship. However, little things bother the women, and they often jeopardize a delicately negotiated agreement to exert control over a minor and replaceable object. Sometimes, it seems that they exercise symbolic control here, as in the marriage, when reality demonstrates how powerless they are really. The women who trusted attorneys who understood their terror and validated their fears of further violence were more likely to stay out of the settlement negotiations and subsequently get a more equitable agreement.

CHILD SUPPORT, CUSTODY, AND VISITATION

The link between the batterer and battered woman that cannot be dissolved during the legal proceedings is the children. The batterer views his children, like his wife, as possessions, and frequently uses them to get back at her. The women tell of constant threats by the men to fight for legal custody (Zorza, 1995). Some, who don't see the courts as an option, kidnap their children, preventing mothers from ever seeing them again. Several in our sample were involved in international child-snatching cases. Women spoke of "voluntarily" giving up physical custody of their children to save their own lives. Some went back to live with the batterer because they couldn't stand to be separated from their children. In fact, Liss and Stahly (1993) found that the most common reason given by women in battered women shelters in California to go back to their abuser was better control over protecting their children. Some men are described as being unable to cope with the loss of both their wife and child. Others merely use the children as a ploy to get the woman back.

The financial and emotional expense of an all-out custody war is one more burden battered women must bear, if they are to get a divorce. Often, joint custody is forced upon them, without reasoning that the coercion does not stop because the power is still balanced in the batterer's favor. Battered women can be so intimidated by court-appointed professionals assigned to complete an evaluation to help the judge decide that they perform poorly and may lose custody. Threats and manipulation are often utilized by the batterer to try to bully court personnel into giving him what he wants. Women fearfully told of losing custody when they ran away from home to escape the abuse, but left their children in the batterer's physical custody while they were gone. In one case, the man had the locks changed and filed desertion charges after he cheerfully drove her to the airport and put her on a plane for a trip that he suggested, so she could relax and visit her relatives. He then told the children that their mother left them and chose not to return rather than let them know of his scheme to keep her away from them. Two years later, the woman was still trying to persuade them that she didn't abandon them voluntarily, simply to get them to agree to go out to dinner together. Once their father won custody, he made it impossible for those children to enjoy being with their mother, even temporarily.

It is frightening to realize that professionals ignorant of how abuse is learned and perpetuated may see men who cannot control their violence against women, and teach that behavioral response to their children, as the better parent. Many professionals ignore the role of exposure to a father's violence (Hodges, 1986) or find ways to rationalize that a particular case is not domestic violence because of a dissimilarity with some peculiarity with their own personalized definition. For example, psychiatrist and father's advocate, Richard Gardner claims that battered women should not be viewed as engaging in behavior that he terms, *parental alienation syndrome* as their fears of their batterer's abuse are legitimate (Gardner, 1987, 1992). However, in one case that I reviewed his report to the court, he stated that a particular battered woman was alienating her children from their father. Even when confronted with police and medical reports indicating injuries from the husband's physical abuse in this case, he challenged their reports and denied that these were true "battering" incidents (Personal communication, 1998). Those who view women as having sinister motives will find some excuse to deny the reality of the abuse they have experienced, even when it is clearly determined by others. For some, there is an over-inflated belief in their own ability to identify a batterer, even when he is not willing to disclose his behavior due to self-interest. The closer the man looks like everyone else, the less likely professionals will be willing to identify him as dangerous to his children. Thus, attorneys advise their clients to dress and act like everyone else in their community. Batterers, who usually have a "good" as well as "bad" side to their personality, are often able to keep the good side in front of evaluators, so they can indeed manipulate the system.

Similarly, judges need to be educated to the emotional trauma and fear unsupervised visitation brings to the abuser's children. Some as young as 2 years old were reported to return from a visit more likely to use aggression against their mothers. Like other weekend fathers, batterers too have difficulties in adjusting to a less intensive and controlling interest in their children's lives. Often they do not pay child support regularly, causing more bitterness, anger, and deprivation. Many of the women believed that the custody struggles were more about money for the man than wanting more contact with his children. New ways of looking at parental access to children are essential if we are to prevent those at risk for damage from exposure to their fathers abuse of their mother from actually developing those problems. Attorneys have been looking at the problem and posing some different solutions including changing the burden of proof from the mother to prove the father is a batterer and therefore, unfit or dangerous for the children to putting the burden of proof on the adjudicated batterer to demonstrate that he has the requisite skills to properly parent his children (Cahn; 1991; Mahoney, 1991; Zorza, 1995).

Mediation programs that have been successful in averting bitter fights in nonviolent families, are not as useful for violent ones. The men can be overpowering in negotiations and the women can feel pushed into settlements simply to avert another violent fight. Some mediators understand this potential and add power to the women so they stay strong, can respond to conciliation, and feel safe from harassment. Sometimes this includes using what is called, *shuttle-mediation,* where each person is in a separate room and the attorneys shuttle back and forth between them. Most mediators, however, have no idea just what kind of terrifying violence is involved and cannot equalize the power differential to make the process fair to the battered woman or the children.

The research seems pretty clear that there are detrimental effects from the bitter fights between parents over access to their children. Johnston's and Campbell's (1993) and Cummings' (1998) research indicates that children placed in the middle of these custody battles have major emotional effects that they will have to spend years to overcome, if at all. Cummings (1999) has studied young children's reactions to parental anger and found that it has a detrimental impact on their development. Liss and Stahly (1993) found that young children who went into shelter with their mothers, particularly boys, were less likely to develop empathy with the emotional state of other people after being exposed to their fathers battering their mothers. The research on the emotional impact of exposure to domestic violence shows significant vulnerability is produced (Peled et al., 1995; Holden et al., 1998; Jaffe et al., 1995; Rossman & Rosenberg, 1998). This is further discussed in Chapter 6. However, it is not known how much of the emotional damage noted is caused by inappropriate custody and visitation arrangements in addition to the exposure to domestic violence in the home.

JUVENILE LAW

Many violent men's children get in trouble with the law. In fact, the APA Task Force on Violence and the Family found that one of the highest risk factors for all forms of behavior problems is abuse in the family! Delinquency and dependency hearings have been sensitive to the issue of child abuse but until recently, did not inquire also about spouse abuse in those same homes. The juvenile section of the court can order parents into counseling programs to remediate their inadequacies or child abuse tendencies. In most districts with separate juvenile divisions, the emphasized philosophy is on remediation and not punishment. However, the rise of youth committing serious crimes including murder, has made the general public less accepting of remediation and more harsh consequences are now being handed out to juveniles. In fact statistics show that there has been a major increase in youth in the punitive criminal justice system rather than in the rehabilitative juvenile section (see Chapter 6 for further discussion and statistics). This situation is occurring at the same time as we are finding more and more youth suffering from some form of PTSD, often from exposure to abuse in their family lives.

CHILDREN WHO KILL PARENTS

Most abused children develop a variety of ways to cope with their situation (Sonkin, 1994). Some do not. These are the children who may end up killing their parents perceiving it as the only way to survive. Perhaps the most famous case during these past 15 years has been Lyle and Eric Menendez, two California men in their early 20s who shot and killed their mother and father after what they described as a lifetime of physical, sexual, and psychological abuse by their father without protection from their mother. Their attorneys presented a *battered child syndrome* defense during their first trial and neither jury was able to reach a verdict. In their second trial, that was not bifurcated this time, the court refused to permit testimony on abuse issues noting how confused the first juries became when such evidence was presented. Both were convicted of first degree murder and are serving life sentences in California prison.

The Menendez brothers actions are not common, but also not isolated examples of children who kill parents. In fact, the Bureau of Justice (1994a, 1994b) statistics on Murder in Families indicate that among murder victims, 1.9% are killed by their children. One-third of family murders involved women as the killer with 18% killing their parents and 15% killing a sibling. However, 41% of the spousal killings were committed by women and 55% of the killings of their own children. Mones (1991) and Morris (1985) describe other "kids" who kill their parents sometimes out of mental illness, sometimes out of fear of further abuse, and sometimes as a combination. One of the major differences between battered women and battered children who kill is that for children, the threat they are protecting themselves from is usually "psychological death," while the women perceive actual death. Perhaps, as our treatment programs become more successful, we can intervene in time to stop these youth from committing violence against others.

CIVIL RIGHTS LAW—VIOLENCE AGAINST WOMEN ACT OF 1996

Despite the advances made in criminal and civil areas of the law, those who want to stop the abuse of male violence against women advocated for a federal statute that would declare violence against women to be a civil rights violation—in other words, a violation of every woman's right to be protected under the United States constitution. After several years of political lobbying efforts (Biden 1993), the Congress passed and President Clinton signed into law the Violence Against Women Act of 1994. This law did several things. By making male violence against women a civil rights complaint, it makes it possible for women to file for compensatory and punitive damages against one or more abusers in federal court without having to prove the nexus between domestic violence and their personal damaged from the abuse. Physical and sexual assault of a woman was declared to have such a potential of harm that it is a violation of her civil rights if it can be proved to have occurred. It also recognized the difficulty abuse victims have in disclosing their victimization and therefore did not place any time restrictions on when the abuse had to be reported. This is important because most state civil tort laws do have a 1- to 2-year statute of limitation that is difficult though not impossible to overcome. The statute can be tolled (stopped) if it can be proved that the woman did not have the ability to know or report what she knew. The time clock starts running again at the point she is deemed able to know what happened. Interestingly, the standard that she must prove is that the man intended to commit whatever action he took; not that he intended to harm her, which is much more difficult to prove when there is also a love bond in the relationship. Recent case decisions suggest that this law will continue to be challenged in the next few years.

There were several other areas that this law covered in addition to the civil rights portion. One major area is in giving police departments more training and equipment so that they can better protect abused women. At the same time, police departments are instructed to make sure that they do not permit any officer who has been convicted of abuse to carry a gun or other weapon. Obviously, in the United States, it is almost impossible to remain a police officer and not carry a weapon. While this is designed to get better law enforcement protection for battered and sexually abused women, in fact, it has caused major difficulties for law enforcement agencies who had many officers in their departments who had convictions on their records from many years earlier. Eventually, it will be easier to enforce this section of the law, as law enforcement departments learn to better screen their potential employees.

Other areas of the civil rights laws have also been used to better protect battered women. The most notable case was that of Tracey Thurman, a severely physically abused battered woman who sued the Torrington, Connecticut police department under the 1963 Civil Rights Act for failure to protect her constitutional rights to be free from violence and her safety protected by them. *Thurman v. Torrington* was filed after the police failed to protect her from a brutal beating from her abusive husband. She won over $2 million in damages in a judgment that also required the police department to change its policies and procedures to better protect all battered women. The award was significant enough to get the attention of police departments across the country and thus, ended up protecting many more battered women.

RISK MANAGEMENT FOR THERAPISTS

Providing therapy and evaluations in this area is one of the more dangerous professionals areas in which to practice today. Both battered women and batterers become unhappy if they do not get precisely what they want, without regard for what may or may not be feasible. It is important for therapists to document their assessment findings and treatment plan. The therapy goals listed in the treatment plan need to be referred to in subsequent notes of therapy sessions. If a situation occurs where the therapist believes that someone may harm another person, after doing a careful risk assessment that includes checking on the specificity of the threat, if it is directed toward a particular individual, and if it appears feasible for the threat to be carried out, then the therapist may be legally mandated to warn the other party or law enforcement of the potential danger. Further, if in the therapist's professional opinion an individual is thought to be in danger of harming her/himself or others, then it may be necessary to make arrangements to have that individual hospitalized—either voluntarily or involuntarily.

Therapists must also take precautions when dealing with clients who have previously engaged in violent actions. These clients should not be seen when the therapist is alone in the building with no one available for assistance, should it become necessary. In fact, it is preferable to see such clients when others are nearby and warned that their help might become needed. A pre-arranged signal might be an important preparation to take. Any precautions that are taken should be carefully documented in the notes.

Finally, it cannot be stressed enough how important it is for therapists who work with violent offenders or women who have been abused to have good training and continued consultation available in this area. Family violence and violence against women are considered specialization areas and those practicing within them without such training are putting themselves in a vulnerable situation. Even offering an opinion in a custody determination where domestic violence is alleged is risky unless special training in this area has been obtained.

CONCLUSIONS

In all of these areas of the legal system, there is an opportunity to make a contribution to stopping men's violence against women. However, despite its formal power, there is great reluctance to use the legal system to interfere in the privacy of people's homes. This reluctance is one of the continuing problems for those working in this field. The best way to stop violence in the home is to expose it, and yet, most women continue to be abused while isolated from the very help they could use to protect themselves better. The issue of isolation as a key factor in the batterer's arsenal of weapons has been addressed throughout this book. It cannot be overemphasized. While historically "rule of thumb" laws discouraged such legal intervention (Martin, 1976), their replacement by some of the best assault laws still hasn't brought about much more protection for the victim. Even after extensive training, law enforcement officials are still reluctant to invoke the only societal consequences available for what they prefer to define as a private family quarrel. The women interviewed in this research project expressed frustration, anger, and disappointment that the legal system seemed to batter them too. Recent newspaper reports indicate that while more women do get protection from all the new laws, there are still many who end up frustrated and seriously harmed.

When we began this research, we believed that helping battered women terminate the battering relationship would result in ending the abuse against them and their children. We had no idea of the tenacity of batterers to use every possible manipulation to keep their women in their power and control. The legal system, even with all the positive changes that have been made, still can be manipulated by the batterer to use it to continue his/her abuse of power. The most obvious area used is in the domestic courts when access to children is at issue. But, in every legal arena it remains a struggle just to get women's voices heard and listened to. Most women who end up dead have tried to use the legal system but it failed them. Most children who have been exposed to violence while growing up, could have been protected from its devastating effects had the courts used their power to keep them safe from a violent and cruel father (or mother, in some smaller number of cases).

CHAPTER FOURTEEN

Conclusions

This research was undertaken in order to identify variables which would identify and assist in understanding battered women and to test two theories specific to understanding the violence. Data were collected from about 400 battered women and analyzed identifying a series of relationships between variables that could be termed a battered women syndrome. Support was found for both theories tested—the application of learned helplessness to battered women and the Walker cycle theory of violence. The women were asked questions relating to both a battering and nonbattering relationship, and comparisons were made to analyze her perceptions of the effect of living in violence. A distinct syndrome was found and named "The Battered Woman Syndrome."

It was concluded that the battered women interviewed behaved in ways that were reactive to the battering. While interactive effects in the relationship were noted, the major control and power seemed to be vested in the man. Descriptions of the violent men indicate that there were sufficient similarities to suggest a violence-prone personality that originates in childhood and becomes more severe as the men grow older. This is in contrast with other criminal patterns that reach a peak in young adulthood and become less violent as men age. More research directly with the men was recommended at the time to confirm this finding. Since then, research has supported the existence of at least three specific types of batterers; those who use violence as a way to gain power and control over the women, those who are mentally ill and may also misuse their power and control; and those who are violent criminals who have an anti-social personality.

Descriptions of the women indicate that their behavior in battering relationships varies directly with what they perceive will be effective in minimizing injuries and staying alive. Indeed, the high risk of lethality

was an important finding. It was concluded that there may be susceptibility factors that originate in childhood and in the battering relationship itself, which cause the women to focus on developing survival
skills rather than escaping early, before the violence escalates to life-
threatening proportions.

The interrelationship between sexism and violence in the environment did have an impact on her reaction to violence. The data indicate
that the woman's current state of functioning is influenced by her earlier
experiences, a finding common in psychological studies. This susceptibility to remaining a victim has been described in the development of
learned helplessness. However, the reality of fear and terror was also
found to be a factor in making it difficult to terminate these violent
relationships. The role of the cycle theory has been found to reinforce
the positive factors in the relationship. The women interviewed were
most likely to terminate the battering relationship when the divergence between the tension-building and loving-contrition phases
begins to widen, and the reinforcement begins to decrease. Thus, studying the costs and benefits of these marital relationships would be a
promising avenue of further research.

A general summary of some of the findings as they relate to some
previous common myths are as follows:

- Less than 15% of the batterers were reported as unemployed during the battering relationship. Thus, our data show no link between
  unemployment and violent behavior.
- The trend for those women who reported on both violent and nonviolent relationships was in the direction of violent pairs being
  less equal on those demographic variables sociologists suggest
  are important in establishing stable marriages.
- Battered women interviewed were less likely to go into another
  relationship and, when they did, it was rarely another violent one.
  However, the batterers did seem to go into another intimate relationship, although it was not generally known by the women if
  there was a repetition of the violence.
- Three-quarters of our sample of battered women were employed
  during the battering relationship.
- The violence always escalated in frequency and severity over time.
- Battered women held attitudes toward women's roles that were
  more liberal than most of the population. They reported that batterers were very traditional in their attitudes toward women.
- Battering was present in two-thirds of the battered women's childhood homes, four-fifths of batterer's homes, and one-quarter of

nonbatterer's homes. Violence in childhood seems to beget more violence as adults.

- One-half of the battered women reported being sexually molested or abused as children. These acts were mostly repeated over time by male members of their families.
- There was a high rate of arrest and convictions for the batterers for offenses other than family violence. Almost three-quarters of the men were reported as having been arrested and about one-half of them were convicted on those charges.
- The women were more likely to be married to their batterers.
- The battered women reported early romantic and sexual involvement with the batterers that resulted in pregnancy and subsequent marriage in one-third of the cases.
- Women were at a high risk to be battered during pregnancy.
- Battered women in general had small families with an average of 1.5 children with the batterer.
- Sex was used as a power weapon to dominate the women in the same manner that they used physical violence. Marital rape was commonly reported.
- The batterer's unreasonable jealousy was almost always reported by the women. It was usually sexual in nature. The man accused the woman of sexual relations with other men and women. Oftentimes the jealousy extended to family and friends.
- Battered women believed that the batterer could kill them. Even though they perceive the danger, they also believe they can help the batterer change. Approximately one-third of the women reported threatening suicide themselves, and in one-half of the cases the batterers threatened suicide. The line between suicide and homicide seemed to be fluid.
- Children in the battering-relationship homes were at high risk for physical child abuse and almost all were psychologically abused by living in the violent atmosphere. The typical child abuse professional's condemnation of the mother for not protecting her children from abuse may be unfair in that it does not take into account that she may be without the ability to control the violence against herself or her children.
- Battered women report experiencing more anger when living with a batterer than with a nonbatterer. While they do not always show this anger directly, three times as many women in a violent relationship were likely to show their anger by using physical violence toward their partner than when they were in a nonbattering relationship. Still the percentage was small with 15% of those in a

violent relationship and 5% of those in a nonbattering relationship reporting the use of violence. These data refute the "mutual combat" or "battered man" problem as being a large one.

- Eight times as many women report using physical discipline on their children while with their batterers than when living alone or in a nonbattering relationship. Again, the theory that violence begets more violence is obvious here.
- Battered women are more socially and financially isolated when living with a batterer.
- Violent acts are most likely to occur on the weekend, during the warm, summer months, from 6:00 P.M. to midnight. Most battering incidents start and end in the home, usually in the bedroom and living room.
- Violence escalates over time. The need for medical attention increases, although only two-thirds of the women who need such medical care actually seek it.
- Use of weapons during battering incidents increases over time.
- The probability that the woman will seek help increases over time, from 14% to 50% at the final incident reported. This still leaves 50% who do not seek help no matter how severe the violence. The women are two times more likely to discuss the last incident with a relative or friend than the first incident.
- Battered women are most likely to leave the relationship when the rewards from the loving kindness phase 3 decrease. The divergence between the tension building phase 1 of the cycle and the loving-contrition phase 3 widens, so that the cost benefit ratio changes and the woman receives less reinforcement for staying in the relationship. Sometimes when she tries to escape, one of them dies. If she kills him, our data indicate it is usually in self-defense, against his escalating violence toward her as an attempt to get her to stay.
- There is more alcohol abuse reported than drug abuse in battering relationships. It was reported that 67% of the batterers frequently abused alcohol. However, only about one-fifth of them abused alcohol during all four battering incidents on which we collected data.
- If a battered woman reported abusing alcohol, she was most likely to be battered by a man who also abused alcohol.
- Violent men who abused alcohol were more likely to be older than men who did not.
- The trend was to support clinical observations that batterers who abuse alcohol inflict more serious injuries on women.

- The trend was that batterers who abuse alcohol were from lower socioeconomic-status homes.
- Battered women rated themselves high on a self-esteem measure, indicating that they do not perceive themselves as having low self-esteem, as professionals in this area tend to think.
- Battered women reported themselves as high on depression indices although they do not report feeling that depressed. Women out of the battering relationship for the longest time seem to have a higher risk of depression than those women still in the relationship.
- Inequality between men and women impacts on the perceptions of violent behavior for the women so that they are unable to develop adequate skills to escape from the relationship. Such sexism also pervades society's institutions, so that women feel that they are unable to receive any assistance to help them or their batterers.

Finally, these research findings demonstrate the heterogeneity of both batterers and battered women. Every day, ordinary people get caught up in the domestic violence cycle causing untold physical and psychological harm to themselves, their children, their families, their co-workers, and their friends. Domestic violence cannot be considered a private family matter. Its painful repercussions extend into the general community. The human and economic cost to help its victims heal is staggering. However, violence is learned behavior that can be unlearned so that the negative psychological effects reported here can be prevented.

Tables 1–36

TABLE 1   Current Sociodemographic Data for Battered Women

Demographic Variable	Battered Women Sample		Comparison Sample (1)
	n	%	
Racial and Ethnic Group			Region 8: Women Aged 20–64
White	321	80	95%
Spanish Surnamed/Chicana	3	8	5%
Black	25	6	1%
Native American	18	4	
Asian American	1	0	
Other	4	1	
Marital Status			(2)
Single	26	6	31%
Married/Living Together	103	24	60%
Separated/Divorced	261	65	6%
Widowed	11	3	2.3%
Employment Status			
Unemployed	192	48	45%
Part-time	49	12	
Full-time	147	37	53%
Other	13	3	
Education			
Less Than High School	66	12	
High School Only	99	25	
Some College	160	40	
College & Post Grad	92	23	
Mean Years of Education 12.7 years			
Religion			(5)
None	85	21	3%
Agnostic/Atheist	10	2	
Protestant	185	46	65%
Catholic	93	23	28%
Jewish	4	1	
Other	25	6	1%
Social Class-Family of Origin			(5)
Lower	53	13	4%
Working	139	35	46%
Middle	177	45	47%
Upper	24	6	1%

TABLE 1   *Continued*

Demographic Variable	Battered Women Sample		Comparison Sample (1)
	n	%	
Age			U.S. –
	X = 32.2 years		X = 30.0 years
	Range = 18–59		Region 8 –
			X = 27.7 years
			Colorado –
			X = 28.6 years
Height Median = 5'4"	Range = 4'6"–6'0"		
Weight	Median = 130.3 lbs.		
	Range = 85–276 lbs.		
Number of Children	X = 2.02		
	Range = 0–10		
By Woman's Age			(4)
18–24	X = .9		X = .4
25–34	X = 1.3		X = 1.6
35–44	X = 3.3		X = 2.9

(1) *Source:* 1980 Census for Region 8, unless otherwise specified.
(2) *Source:* U.S. Census P-Series (P-20) #338 for March 1978, issued May 1979.
(3) *Source:* 1970 Census Data.
(4) *Source:* U.S. Census P-Series (P-20) #325 for June 1977, issued September 1978.
(5) *Source:* National Opinion Research Center, July 1976.
(6) *Source:* Compiled from General Social and Economic Characteristics, U.S. Census, 1970 for each state of Region 8.

TABLE 2 Sociodemographic Data for Batterers and Nonbatterers at Time of Relationship as Reported by Women

Variable	Battered		Nonbatterer		Comparison Sample (1)
	n	%	*n*	%	
Racial and Ethnic Group					Region 8 (2)
White	286	71	152	75	91%
Spanish Surnamed/Chicana	37	9	19	9	1.6%
Black	50	12	21	10	5.6%
Native American	23	6	7	3	
Asian American	2	0	2	1	
Other	3	1	2	1	
Current Marital Status					(3)
Single	36	10	Information		31%
Married/Living Together	177	49	Not Asked		63%
Separated/Divorced	100	26			6.2%
Widowed	2	1			2.4%
Other	23	6			
Don't Know	30	8			
Employment					
Unemployed	55	14	20	10	
Employed	342	85	179	88	
Other	6	1	5	2	
Religion					(4)
None	114	29	71	37	3%
Agnostic/Atheist	16	4	6	3	
Protestant	147	37	64	32	65%
Catholic	110	28	42	21	28%
Jewish	4	1	3	2	2%
Other	9	2	10	5	1%
Education					
Less than High School	103	24	30	17	
High School Only	113	28	56	28	
Some College	95	24	55	28	
College & Post Grad	91	22	58	29	
Mean Years of Education	12.1 years		12.7 years		

TABLE 2 *Continued*

Variable	Battered	Nonbatterer	Comparison Sample
Height	X = 5'8" Range = 5'1"–6'3"	X = 5'8"	
Weight	X = 174 lbs. Range = 110–285 lbs.	X = 172 lbs.	

(1) *Source:* 1970 Census Data.
(2) *Source:* Compiled from General Social and Economic Characteristics, U.S. Census, 1970 for each state of Region 8.
(3) *Source:* U.S. Census Data P Series 20, #338, May 1979.
(4) *Source:* National Opinion Research Center, July 1976.

TABLE 3 Education Levels of Battered Women, Batterers, and Nonbatterers

Battered Women vs. Batterer (n = 400)*	Woman	Batterer
Some High School	12.3%	25.8%
Graduate High School	24.8%	28.3%
Some College	40.0%	23.3%
Graduate College	23.0%	22.8%

Battered Women vs. Nonbatterer (n = 199)**	Woman	Nonbatterer
Some High School	8.5%	15.1%
Graduate High School	22.1%	28.1%
Some College	42.7%	27.6%
Graduate College	26.6%	29.1%

Batterer vs. Nonbatterer (n = 198)***	Batterer	Nonbatterer
Some High School	23.7%	15.2%
Graduate High School	28.8%	28.3%
Some College	26.3%	27.3%
Graduate College	21.2%	29.3%

* $\chi^2(9) = 118.34$ p < .001
** $\chi^2(9) = 22.36$ p < .001
*** $\chi^2(9) = 20.95$ p < .013

TABLE 4 Family Background of Battered Women

Variable	n	%
Social Class—Family Origin		
Lower Class	53	13
Working Class	139	35
Middle Class	177	45
Upper Class	24	6
Parents in Home		
Mother and Father	306	76
Mother Only	33	8
Father Only	2	0
Parent/Stepparent	21	5
Other Relative	19	5
Other	20	5
Birth Order		
Youngest	88	22
Middle	166	42
Oldest	117	30
Only	24	6
Mother Employed	159	41
Battering in Home	267	67
Critical Periods While Growing Up	360	91
Physical Health		
Poor	42	10
Average	130	32
Above Average	231	57

Variable	Mean
Family Size	X = 6.54
Number of Siblings (Including Self)	X = 4.2
Age Leaving Home	X = 17.78
Number of Critical Periods	X = 2.1

TABLE 4 *Continued*

Variable	Mean
Attitudes Toward Women	
Battered Women	X = 58.48
Mother	X = 40.16
Father	X = 27.06

Childhood Health Problems	Never Rarely		Sometimes		Most of the Time	
	n	%	*n*	%	*n*	%
Migraines	324	82	35	9	41	10
Hospitalization	339	84	41	10	21	5
Eating Problems	244	61	57	14	101	25
Depression	147	36	110	27	145	36
Serious Injury	364	91	28	7	8	1
Weight Problems	230	57	58	14	114	29
High Blood Pressure	386	97	8	2	6	1
Sleep Problems	239	60	75	19	87	22
Allergies	279	70	44	11	74	18
Menstrual Problems	233	58	56	14	112	27

TABLE 5   Family Background for Batterers and Nonbatterers as Reported by the Women

Variable	Batterers		Nonbatterers	
	n	%	*n*	%
Battering in Home	281	81	41	24
Discipline in Home				
Mother – Strict	149	41	46	27
– Fair	30	8	70	41
– Lenient	179	50	54	31
Father – Strict	221	65	65	44
– Fair	24	7	42	29
– Lenient	89	27	39	26
Dependency				
Mother – No	137	35	94	49
– Somewhat	59	15	48	25
– Yes	190	49	49	25
Father – No	180	50	100	60
– Somewhat	70	20	41	25
– Yes	108	39	25	15
Social Class for Family of Origin				
Lower Class	114	29	26	13
Working Class	148	38	75	38
Middle Class	102	26	75	38
Upper Class	28	7	21	11
Mother Employed	160	41	68	35
Family Size	X = 6.10		X = 5.10	
Number of Siblings (Including Self)	X = 4.35		X = 3.15	
Attitudes Toward Women	X = 25.67		X = 42.88	

TABLE 6 Battering History for Battered Women, Batters and Nonbatterers

Battering Relationship	Battered Women		Batterers		Nonbatterers	
	n	%	n	%	n	%
Battering in Childhood Home	267	67	281	81	41	24
Battered by Mother	147	41	135	44	13	13
Battered by Father	144	44	187	61	24	23
Father Battered Mother	156	44	190	63	26	27
Mother Battered Father	104	29	103	35	13	13
Mother Battered Siblings	–	–	91	32	6	6
Mother Battered Sisters	62	21	–	–	–	–
Mother Battered Brothers	61	20	–	–	–	–
Father Battered Siblings	–	–	129	47	16	17
Father Battered Sisters	85	29	–	–	–	–
Father Battered Brothers	97	32	–	–	–	–
Battered Own Children	91	28	155	53	–	–
Spanked as Young Child (Age 0–6)	353	89	–	–	–	–
Spanked as Older Child	332	83	–	–	–	–
Hit with an Object	317	78	–	–	–	–

TABLE 7 Racial and Ethnic Background of Women Reporting Childhood Sexual Assault

Total Sample	Total N	n Reporting Childhood Sexual Assault	% of Each Racial Group Sexually Assaulted
White	321	144	45
Chicana	33	23	68
Black	25	14	56
Native American	8	8	44
Asian American	1	1	100
Other	4	2	50
Woman Reporting Childhood Sexual Assault (N = 192)		n	%
White	144	75	
Chicana	23	12	
Black	14	7	
Native American	8	4	
Asian American	1	5	
Other	2	1	

TABLE 8 Frequency of Childhood Sexual Assault Acts (n = 192)

Sexual Assault Act	Attempt But Resist		Single Incident		Several Times	
	n	%	*n*	%	*n*	%
Child Fondled						
By Father	1	.5	5	3	22	12
By Brother	7	4	13	7	22	12
By Other Male Relative	13	7	18	9	44	23
By Female Relative	0	0	3	2	8	4
By Other	0	5	37	19	45	23
Child Fondles						
Father	1	.5	2	1	4	2
Brother	4	2	1	.5	10	5
Other Male Relative	0	0	4	2	14	7
Female Relative	0	0	1	.5	6	3
Other	5	3	3	2	10	5
Oral Sex						
With Father	2	1	0	0	1	.5
With Brother	2	1	0	0	3	2
With Other Male Relative	3	2	1	.5	5	3
With Female Relative	0	0	1	.5	3	2
With Other	6	3	5	3	6	3
Sexual Intercourse						
With Father	3	2	2	1	8	4
With Brother	7	4	3	2	5	2
With Other Male Relative	6	3	6	3	9	5
With Female Relative	0	0	0	0	0	0
With Other	11	6	21	11	11	6
Asked/Forced to Watch Sex Acts						
With Father	0	0	1	.5	2	1
With Brother	2	1	2	1	1	.5
With Other Male Relative	1	.5	3	2	6	3
With Female Relative	0	0	0	0	1	.5
With Other	2	1	5	3	4	2
Other Abuse						
By Other	3	2	12	6	8	4

TABLE 9   Reported Perpetrators of Childhood Sexual Abuse Acts (n = 192)

Sexual Act/Perpetrator	n	%
Child fondled by father	28	15
Child fondles father	7	4
Oral sex with father	3	2
Sexual intercourse with father	13	7
Watch sex acts with father	3	2
Other with father	7	4
Child fondled by brother	42	22
Child fondles brother	17	9
Oral sex with brother	5	3
Sexual intercourse with brother	15	8
Watch sex acts with brother	5	3
Other with brother	8	4
Child fondled by other male relative	75	39
Child fondles other male relative	18	9
Oral sex with other male relative	9	5
Sexual intercourse with male relative	21	11
Watch sex acts with other male relative	10	5
Child fondled by female relative	11	6
Child fondles female relative	7	4
Oral sex with female relative	4	2
Sexual intercourse with female relative	0	0
Watch sex acts with female relative	1	.5
Other with female relative	1	.5
Child fondled by other	91	47
Child fondles other	18	9
Oral sex with other	17	9
Sexual intercourse with other	43	22
Watch sex acts with other	11	6
Other with other	23	12

TABLE 10   Military and Criminal History for Batterers and Nonbatterers

Military History	Batterer		Nonbatterer	
	n	%	*n*	%
Was He in the Military?	229	58	87	46
Drafted?	51	23	28	32
Combat Experience?	86	37	32	37
Number of Years in Military*	X = 3.2		X = 1.9	
Criminal History				
Was He Ever Arrested?	240	71	53	34
Was He Convicted?	140	44	29	19
Woman Obtained Restraining Order	131	39	4	1
Number of Restraining Orders**	X = 1.12		X = .01	

* $p < .01$
** $p < .001$

TABLE 11 Profile of Four Battering Incidents as Reported by Battered Women

Variable	First		Second		One of Worst		Last prior to Interview	
	n	%	n	%	n	%	n	%
Month								
January	32	8	27	7	20	6	35	9
February	21	5	30	8	25	7	29	8
March	24	6	29	8	24	7	27	7
April	28	7	22	6	27	7	30	8
May	35	9	25	7	28	8	27	7
June	37	10	36	10	34	9	36	10
July	43	11	38	10	40	11	25	7
August	32	8	18	5	35	10	37	10
September	41	11	36	10	27	7	35	9
October	27	7	44	12	32	9	27	7
November	32	8	34	9	32	9	35	9
December	33	9	34	9	38	10	26	7
Day								
Monday	10	4	7	3	12	4	17	6
Tuesday	9	3	10	4	4	1	23	8
Wednesday	11	4	21	8	18	7	22	8
Thursday	18	6	10	4	17	6	23	8
Friday	34	12	41	15	37	13	31	11
Saturday	42	15	39	14	59	21	52	18
Sunday	21	7	15	5	31	11	41	14
Weekday	97	34	93	34	60	22	56	20
Weekend	41	14	38	14	38	14	18	6
Time								
6 a.m.–12 noon	29	9	27	9	35	11	50	16
12 noon–6 p.m.	103	32	109	35	101	33	98	32
6 p.m.–12 midnight	135	42	138	44	126	41	129	42
12 midnight–6 a.m.	53	17	41	13	42	14	31	10
Where Incident Started								
At Home	297	75	311	81	290	79	302	79
Not at Home	99	25	72	19	78	21	77	20
In What Room Started?								
Basement	1	0	3	1	1	0	3	1
Outside (front or side)	10	3	5	2	7	3	10	3
Outside (back)	4	1	0	0	2	1	5	2
Living Room	123	42	126	41	117	42	117	39
Bathroom	8	3	8	3	6	2	11	4
Family Room	3	1	7	2	2	1	7	2

TABLE 11 Profile of Four Battering Incidents as Reported by Battered Women *(Continued)*

Variable	First		Second		One of Worst		Last prior to Interview	
	n	%	n	%	n	%	n	%
In What Room Started? *(Continued)*								
Kitchen	42	14	4	16	48	17	56	19
Bedroom	82	28	82	27	71	25	66	22
Other	21	7	29	9	26	9	24	8
Where Started?								
Car	23	28	16	26	25	35	13	19
Relative's Home	11	13	9	15	8	11	11	16
Friend's Home	11	13	7	11	7	10	4	6
Other Private Setting	14	17	7	11	6	8	8	12
Public Setting	22	17	17	27	20	28	27	40
Other	2	2	6	10	6	7	2	3
Where Incident Ended?								
At Home	310	78	318	83	301	82	311	82
Not at Home	86	22	63	17	67	18	67	18
Room Ended?								
Basement	1	0	1	0	1	0	2	1
Outside (front, side)	22	7	15	5	17	6	29	9
Outside (back)	4	1	0	0	5	2	3	1
Living Room	105	34	105	33	87	30	92	30
Bathroom	17	6	13	4	15	5	13	4
Family Room	1	0	4	1	3	1	7	2
Kitchen	27	9	32	10	35	12	32	10
Bedroom	107	35	120	38	104	36	105	34
Other	22	7	24	8	25	9	23	8
Where Ended?								
Car	24	33	12	20	12	18	10	16
Relative's Home	11	15	13	22	11	17	11	18
Friend's Home	9	12	4	7	3	5	4	7
Other Private Setting	12	16	6	10	13	20	12	20
Public Setting	14	19	18	30	25	38	18	30
Other	3	4	7	12	2	4	6	11
Batterer Using Alcohol								
Yes	194	50	191	52	199	56	190	58
Not Sure	14	4	9	2	7	2	20	6
No	179	46	168	46	150	42	150	42

TABLE 11 *Continued*

Variable	First		Second		One of Worst		Last prior to Interview	
	n	%	n	%	n	%	n	%
Woman Using Alcohol								
Yes	88	22	64	17	61	16	71	19
Not Sure	0	0	2	1	2	1	2	1
No	308	78	316	83	303	83	306	81
Batterer Using Drugs								
Yes	55	15	53	14	61	17	57	16
Not Sure	16	4	19	5	17	5	21	6
No	297	81	294	80	176	78	269	78
Woman Using Drugs								
Yes	30	7	31	8	30	8	18	4
Not Sure	1	0	5	1	0	0	1	0
No	363	91	347	91	383	92	355	95
Forced Sex								
	22	6	41	11	33	9	30	8
Medical Treatment Required								
	68	19	96	28	15	45	127	37
Medical Treatment Sought								
	45	12	68	18	117	32	104	28
Weapon Used								
None	347	91	317	86	269	77	291	80
Household Item	23	6	33	9	45	13	39	11
Actual Weapon	13	3	18	5	37	11	34	9
Immediately After, Leave								
Temporarily	88	23	81	22	108	29	94	25
Permanently	1	0	2	1	9	2	93	25
Immediately After, Seek Outside Help								
	54	14	81	22	113	31	182	49
Whom She Told								
Neighbor	337	7	37	10	66	19	80	22
Relative	69	19	75	21	87	25	112	31
Friend	95	26	94	26	112	31	157	43
Police	30	8	52	15	92	26	126	34
Doctor	35	10	43	12	77	22	80	22

TABLE 11   Profile of Four Battering Incidents as Reported by Battered Women *(Continued)*

Variable	First		Second		One of Worst		Last prior to Interview	
	n	%	n	%	n	%	n	%
Whom She Told *(Continued)*								
Minister	7	2	15	4	30	9	29	8
Safehouse	2	1	3	1	16	5	76	21
Psychologist	15	4	14	4	30	9	29	8
Psychiatrist	11	3	14	4	14	4	24	7
Parent	53	15	63	18	42	20	108	30
Lawyer, Other	12	3	22	6	43	13	107	29
Did He Justify, Rationalize, Explain or Apologize Afterward								
	316	82	280	75	244	67	218	59
Women's Perception of Responsibility								
Batterer's	315	80	311	82	294	81	301	84
Both	47	12	45	12	43	12	38	11
Woman	29	7	22	6	25	6	18	5
Sensed It Would Happen?								
	42	13	122	38	139	46	147	48

TABLE 12   Social Isolation of Battered Women

Variable	With Batterer		With Nonbatterer	
	n	%	*n*	%
Get Together With Neighbors				
Never	122	31	52	26
Occasionally	176	44	60	31
Frequently	102	26	86	53
Location of Women's Nearest Relative				
Another State	158	39	79	39
Another City	32	8	27	14
Same City	166	41	84	41
Location of Woman's Nearest Friend				
Another State	55	15	19	10
Another City	32	8	27	14
Same City	285	75	153	77
Own a Phone				
No	61	15	24	13
Part of the Time	64	16	8	4
Most of the Time	276	69	160	83
Type of Housing				
Rent	256	63	123	65
Own	133	33	58	30
Other	13	3	8	4
Frequency of Women Reporting They DID NOT Have Access to:				
Checking Account	134	34	49	26
Charge Accounts	204	51	99	53
Cash	108	27	16	8
Automobiles	89	22	24	13
Public Transportation	116	30	41	22
Mean Number of Relatives Within Visiting Distance				
Woman's	4.5		4.1	
Man's	5.9		3.6	
Mean Number of Moves	6.2		2.2	
Mean Number of Years in Last or Present Residence	2.0		1.1	
Mean Number of Voluntary Organizations in which the Woman was a Member	.98		.81	
Mean Number of Organized Recreational Activities of which the Woman was a Member	.39		.45	

TABLE 13 Women's Reports on Controls on Behavior in Battering and Nonbattering Relationships

Variable	With Batterer		With Nonbatterer	
	n	%	*n*	%
How often did *he* know where *you* were when you weren't together?				
Never	3	1	4	2
Occasionally	23	6	53	26
Frequently	376	94	146	71
How often did *you* know where *he* was when you weren't together?				
Never	44	11	6	3
Occasionally	180	45	52	25
Frequently	179	45	145	71
Were there places *you* wanted to go, but didn't because of him?				
Never	51	13	158	78
Occasionally	129	32	36	18
Frequently	223	56	8	4
Did you generally do what he asked?				
Never	0	0	13	2
Occasionally	44	11	43	22
Frequently	359	89	151	77
Did you emotionally withdraw to get what you wanted?				
Never	82	21	116	57
Occasionally	233	58	75	37
Frequently	85	21	12	6
Did you restrict his freedom to get what you wanted?				
Never	293	74	176	86
Occasionally	94	24	23	11
Frequently	11	3	5	2
Did you stop having sex to get what you wanted				
Never	215	54	166	82
Occasionally	142	36	33	16
Frequently	43	11	4	1

TABLE 13 *Continued*

Variable	With Batterer		With Nonbatterer	
	n	%	*n*	%
Did you threaten to leave to get something you wanted?				
Never	105	26	148	73
Occasionally	211	52	48	24
Frequently	84	21	8	3
Did you use physical force to get something you wanted?				
Never	304	77	196	96
Occasionally	91	23	8	4
Frequently	2	1	0	0
Did you use physical force against the children to get something from him?				
Never	313	96	156	99
Occasionally	12	6	1	1
Frequently	0	0	0	0
Did you say or do something nice to get what you wanted?				
Never	37	9	54	26
Occasionally	180	45	80	39
Frequently	184	46	70	34
Who wins major disagreements?				
Always him	159	40	9	5
Usually him	130	33	21	11
Equal	37	9	117	59
Usually her	29	7	30	15
Always her	0	0	4	2
Other	45	11	18	9
How Woman Shows Her Anger: (May choose more than one response)				
Doesn't show	101	26	31	18
Curses or shouts	198	52	78	45
Sulks, no speaking	279	73	98	57
Directed at children or pets	63	16	5	3
Directed at objects	132	35	26	15
Physical violence toward him	58	15	9	5
Physical violence toward child	18	5	1	.6
Other	72	19	184	49

TABLE 14   Women's Emotional Reactions to First and Third Significant
Battering Incidents Reported

INCIDENT 1:	None	A Little	Moderate	A Lot	Overwhelming
Fear	13%	13%	13%	34%	27%
Anxiety	16%	12%	16%	39%	17%
Depression	22%	14%	17%	31%	16%
Shock	7%	7%	8%	36%	41%
Anger	17%	19%	17%	29%	17%
Hostility	34%	19%	13%	23%	12%
INCIDENT 3:	None	A Little	Moderate	A Lot	Overwhelming
Fear	10%	7%	8%	27%	48%
Anxiety	13%	7%	11%	32%	38%
Depression	14%	7%	13%	31%	35%
Shock	22%	13%	12%	25%	29%
Anger	12%	6%	12%	33%	37%
Hostility	18%	10%	9%	30%	33%

TABLE 15   Passivity-Activity during the Period Before and After the
Battering Incident

BEFORE BATTERING	INCIDENT 1	INCIDENT 3
Very passive; low profile	12%	16%
More passive than active	18%	20%
Mixed or ambivalent behavior	9%	16%
More active than passive	48%	35%
Very active; assertive	13%	13%
AFTER BATTERING	INCIDENT 1	INCIDENT 3
Very passive, resigned	26%	21%
More passive than active	28%	23%
Mixed or ambivalent behavior	22%	17%
More active than passive	14%	23%
Very active; assertive	9%	17%

TABLE 16   Women's Perception of Danger With the Batterer

Variable		n	%	
Did you think *he* ever would or could kill *you?*				
Never		32	8	
Maybe		22	6	
Yes, accidentally		46	12	
Yes, if mad enough	329	99	26	86
Yes		184	48	
Did you think *you* ever would or could kill *him?*				
Never		181	45	
Maybe		37	9	
Yes, accidentally		14	4	
Yes, if mad enough	181	75	19	46
Yes		92	23	
If someone were to die during a battering, who would it be?				
Neither		14	4	
Him		24	6	
Me		341	87	
Both		10	3	
Do you ever think about dying?				
Never		99	25	
Occasionally		136	34	
Frequently		160	40	
Have you ever tried to kill him?				
Never		356	89	
Yes, accidentally		10	3	
Yes		33	8	
To what extent do you think you can control his behavior?				
Never		238	60	
Occasionally		114	29	
Frequently		47	13	

	Yes		Did You Believe Him	
Variable	n	%	n	%
Did he ever threaten to:				
Commit suicide	197	50	120	48
Kill someone	228	57	198	71
Batter children	109	33	122	69

TABLE 16   Women's Perception of Danger With the Batterer *(Continued)*

Variable	Yes		Did You Believe Him	
	n	%	*n*	%
Did *you* ever threaten to:				
Commit suicide	141	36		
Kill someone	41	11		
Batter children	20	6		
Will he continue to be a batterer?				
Yes	247	65		
Yes, but used to think he'd change	49	13		
No, he'll change eventually	38	10		
No, he'll change soon	28	7		
Do you think he'll batter another woman?				
No, very unlikely	35	9		
Not sure	36	10		
Yes, very likely	305	81		

TABLE 17   Violence Prone Characteristics of Batterers Compared to Non-batterers as Reported by the Women

Variable	Batterers %	Non-Batterers %
Battering in Childhood Home	81	24
Battered by Mother	44	13
Battered by Father	61	23
Father Battered Mother	63	27
Battered Own Children	53	N/A
Was In Military	58	46
Drafted	23	32
Combat Experience	37	37
Number of Years	X = 3.2	X = 1.9
Was he ever arrested?	71	34
Was he convicted?	44	19
Women Obtained Restraining Order	39	1
Frequent Alcohol Abuse	67	43

TABLE 18   Women's Report of Pattern of Abuse Over Time

	Decrease	Increase	Same	Other Pattern
Frequency of abuse	12%	66%	5%	16%
Physical aspect of abuse	12%	65%	15%	8%
Psychological aspect of abuse	7%	73%	15%	5%
Length of time of abusive incidents	8%	37%	—	55%

TABLE 19   Violent Acts Scale

Please give each of the following acts a severity rating, any number from 1–100. A 0 rating would mean that the act is not at all severe. A 100 would mean that the act is extremely severe. Please rate each act under three conditions — 1. threatened, 2. committed briefly, and 3. committed repeatedly. Write your rating for each condition in the appropriate box. Thank you.

Violent Act	Threatened	Committed Briefly	Committed Repeatedly
Push, Shove	31	58	77
Burn	60	85	97
Claw, Scratch	39	64	83
Verbal Abuse	43	63	83
Hit with Object	60	86	96
Used Knife	79	96	99
Throw Object At	53	85	94
Try To Hurt With Motor Vehicle	81	96	100
Slap, Hit, Spank	54	76	90
Kick	55	79	94
Throw Bodily	62	86	95
Used Gun	88	97	100
Wrestle, Twist Arm	52	72	89
Tried to Drown	78	97	100
Strangle	76	97	100
Punch	68	84	95

TABLE 20   Injury Severity Scale

Please give each of the following injuries a severity rating, any number from 0–100. A 0 rating would mean that the injury is not at all severe. A 100 would mean that the injury is extremely severe. There are no right or wrong answers. We just want your opinion as to how severe you think these injuries are.

Injury	Rating	Injury	Rating
Lost Teeth	91	Severe Cut or Burn	95
Concussion	91	Lost Hair	78
Joint or Spinal Injury	96	Internal Injury	96
Break Jaw or Nose	96	No Real Hurt	40
Bruises	75	Permanent Head Injury	100
Permanent Eye Injury	98	Break Eyeglasses	66
Tear Clothing	51	Permanent Internal Injury	99
Black Eye	78	Cut or Burn	85
Psychological Harassment	85	Break Eardrum	96
Splinters or Fragments	85	Severe Bruises	87
Other Broken Bones	93	Other Permanent Injury	99
No Visible Injury But Painful	77		

TABLE 21 Women's Report on Sexual Relationship With Batterer and Nonbatterer

Variable	With Batterer		With Nonbatterer	
	n	%	*n*	%
Who Initiates Sex?				
Neither	1	0	2	1
Man	257	64	68	34
Both	115	29	106	53
Woman	29	7	25	12
Sex Unpleasant for Woman?				
Never	59	15	142	71
Occasionally	186	46	41	20
Frequently	155	38	18	9
Sex Unpleasant for Man?				
Never	200	53	173	87
Occasionally	122	32	19	10
Frequently	50	13	8	5
Woman Feels Guilt or Shame?				
Never	179	45	147	74
Occasionally	167	42	46	24
Frequently	56	14	7	4
Man Feels Guilt or Shame?				
Never	232	61	152	78
Occasionally	107	28	36	18
Frequently	44	11	8	4
Woman Asked to Perform Unusual Sex?				
Never	236	59	192	95
Occasionally	114	29	8	4
Frequently	48	12	2	1
Woman was Forced to Have Sex?				
No	163	41	187	93
Once	41	10	4	2
Often	197	49	11	5
How Often Does He Have Affairs with Other Women?				
Never	140	35	130	66
Occasionally	210	53	64	33
Frequently	50	13	4	20

TABLE 21 Women's Report on Sexual Relationship With Batterer and Nonbatterer *(Continued)*

Variable	With Batterer		With Nonbatterer	
	n	%	*n*	%
Men?				
Never	277	88	149	99
Occasionally	36	11	1	1
Frequently	1	1	0	0
How Often Are You Jealous of His Affairs?				
Never	128	32	102	50
Occasionally	163	40	68	34
Frequently	112	27	32	15
How Often is he Jealous of You having Affairs with Other Men?				
Never	26	6	82	41
Occasionally	101	25	92	45
Frequently	275	68	27	13
Women?				
Never	242	77	144	97
Occasionally	42	13	5	3
Frequently	29	10	0	0

TABLE 22 Pregnancy in Battering and Nonbattering Relationship

Batterers' Reactions to the Pregnancy	Pregnancy 1 (N = 304)		Pregnancy 2 (N = 205)		Pregnancy 3 (N = 112)	
	n	%	n	%	n	%
Unhappy	104	34	66	32	38	34
Didn't Seem to Care	34	11	35	17	22	20
Happy	163	54	104	51	52	45
Didn't Know About It	3	1	—	—	—	—
Battered During Pregnancy	(N = 308)		(N = 206)		(N = 111)	
	125	59	131	63	62	55
Battered During Which Trimester	(N = 185)		(N = 135)		(N = 65)	
First Trimester	52	28	26	19	15	23
Second Trimester	20	20	15	11	6	9
Third Trimester	23	12	17	13	9	14
Any Two	30	16	16	13	10	15
All Three	60	32	60	44	25	38

Pregnancies During Battering Relationship
   Pregnancies with Batterer: 23% report none (N = 402)
                                      Mean = 2.0

   Mean Age of First Pregnancy: 22.5 years

   Married at Time of First Pregnancy: 64% (N = 311)

TABLE 23   Birth Control in Battering and Nonbattering Relationships

Variable	With Batterer		With Nonbatterer	
	n	%	*n*	%
Birth Control Method Most Consistently Used				
none	80	20	49	24
withdrawal	7	2	1	0
rhythm	12	3	2	1
foam	13	3	2	1
condom	12	3	5	2
foam and condom	3	1	1	0
diaphragm	30	7	9	4
pill	146	36	63	31
vasectomy	7	2	7	3
tubal ligation	15	4	13	6
abortion	0	0	0	0
abstaining	1	0	3	1
I.U.D.	60	15	36	18
other	16	4	10	5
Responsibility for Birth Control				
Man	29	8	15	8
Both	13	3	7	4
Woman	270	70	176	66
Other	71	18	42	22
Mean Number of Children	1.5		.4	

TABLE 24 Relationship History for Battered Women, Batterers, and Non-batterers

Number of Intimate Relationships for Women				
Marriages	X = 2.1			
Living Together	X = 1.3			
Total Battering	X = 1.3			
Total Nonbattering	X = .7			

Variable	Batterers		Nonbatterers	
Age of Women When Couple Met	21.2		23.0	
Age When Relationship Became Romantic	21.8		24.0	
Couple Dated How Long?*	88% 5.9 months		87% 5.9 months	
Couple Lived Together How Long?*	59% 10 months		59% 9.2 months	
Couple Married How Long?	82% 6 years		97% 6 years	

Order of Relationship for Women	*n*	%	*n*	%
First	227	56	85	42
Second	120	30	69	34
Third	38	9	38	19
Fourth	11	3	5	2
Fifth	6	1	4	2
Children from Relationship	X = 1.5		X = .4	

* Median reported due to wide distribution.

TABLE 25   Women's Report of Child Abuse for Herself and the Batterer

Variable	n	%
Did *batterer* abuse the children?	155	53
Did *he* threaten to abuse the children?	228	33
Did *you* abuse the children?	91	28
Did *you* threaten to abuse the children?	41	11
Did *you* use physical force on the children to get what you wanted from him?	12	6
When *you* were angry with the batterer, did *you* use physical force directed toward the children?	18	5
Did children know about the battering?	278	87

TABLE 26   Report of Batterer's and Nonbatterer's Substance Abuse During Relationship

Drug	Batterer		Nonbatterer	
	n	%	n	%
Alcohol				
Never	40	10	42	21
Occasionally	92	23	89	36
Frequently	269	67	89	43
Prescription Drugs				
Never	188	8	149	78
Occasionally	125	32	32	17
Frequently	81	20	11	6
Marijuana				
Never	154	40	103	52
Occasionally	143	37	27	14
Frequently	91	23	67	35
Street Drugs				
Never	249	65	163	83
Occasionally	75	20	25	13
Frequently	57	15	8	5

TABLE 27 Women's Report of Alcohol and Drug Use During Four Battering Incidents

	First		Second		One of the Worst		Last	
Alcohol Use	BW	BM	BW	BM	BW	BM	BW	BM
Yes	22	50	14	52	16	56	19	53
Not Sure	0	4	5	2	1	2	1	5
No	78	46	80	46	83	42	81	42
Drug Use								
Yes	7	15	8	14	8	17	4	16
Not Sure	0	4	1	5	0	5	0	6
No	92	81	91	80	92	78	95	78

BW = Battered Woman
BM = Batterer

TABLE 28 Battered Women's Perceptions of the Attitudes Toward Women for Themselves, Their Mothers, Fathers, Batterers, and Nonbatterers

Group	N	Mean	S.D.	Normative Sample	Mean	S.D.
Mothers	384	40.16	14.87	Mothers(1)	41.86	11.62
Fathers	371	27.06	14.59	Fathers(1)	39.22	10.49
Batterers	391	25.67	14.27	College Males(1)	44.80	12.07
Nonbatterers	199	42.88	14.57			
Ss Short AWS	383	58.48	11.82	College Females(1)	50.26	11.68
Ss Full AWS	362	118.24	22.84	College Females(2)	98.21	23.16

(1) Norms reported in Spence, Helmreich, & Stapp (1973).
(2) Norms reported in Spence & Helmreich (1972).

TABLE 29 Battered Women's Attributions of Locus of Control as Measured by the Levinson IPC Scale

	Battered Women			Comparison Norms			
	N	M	SD	N	M	SD	*t* Value
Internal Scale				48	35.46	7.41	
Total Sample*	386	41.46	6.88				6.12
Total Out*	292	41.33	6.79				6.51
Out 1 Year*	112	41.62	6.44				5.26
Out 1 Year*	180	41.14	7.01				4.62
In*	94	41.87	7.13				5.09
Powerful Others Scale				48	14.64	6.87	
Total Sample*	383	18.01	9.73				9.36
Total Out**	291	18.17	9.39				2.76
Out 1 Year**	117	18.43	8.92				2.61
Out 1 Year***	174	17.99	9.72				2.09
In	92	17.52	10.78				1.72
Chance Scale				48	13.38	9.05	
Total Sample**	383	17.37	9.48				3.14
Total Out**	289	17.41	9.32				3.08
Out 1 Year**	113	18.01	8.73				3.03
Out 1 Year***	176	17.03	9.70				2.28
In	94	17.25	9.995				2.30

*p < .001
**p < .01
***p < .05

TABLE 30   **Mean Scores for Battered Women, Women In General, and Men In General on the Semantic Differential for Self-Esteem as Reported by Battered Women**

Adjective Pair		Women Battered	Women In General	Men In General
1	7			
Modest	Boastful	3.15	3.44	5.48
Poised	Awkward	3.16	2.81	3.95
Warm	Cool	2.12	2.64	4.02
Sexual	Nonsexual	2.57	2.53	2.43
Sensitive	Insensitive	1.57	2.32	4.24
Calm	Excitable	3.84	3.66	3.94
Dominant	Submissive	3.71	3.81	2.25
Witty	Humorless	2.88	3.00	3.21
Rational	Irrational	2.64	3.00	3.55
Sexy	Sexless	3.05	2.63	2.60
Moral	Immoral	2.31	2.84	4.14
Mature	Immature	2.25	2.82	4.15
Intelligent	Unintelligent	2.12	2.36	2.77
Normal	Emotionally Disturbed	2.48	2.49	3.23
Good	Bad	2.06	2.47	3.27
Just	Unjust	1.97	2.55	3.72
Attractive	Unattractive	2.77	2.49	2.65
Helpless	Independent	5.45	4.70	5.20
Weak	Strong	5.36	4.93	5.02

TABLE 31   Average Depression Scores (CES-D) for Battered Women by Age, Marital and Employment Status

Variable	N	Mean	S.D.	Comparison Sample Mean	% at or above cut off score of 16
MARITAL STATUS					
Married and Living Together	98	16.86	11.62		
Living Together	22	17.05	12.20		
Married	76	16.80	11.53	9.53	
Not Married	275	18.67	12.70		
Never Married	23	17.13	11.10	12.79[a]	
Separated/Divorced	243	18.58	12.60	13.71	
Widowed	9	18.19	12.44	10.26	
Total	373	18.19	12.44	10.10	
EMPLOYMENT STATUS					24.7 WC[c]
Unemployed*	176	21.86	13.14	11.44[b]	33.6 KC
Employed*	186	14.78	10.86	9.61	
AGE					
18–24**	66	21.89	12.48	13.48[b]	
25–34	197	18.14	12.55		
35–44**	72	15.65	10.52		
45–49	41	16.95	14.44		
25 & Up				9.62	
TOTAL CES-D					
	376	18.19	12.50	KC 9.62	21.6[c]
				WC 9.13	18.1

* $p < .000$
** $p < .026$
[a] Reported in Radloff (in press) Table 5.2
[b] Reported in Radloff (in press) Table 5.3
[c] Reported in Radloff (1975) Table II

TABLE 32   Correlation Matrix: Battered Women's Mental Health Measures at Time of Interview

Current State Measure	ANOMIA	INT	PO	C	CES-D	AWS	HLTH	SELFEST
Anomia								
Levinson Internal	.28							
Levinson Powerful	.30	.27						
Levinson Chance	.39	.23	.60					
Radloff CES-D	.40	.18	.35	.36				
AWS	.26	.18	.28	.35	.25			
Health Scale	.23	.13	.22	.22	.46	.17		
Self-Esteem	.27	.30	.25	.21	.36	.19	.25	

TABLE 33   Childhood Learned Helplessness Scale Items for Battered Women

Variable Name	Description of Question or Item	Correlation
CRITPER Number of criticalperiods experienced as a child.	When you were growing up, were there any years that were particularly important? Do any times stand out in your mind as being especially critical? 1 = yes 2 = no	
MAWSTOT	25 item AWS for Mother	Alpha .90914
FAWSTOT	25 item AWS for Father	Alpha .92754
TTYBATH	Would you say there was battering in the home you grew up in? Add "1" for each of the following variables:	

	FBATM	Father battered mother
	MBATF	Mother battered father
	MBATB	Mother battered brother
	MBATS	Mother battered sister
	MBATW	Mother battered subject
	FBATB	Father battered brother
	FBATS	Father battered sister
	FBATW	Father battered subject
	BATOTHS	Any other person battered in home

Variable Name	Description of Question or Item	Correlation
MOTHTOT	Woman's report of her relationship with her mother as a child.	Alpha .83179
FATHTOT	Woman's report of her relationship with her father as a child.	Alpha .83518

Questions
1. I wanted to be just like my mother/father.
2. My mother/father liked my appearance.
6. My mother/father was very responsive toward me as a person.
9. My mother/father did lots of little things for me like combing my hair, grooming, and so on.
10. My mother/father initiated conversation with me.
11. My mother/father shared family problems with me.

TABLE 33 *Continued*

Variable Name	Description of Question or Item	Correlation
	12. I felt I could share intimate things with my mother/father.	
	13. My mother/father displayed physical affection with me.	
	14. My mother/father protected me more than I wanted.	
	19. I felt I had a lot of control over what happened to me at home.	
	20. My mother/father talked to me about my career.	
	21. My mother/father wanted me to get married and have grandchildren for her/him.	
	22. I felt my mother/father could help me figure a way out of trouble.	
	23. My mother/father expected me to be very feminine.	
	25. When I was a teenager, my mother/father warned me about getting too romantically or sexually involved.	
	26. My mother/father protected me from boys or men who were interested in me romantically or sexually.	
HLTSCAL	Women's health in childhood (see Table 5 for items).	Alpha .7250
MSEXAS	Women's experiences with attempted or forced sexual assaults as a child (see Table 9 for items).	

TABLE 34   Relationship Learned Helplessness Items in Battered Women

Variable Name	Questions or Items
RAPEB	"Has he ever forced you to have intercourse (sex)?"
FREQ	"About how often do these batterings occur?"
KILLYOU	"Do you think he would or could kill you?"
CONTROLB	"Generally, to what extent do you think you can control him or his behavior?"
MBACTS	Abusive acts done to the woman by the batterer during battering incidents.
	Exactly what did he do to you? Tell me if he threatened to do any of the following:
	Push, shove Slap, hit, spank Claw, scratch Wrestle, twist arm Throw object Punch Kick Hit with object Strangle attempt Throw bodily Sexual abuse Burn Tried to drown Used knife Used gun Used motor vehicle
	1 = no 2 = threatened 3 = yes, briefly 4 = yes, repeatedly
	Injuries suffered by woman during the battering.
NOHURT	No real hurt Tear clothing Break eyeglasses
LESSINJ	No visible injury but painful Lost hair Splinter or fragments

TABLE 34 *Continued*

Variable Name	Questions or Items
MININJ	Bruises Cut or burn Black eye
MAJINJ	Severe bruises Severe cuts or burns Lost teeth
SEVINJ	Break eardrum Joint or spinal Injury Break jaw or nose Other broken bones Concussion Internal injury
PERMINJ	Permanent head injury Permanent joint or spinal injury Permanent internal injury Permanent eye injury Other permanent injury
MREACT	Emotional reactions to battering incident: Fear Depression Anxiety Anger Disgust Hostility
PASACTB	Whether the woman was more passive or active *before* the battering incident.
PASACTA	Whether the woman was more passive or active *after* the battering incident. 1. Very passive, low profile, resigned 2. More passive than active 3. Mixed 4. More active than passive 5. Very active
MPLACAT	What the woman did in daily life to avoid the batterer getting angry.

TABLE 35 Current State Scale Items

Variable Name	Description of Question or Item	Correlation
RADDEP	Radloff CES-D Depression Scale	Alpha .92580
AWSGTOT	Attitude Toward Women Scale	Alpha .93711
HLTSCALN	Health Scale for woman's current health. Same items as in childhood health scale on Table 5.	Alpha .7176
SELFEST	Semantic differential on woman's self-image at the time of interview.	Alpha .87503
ANOMIA	"Please look at these statements. Some people agree with each statement, others disagree. For each one tell me whether you more or less agree or disagree with it."	
	a. I sometimes can't help wondering whether anything is worthwhile. b. Nowadays, a person has to live pretty much for today and let tomorrow take care of itself. c. In spite of what some people say, the lot of the average person is getting worse, not better. d. It's hardly fair to bring a child in the world with the way things look for the future.	
SEVINT	Women's score on the internal dimension of the Levinson Internal-External Scale.	
LEVPOW	Women's score on the powerful others dimension of the Levinson Internal-External Scale.	
LEVCHA	Women's score on the chance dimension of the Levinson Internal-External Scale.	

TABLE 36   Mean of Learned Helplessness Scores for Battered Women In and Out of Relationship*

Status of Battering Relationship	CHILD Score	REL Score	–CSTATE Score
In Relationship	.2708	–.2904	–.7136
Out Less Than One Year	–.1451	.2087	.3476
Out More Than One Year	–.0454	.0145	.1922

* A higher score indicates a greater degree of Learned Helplessness. Scores were normalized z-scores.

Sample Selection Procedures

SELECTION CRITERIA

The sample for this study consisted of approximately 400 self-identified battered women who lived in the six-state region composing the federally defined Health and Human Services Region VIII. A woman was considered eligible to participate if she reported that she was battered at least two times by a man with whom she had an intimate or marital relationship. The criterion for physical abuse was any form of a coercive physical act, with or without resultant injury. The criteria for psychological abuse included excessive possessiveness or jealousy; extreme verbal harassment like constant name calling; restraint of freedom of movement by restricting activities, withholding money, or constant surveillance; and threats of future abuse. The criteria for psychological abuse proved too difficult to measure without accompanying physical abuse. Thus, after the first several months, women who did not report physical abuse too were no longer interviewed. It would take a separate study to quantify the subjective impressions of the seriousness of each psychologically abusive act and consequent injury. Such precision in measurement is needed because the women's ratings showed that the psychological abuse created longer-lasting pain than did many of the physically induced injuries. Several definitions were operationalized for this project.

Definitions

"A battered woman is a woman, 18 years of age or over, who is or has been in an intimate relationship with a man who repeatedly subjects or subjected her to forceful physical and/or psychological abuse." (We used 18 years or older because of the need to avoid possible overlap with child abuse in younger women, given our state's child abuse statutes. Obviously, a younger woman in an intimate sexual relationship is also a battered woman if it fits the pattern.)

"Intimate" means a relationship having a romantic, affectionate, or sexual component. (The sexual intimacy turned out to be more important than actually living together.)

"Repeatedly" means more than one assault. Our minimum number was two acute battering incidents although most reported more than the four we used for a complete battering history.

"Abuse" within the context of such relationships differs from the typical marital or partner conflict by evidence of any of these behaviors:

- excessive possessiveness and/or jealousy
- extreme verbal harassment and expressing comments of a derogatory nature with negative value judgments
- restriction of her activity through physical or psychological means
- nonverbal and verbal threats of future punishment and/or deprivation
- sexual assault whether or not married
- actual physical attack with or without injury

Control Group

No control group was utilized for comparisons because of the time and expense involved in carefully matching so large a sample. The purpose of this study was to learn more about intrafamily violence from battered women themselves. It was seen as an opportunity to empirically identify relevant variables in preparation for subsequent research that could then utilize control of meaningful variables. Some comparisons were possible through the use of published norms on psychological scales. In addition, each woman served as her own control for identical questions asked about both battering and nonbattering relationships. Approximately one-half the sample reported on both kinds of relationships.

SAMPLING TECHNIQUES

The sample size of 400 was chosen to allow for some stratification to partially deal with the difficulty of a nonrandomized, self-selected sample and to have enough subjects to perform intragroup statistical comparisons.

Geographic distribution was constructed to allow for natural selection, but with ability to correct for underrepresentation of groups, if it occurred. While the largest number of subjects came from the metropolitan Denver area, other areas of Colorado, Montana, South Dakota, North Dakota, Wyoming, and Utah accounted for almost one-third of the final sample. This procedure resulted in adequate regional representation of urban, suburban, rural, and mountain women.

Direct contact with minority groups was made so as to encourage their participation rather than expect these groups to volunteer. It is important to pay attention to longstanding biases that some subgroups have developed against research because of a history of previous exploitation. Such unfortunate biases can be overcome when it is demonstrated that the current project is different. Women were interviewed on several Indian reservations, in high-energy impact areas, in battered women shelters, and in prisons. A special group of women who had killed their batterers was also obtained. About three-quarters of the way through the data collection phase of the study, the naturally self-selected sample was analyzed and a concerted effort was made to attract specific underrepresented groups. In particular, we needed more rural women, more women still in the relationship at the time of the interview, and more older women (defined as over 60 years old).

PUBLICITY AND REFERRALS

The sample was generated by a variety of techniques, using both referral sources and direct advertising. Referrals came from human service agencies, battered women shelters and task forces, mental health centers, private practitioners, hospital emergency rooms, legal service agencies, private attorneys, judges, police, prosecutors, probation and welfare caseworkers, church leaders, community groups, corporate medical services, and other community groups. Subjects could also refer themselves by responding to public service announcements on television, radio, newspapers, women's magazines, and posted signs. The entire staff took part in publicizing the project through speaking engagements, workshops, radio and television spots, and distribution of posters and fliers. Most of the staff had contacts within the battered women's movement, as well as human service delivery systems, thus facilitating ongoing advertisement.

These efforts were successful in generating the required sample pool. Approximately 40 calls per week were received from potential volunteers. About 20 of these needed referrals to direct services and did not meet the criteria to participate in the research. An example would be an 80-year-old woman who needed resources to assist her in becoming free from her son who was battering her. Of the remaining 20 calls per week, about 17 eventually completed the interview process.

SCHEDULING PROCEDURES

Scheduling battered women for interviews proved to be a very difficult and time-consuming task. It necessitated our developing more elaborate procedures than originally anticipated, and we spent a great deal of time searching for successful solutions. Despite the fact that we received a steady number of telephone calls from the potential subjects, the problem of "no-shows" and cancellations was as high as 60% during the first months of the project. It was decided to assign responsibility for the intake, screening, and scheduling process to one person, the administrator. The scheduling process (described in more detail in the Appendix, below) was implemented, and the "no-show" rate dropped to 10% and cancellation rate to 33%. If we allowed a woman to cancel and reschedule when she felt it was necessary, then the cancellation rate dropped and we lost very few subjects.

We conclude the following rationale for why the population of battered women needs special scheduling procedures:

- Battered women's lives are chaotic. They live in constant crisis. Often they are forgetful. They cannot meet the expectation that they will remember to keep an appointment scheduled some six weeks in advance. Many are ambivalent about exposing their violent lives to interviewers and to themselves. Appointments with professionals should be expected to have low priority for battered women.
- Battered women tend to be very suggestible and want others to think well of them. They may agree to an appointment, even if they know it will be difficult or impossible to keep, because they want to please the intake person.
- Battered women may be in transition periods of their lives. Thus, it should be expected they are transient, move frequently, change jobs, leave town without notice, and display other characteristics of a transitory population.
- Battered women change telephone numbers frequently; they get unlisted numbers, have their phones disconnected, and become difficult to locate as they try to hide from or avoid their batterers. Sometimes they purposely isolate themselves as a way of controlling the escalation of violence in their relationship.

- Battered women who have just been in a shelter and are setting up an apartment often cannot afford a telephone, are looking for a job, don't know when they will have a free day, or have similar reasons for not being willing to set up any interview far in advance.
- Battered women are easily frightened, sometimes exhibiting paranoid-like survival behaviors. Their fear reactions make them hard to reach. Their well-practiced ability to use denial or forgetting mitigates against easy scheduling.
- Constant involvement in legal hassles makes unscheduled court appearances necessary, which sometimes conflict with professionals' appointments.

Thus, battered women, for many reasons, wanted and needed to change the date of appointment frequently. Part of these problems came from our need to make appointments in advance. Since we used part time interviewers, we needed to know how many to have available on any particular day. Each interview took one interviewer the entire day, so if a woman cancelled or didn't show up, the interviewer was without work for the day.

It simply was not possible to set up an appointment for an interview and assume that the woman would be there. Rather, constant contact, reminders, arrangement to call 24 hours before the appointment date, repetitive instructions, and an atmosphere of caring concern communicated via telephone was essential to insure that subjects would keep appointments.

These procedures are also necessary to assist a battered woman in learning to utilize psychotherapy on a weekly schedule. It has been found that it takes about 8 weeks of regular appointments before these problems are overcome. I believe that a drop-in or crisis center would probably be most effective in meeting the battered women's needs.

INCENTIVES

The battered women who participated in the research project all felt that they wanted to help other women by telling their stories. Many felt it would be a good emotional experience for them to sort out their feelings about having been battered. Others used it as a way to help them terminate their relationship with the batterer. Whatever the subject's personal reasons, most women were appreciative of the $24 in cash we gave them at the end of the interview. The cash made it easy for her not to have to explain extra money. One woman in Colorado Springs actually used that money to buy a bus ticket so she could escape another beating. By paying the subjects, it made everyone feel respectful of each other's time and usefulness.

PRISON SAMPLE

The method used to obtain volunteers from the prison was so successful, it can be used as a model for other hard-to-reach sample groups. Permission to interview at the Colorado State Prison was granted by the head of the State Department of Institutions. However, when contact was made with the administrators at the prison—after numerous telephone calls—they insisted that there were no battered women inmates and, thus, we needn't bother to come there. The prison psychologist, who was male, confirmed the administration's findings; none of the approximately 80 inmates had been a battered woman! Armed with statistics that made it impossible to believe this, one of the WICHE (Western Interstate Consortium for Higher Education) interns undertook this as her special project. After many more hours of phone calls, she managed to allay the administrator's fears sufficiently to get permission to visit the prison and talk with the inmates directly. It meant agreeing to stay for only 3 days, working within prison routines, and not offering the $24 expense money directly to the women. We agreed but offered to have the money placed in a petty cash fund that they all could use.

Five interviewers drove the 125 miles to Canon City confident they would find enough volunteers to interview. When they arrived, they were introduced to all the inmates at a meeting in the cafeteria. There, they explained the project, the criteria for acceptance as a participant, and answered their questions. The interviewers' training in understanding group process was of great assistance in identifying the informal leaders with whom they spent additional time, giving assurance that the research would not harm nor exploit them. The interviewers then waited for inmates to volunteer. By midafternoon, over two-thirds of the inmates were found to have met the criteria; they had been battered women. Interestingly, most claimed that they had committed the crimes for which were now imprisoned at the demand of an angry batterer. Many said they preferred prison to living in fear of another beating.

As was expected, the prison administrators expressed surprise at the number of volunteers. They insisted we keep to our original commitment of 3 days of interviewing and, so, we were only able to choose 15 inmates for the sample. However, had we not taken the time to gain entrance, none would have been studied. (Since that time, I was appointed by the Colorado Legislature to chair a committee that went into the women's prisons to assess those inmates who had previously experienced abuse and assist in the recommendations for programs to assist them when they left the prison. Interestingly, there were over 650 women in the Colorado prison system in 1996 as compared to under 100 women inmates 20 years earlier. Over two-thirds of them said that they had been abused as children or adults and wanted programs to help them learn how to deal with the psychological effects. Unfortunately, the report stayed in the legislature and no interventions have been developed or funded as of this time.)

Communication with women in other state prisons confirms that our experience was not unusual. Typically, male psychologists are employed to work in prisons. They do not understand the differences between male and female prisoners and tend to discount the women's statements. Jones (1980) describes the impact of such sexist attitudes in her book, *Women Who Kill.* At this time women inmates in two state prisons, Wyoming and Missouri, have organized their own battered women support groups to help them deal with abuse when they are released. More unbiased information about women and crime is needed.

It is also interesting that during the intervening 20 years, there has been a movement towards granting clemency for battered women who are imprisoned and serving long sentences for killing their abusive partners, probably in self-defense. The introduction of self-defense for battered women became possible in the middle 1980s after several state Supreme Courts and Federal court ruled such testimony from an expert as admissible (see Walker, 1989a for a full discussion of the history and cases as well as Browne, 1987, and Ewing, 1987). The Domestic Violence Institute has been involved in clemency efforts in several other countries including one case in Greece. After review, governors of several states released women who they believed had not received a fair trial. It has become very clear that large numbers of women in prisons all over the world have been battered in their childhood and adult families and many of them committed the crimes for which they are serving time at the behest of the batterer to whom they didn't believe they could say, "no."

FINAL SAMPLE CHARACTERISTICS

A total of 435 interviews were conducted within 18 months, during the research project. Twenty (20) of these were pilot interviews conducted during the initial testing and revision of instruments period. Four (4) interviews were aborted when it became apparent that the women were not sufficiently lucid to respond to the interview questions. One interviewer was unable to learn how to accurately complete eight interviews, and these had to be deleted for insufficient data. The final number that were analyzed was 403.

Demographic distribution of the sample was highly representative of the region from which the sample population was drawn. Table 1 indicates the specific frequencies. Geographic distribution had almost 30% of the sample living outside of the metropolitan Denver area. Approximately 25% of the sample were still in the battering relationship at the time of the interview. This was the most difficult group to get to keep an appointment, as they were always rescheduling. In order to recruit subjects in this group, we had to continue interviewing several months beyond the original time allotted.

The racial and ethnic characteristics of our sample closely approximated the percentages for each group in the total regional population. We made special efforts to become known in the various minority communities, which assured us of reaching a proportionate sample. While we cannot make specific predictions about the incidence levels of wife abuse in our region, from the final sample it is obvious that such battering is found across all demographic lines.

SPECIFIC INTAKE PROCEDURES

INTAKE SHEETS AND NUMBER ASSIGNMENTS

In order to record and keep track of each potential volunteer's information and to maintain our strict confidentiality procedures from the time of her first contact with us all the way through scheduling, interviewing, and data analysis, we developed and used a system of five color-coded notebooks.

A. Yellow INTAKE Notebook

1. Blank intake forms. These forms were filled out for each woman who called. They were prenumbered so there is a record of every potential volunteer who called. This form was filled out as an intake/screening was done. At that time, the subject received an intake number, or master code number. This number identified the subject all the way through the research process, eliminating the need to use names or other identifying data. It met our confidentiality and human subjects' protection assurances. After the intake form was completed, if the woman was scheduled, the form went into the green INTERVIEWS

PENDING notebook (See section B). If she wasn't scheduled, it went into one of the following tabbed sections.

2. "Hold" section. This section held intake sheets for subjects whom we had not yet scheduled, but might do so at a later date. For instance, the woman:

   a. Didn't want to set a firm date, for a variety of reasons (waiting for a vacation day or until her husband is out of town, or until she has gotten over the shock of her husband killing himself, etc.).
   b. Had not shown up for a scheduled appointment, but we had reason to believe she did want an appointment and would call us again.
   c. Had set up and cancelled two or three appointments and may not really have wanted an appointment.
   d. We had not been able to reach her to confirm for some reason:

      (1) Only had her work number and she didn't work there anymore
      (2) Had her phone number unlisted
      (3) Never able to reach by phone
      (4) We had other incorrect information, but felt she might call again.

3. "Out of town" section. This was for volunteers who couldn't be given an appointment immediately because of their location (Salt Lake City, Phoenix, etc.). Many women traveled through Denver and made plans to visit when they arrived.

4. "Questionable" section.

   a. Information given on intake suggested that she did not fit our definition of a battered woman.
   b. The intake worker sensed the woman was emotionally disturbed:

      (1) "ESP battering her 24 hours a day."
      (2) "Conspiracy of all minority groups to batter her and take over the world."
      (3) Too upset or angry to be able to answer structured questionnaire and/or make it through the interview.

   c. Had not shown up for two or three scheduled appointments and seemed too risky to schedule again.

5. "Lost" section. Woman moved out of state and left no forwarding address. Efforts to reach woman were unsuccessful. Woman chose not

to participate. Data from each category on the intake form was coded and prepared for computer analysis so the "incompleted sample" could be compared with those who completed the entire interview.

B. Green PENDING INTERVIEWS Notebook

1. When the woman was assigned a firm interview date, her intake sheet was placed in this notebook by chronological appointment date.

C. Red INTAKES FROM COMPLETED INTERVIEW Notebook

1. When the woman came in for the interview, she was assigned a computer number, in addition to her intake, or master code number. The interviewer was given the woman's first name, her master code number, and her computer number. The white intake sheet was then separated from the rest of the data form. This form was then filed according to the master code number in the red notebook for future analysis. The white section, then, was the only place where the woman's name appeared. It was also filed according to the master code number and stored separately. Thus, from the time the woman appeared for her appointment, her name never again appeared with any of her information.

D. Blue COMPLETED INTERVIEWS BY COMPUTER NUMBER and DATE Notebook

1. Entries in this notebook were filed by computer number and date, as well as intake number. Computer numbers were assigned, without a skip in numbers, and reflected the exact sequence of administration of each interview. Each entry had the assigned computer number, the master code number, the date of the interview, and the interviewer's name.

E. Tangerine COMPLETED INTERVIEWS ACCORDING TO THE INTERVIEWER Notebook

1. The same information contained in the blue notebook (see section D) appeared here. In addition, there were columns for the interviewer to check as she completed her coding for each questionnaire. This notebook also had other columns headed "Coded," "Cleaned," "Keypunched," and "Comments." This facilitated communication between the interviewers and the research staff as to the status of the completed interviews.

INITIAL CONTACT INTAKE

An average intake took approximately 30 minutes. It was necessary to generate at least double the number of volunteers than would actually be studied. Through the following carefully worked-out process, we were able to avoid last-minute cancellations and "no-shows," which plagued us in the first few months of data collection.

SCREENING PROCESS

When the potential volunteer telephoned, a staff member trained in intake/screening procedures responded, usually the administrative assistant. The woman was frequently hesitant and uncomfortable on the telephone. For this reason, it was necessary to convey to her a feeling of acceptance and to establish rapport with her. A higher follow-through rate resulted, as well as no difficulties with threats of violence to our project or staff. Interestingly, another research project in Denver had two serious violence threats and was discontinued during this time. One difference is that they did not do as careful a job in intake procedures. Our subject was not asked to identify herself immediately. Rather, we started off by telling her about the project, asked her how she heard about us and so on, until she was more comfortable. We then asked her questions, based upon our definition of battering, to ascertain if her experiences met the following criteria:

- Did her experience fall into the project's definition of battering?
- Was she emotionally stable enough to handle an entire day of very structured interviewing?
- What was her motivation to participate in the study? Was it strictly voluntary? Might she be saying she's battered just to make some money?
- Did she have any special needs which should be taken into consideration (i.e., language problems, need for a particular style of interviewing)?

These questions were printed on each intake form. If she fit the criteria, she was then asked if she would like to participate. Only after she agreed, did we ask her for her name, address, and home telephone number. We also asked if she was still living with the batterer and determined if she was at risk. If so, we developed safety precautions with her, for example, saying "Sears calling" or some other agreed-upon code when we called.

The woman was then told about the interview itself—how long a time she would be expected to spend, financial remuneration, and lunch procedures. The interviewer's qualifications were explained, as was the availability of referral to other services. It was important to differentiate between research and clinical services from the outset. We provided referral sources as one way to meet our ethical responsibility to take care that the research intervention did not place the subject in greater physical danger or emotional distress, and the clinical director was available for crisis counseling and referral, if necessary, but we did not provide other clinical services. Total confidentiality was emphasized. She was then given an appointment and instructions on how to find the Center.

ACCOMMODATIONS

ACCOMMODATIONS

If the woman was an appropriate candidate, we scheduled her for an appointment, often 6 weeks in advance.

The interviewers all worked on a part-time basis, and most conducted one interview per week. For the most part, they were able to select the days on which they wanted to interview. This posed some problems, as some days were more popular than others and we were limited in the number of adequate interviewing rooms and taping equipment. But, with flexibility, it did work out. A very large monthly calendar was posted on the wall by the administrator's desk. The interviewers were asked to place their names, at least 2 months in advance, on the dates on which they preferred to interview.

The person who did the intake and scheduling checked this calendar for potential dates and interviewers and attempted to find a convenient day for the subject, while also matching interviewer to subject (i.e., Spanish-speaking women with Spanish-speaking interviewer).

Once an agreeable date and interviewer was determined, the subject's intake, or master code number, was placed on the calendar next to the interviewer's name on the agreed-upon date. This information was also put on the subject's intake sheet and was placed according to date in the green PENDING INTERVIEWS notebook. The subject was then considered officially scheduled.

In order to eliminate "no-shows" and last-minute cancellations, several other procedures were developed.

When a woman was scheduled she was told we must confirm her interview the day before it is scheduled, or we would have to give it to someone else; that we would call her, but if she should be unreachable she must call us. This confirmation phone call proved to be a critical element in overcoming some of the natural barriers to getting this population to present themselves. We also asked if she would be interested in filling a cancellation should we have one earlier than her scheduled date. Very often that was the case. She specified which dates she would be available, and a note indicating the dates was clipped on the intake form. In this way, when a woman canceled an appointment or could not be confirmed the day before, we had about 15 women who could be called upon to fill in.

This procedure proved to be very time-consuming, but it was also very effective. Although we still had some early morning cancellations and "no-shows," they were reduced to less than 10% per month.

The local battered women shelters, with whom we had close working relationships, were also fairly good sources of last minute fill-ins. Shelter residents' lives are often in chaotic turmoil; they are unable to make a commitment to an interview in the future; and they sorely need immediate funds. If they had no plans for the day, shelter residents were often grateful for the chance to be interviewed without advance notice. The problems we encountered in using shelter residents to fill a cancellation were often those of time and transportation. Our interviews lasted 6 or more hours, so if we didn't begin an interview by 10:30 A.M., it was usually not possible to finish in 1 day. The shelter women usually didn't have available transportation. Cabs took too long and often did not respond to a call from a particular neighborhood, especially on bad weather days, when last minute changes were most likely. Shelter women were often so upset and frightened that they shied away from public transportation. Sometimes, interviewers did go and pick up women, rather than have to make up the interview at another time. In spite of these problems, the shelters were good sources of regularly scheduled and last-minute volunteers.

RESCHEDULING

The issues discussed earlier required us to reschedule women many times. This was a time-consuming effort, but we felt our willingness to do this helped ensure a full interviewing schedule.

Staff Selection and Training

STAFF SELECTION

The data collection for this project was done by a staff of carefully chosen interviewers, who were trained in special interviewing techniques for the population, and supervised during the entire time. Interviewers were supported by administrative and data analysis staff. They were the key people, however, because of the length of the interview and need for them to code the subjective information into usable categories.

The original project design called for four (4) part-time interviewers. Within several months, a fifth interviewer was hired using funds available from a "phasing-in" period. Within the first year, over 20 more women volunteered to be trained as interviewers, usually for academic course credit. Several simply wanted the opportunity to learn new skills by working on a feminist research project about battered women. During the second year, six additional interviewers, who lived out of state, were hired on a part-time basis. Their training expenses, including two trips to the Battered Women Research Center in Denver, were paid, as were other data collection expenses. Interviewers varied in age; ethnic, racial, and educational backgrounds; sexual preferences; and socioeconomic levels. They were carefully screened and were required to have some previous knowledge about battered women, some political awareness of the women's movement, and clinical sensitivity to the individual women whom they interviewed. They were trained in advocacy skills and in using referral sources. This philosophy seemed to be a critical factor in obtaining accurate self-reports from the women.

SELECTION CRITERIA

The following criteria were established prior to hiring:

- An all-woman staff was required as part of the written grant philosophy. It was felt that a woman interviewer would be more likely to elicit accurate information from the battered women. The high risk nature of this population also required that the day-long interview be as comfortable as possible. Experience from clinicians and shelter workers indicated that battered women felt better about being with other women. Thus, being a woman was an important criteria.
- A racial, ethnic, and age balance in the interviewing staff was another criteria for hiring. This was also a consideration of the peer review committee who approved the grant. We had no difficulty in finding qualified people, particularly when recruitment was extended directly into minority group communities. This meant we had to identify the formal and informal leaders within the minority communities in the region and personally contact them to explain the project. My experience as an elected delegate from Colorado to the National Women's Conference and active participation in the women's movement for our region proved invaluable in identifying and establishing the appropriate liaisons.
- Interviewing experience. Although the questionnaire was predominantly structured, we wanted interviewers who had already developed the skills of establishing rapport, active listening, ability to set limits, sensitivity while probing for emotionally charged data, understanding of the need for strict confidentiality, and ability to sustain a long interview process.
- Clinical sensitivity was also an essential skill for our interviewers. Acquaintance, experience, and sensitivity to the nature of the battered woman were found to be useful. Women who had done some reading, taken academic courses, had previous experience in community crisis intervention (i.e., rape, battered women shelters, women's center) were given higher priority in selection. While we did not control for individual interviewer's experience in a battering relationship, none of those we hired self-disclosed current battering in their lives. Several discussed their previous experiences with violence. Their personal experiences seemed to have less impact than their ability to be clinically sensitive to the subject's experiences. Our experience indicates that formerly battered women are able to effectively separate their personal issues from their work with other battered women.

- Ability to handle high stress material and interactions was another critical factor because of the nature of data collected. Listening to so many violent acts produced emotional reactions in interviewers that caused stress reactions. While we looked for interviewers with a high stress tolerance, potential burnout was an issue with which we struggled throughout the 18 months of interviewing. Consultations with other professionals who deal with battered women indicate that this is a difficult area that mandates special attention to the staff's as well as the battered women's mental health.
- Interviewers were required to have the respect for data collection that resulted in careful attention to the details of the process. Although empathy and support were required as interview skills, it was important to differentiate the work from therapy or counseling. Evidence of meticulousness in paper work, past experience with data analysis, and training in research were high priority qualities.
- The ability to work part-time was another requirement for selection criteria. Grant funding originally placed this constraint, but as the project progressed, we found that interviewers could not complete more than two interviews per week without fatigue and burnout symptoms. Students and women with other commitments were ideal in this regard.
- The ability to work with an all-woman staff was another important criteria. We accurately predicted that this would be an unusual experience for most of our staff. Evidence of competition with women, antifeminist attitudes, joking about the plight of battered women, and the inability to work for "women bosses" were attitudes felt to be inconsistent with smooth staff relations.
- Flexibility and tolerance for all kinds of lifestyles was also considered a high priority. Experiences in the women's movement or feminist psychology were seen as facilitating the growth of these positive attributes. Thus, most of the interview staff were highly politicized and feminist-oriented in their own philosophy. This created some of its own unexpected problems, discussed later on.
- A final criteria for interviewers was to have a good sense of humor. The ability to nurture oneself and one's sister staffers with humor and camaraderie was essential for morale. In fact, our subjects remarked that the positive, friendly atmosphere, and the ability to laugh in the midst of painful stories was one of the most beneficial aspects of spending the day with us.

Thus, while technical competence was certainly an important part of the criteria for the job of interviewer, equally essential was the ability to create an atmosphere of warmth, trust, and respect for our subjects and other staff members. The clinical director, Dr. Majorie Leidig, was responsible for the selection, training, and supervision of all interviewers. In every case, except one, the interviewers hired met every criteria. The one exception did not have the technical competence in data collection and was unable to obtain sufficient information in her interviews for analysis. Having one person responsible for all hiring reduced the problems inherent in such complex staff needs.

TRAINING

INITIAL STAFF

From the time the initial positions were filled in late August, 1978, until we began pre-testing in October, interviewers were paid on a quarter-time basis. Each interviewer was expected to work 10 hours per week. Prior to the two-day training program, which took place in October, 1978, the interviewers became involved in the construction of the questionnaire.

The purpose of the formal two-day training was threefold: First, it assured that all staff were acquainted with existing findings regarding battered women; second, it enabled us to train and practice interviewing skills before working with a high-risk population; and third, it facilitated a working relationship with each other. A leader-facilitated group consciousness-raising session regarding personal stereotypes and experiences regarding battering was also included as was a film on battering. An entire morning was devoted to role-playing (and video taping) potentially troublesome types of interview situations. One afternoon was devoted to methodological aspects: how the particular standardized tests were selected, how to administer each test, and instructions from the methodologist on scoring and coding of the questionnaire.

Once several pretests were administered, the clinical and methodological data they obtained were utilized in further revisions of the questionnaire. Interviewer impressions of the task were essential in some revisions made during this period. They asked for more structure in some areas and less in others. They also quickly learned how much they could do without becoming too fatigued.

ADDITIONAL STAFF

Although training done on an all-staff group basis was considered preferable, as new interviewers joined the staff, it often needed to be done on an individual basis. In either case, a similar training procedure was completed prior to administration of their first interview.

TRAINING PROCESS OF INTERVIEWERS

The first step in the training process was to familiarize the interviewer with the current literature and information about battered women. We utilized films, books, and journal articles available at the time including:

- Viewing the film, *Behind Closed Doors,* produced by Gary Mitchell.
- Reading at least four of the following books:

    Davidson, T. (1978). *Conjugal Crime.* New York: Hawthorne Books, Inc.
    Martin, D. (1976). *Battered Wives.* San Francisco: Glide Publications.
    Pizzey, E. (1974). *Scream Quietly or the Neighbors Will Hear.* Middlesex, England: Penguin Books.
    Roy, M. (1978). *Battered Women.* New York: Van Nostrand & Co.
    Seligman, M. E. (1975). *Helplessness: On Depression, Development and Death.* San Francisco: Freeman.

- Reading at least three of the following paper presentations and journal articles:

    Leidig, M., Flick, D., Groth, G., and Walker, L. *Psychotherapy in a Changing World: Rethinking Theories and Practice Toward Women Victims of Violence.* Panel presented at American Psychological Association Division on Psychotherapy MidWinter Meeting. Mexico City, March 1979.
    Walker, L.E. (1977–1978). Learned Helplessness and Battered Women. *Victimology: An International Journal, 2,* 525–534.
    Walker, L.E. (1978). Treatment Alternatives for Battered Women. In R. Chapman and M. Gates (Eds.), *The Victimization of Women.* Beverly Hills, CA: Sage.

- Reading:

    Walker, L.E. (1979). *The Battered Woman.* New York: Harper & Row.

To facilitate their reading, a packet of materials was prepared and given to the new interviewers. Books were available in our library. Today, the mandatory reading list would be much longer. Other films now available would also be shown. Actually, as the regional Technical

Assistance Center for Battered Women was also located within our office complex at CWC, staff did have an unusual opportunity to become familiar with new developments in the field as soon as they became available for dissemination.

The second step in the process included familiarization with the interview procedure. This included:

- Reading the NIMH grant proposal narrative
- Learning the Interview Questionnaire
- Learning coding procedures from the Coding Handbook
- Receiving coding instructions and training from the data analysis staff
- Observation and discussion with other interviewers
- Listening to tapes of previously completed interviews

The third step in the process was supervised administration of an interview until technical competence was achieved. This included:

- Completing a mock interview with another staff person
- Critique by the clinical director
- Direct observation of an interview with a subject
- Critiques of taped portions of interviews with subjects

Finally, continued spot checks of tapes were done on a regular basis throughout the project as each subject's complete interview was tape recorded.

ONGOING SUPERVISION

Biweekly supervision meetings were held with the clinical director in an effort to establish quality control and to offset potential interviewer burnout from listening to so many horror stories. There were two different groups, meeting at different times, to accommodate everyone's schedules. The group sessions lasted 1½ hours. The group selected issues and problems to discuss, including areas to refine interviewing and coding techniques. The principal investigator and the methodologist often joined these groups. There was a need for a mutual support system given the violent nature of the data.

Some of the issues raised in these meetings were:

- More careful delineation of research definitions in order to collect more reliable data (e.g., how do we define tension-building? How do we operationally define learned helplessness?).

- Interactional problems with the subject (e.g., how to handle the battered woman subject who is manipulative, resistant, or "passive-aggressive").
- Interviewer's own personal reactions to the women subjects. At one point, there was concern about the emotional health of our interviewers after a rush of fairly sordid stories. The interviewers seemed to be "infecting" each other (and us) with their depression, sorrow, anger at the batterer, and feelings of hopelessness for these women. These sessions were used as emotional nurturing times when bonding, support, and sharing of their own experiences were encouraged. Staff had a listing of everyone's telephone number and a phone call support system was begun.
- Specific clinical problems that emerged with the research subjects were: suicidal threats by the subject; severe psychological problems noted in the subject; additional advocacy or therapy needed by the woman subject; and issues of when the interview should be "aborted."

OTHER STAFF

ADMINISTRATORS

The project proposed three administrators to head each of the major areas, in addition to the project director, who was also the principal investigator. The clinical director was the administrator with responsibilities of hiring and supervising the interviewers. Her position was for 16 hours time the first year and increased to 20 hours the second year. A new psychologist, who also had research skills, was hired in the middle of the second year. The methodologist was the administrator with responsibilities for hiring and supervising the data analysts. She also was part-time at 25% time. While she did not have direct supervisory responsibility of the interviewers, she did the training and some supervision of the data coding process. A schism developed between the clinical and methodology staff that eventually culminated in the resignation of the methodologist and the hiring of a new research staff halfway through the second year.

The third administrator, the administrative assistant, was the only full-time person employed on the project. She was responsible for all scheduling, as well as supervising the office staff and work-study students. This was a critical position in keeping the operation smooth.

METHODOLOGICAL ISSUES IN TRAINING AND SUPERVISION

Early in the project the question of how "blind" the interviewer should be was discussed. Ideally, of course, those who collect data should be unaware of the hypotheses being tested. However, anyone who had the qualifications for interviewing on this project necessarily had to have some psychological and sociological knowledge or background. We couldn't hire "blind" uninformed undergraduate students, for example, since the interview itself required sensitivity, ability to discriminate between useful and unimportant information, ability to probe without bias, and so on. Furthermore, those who qualified for the job had varying amounts of knowledge and information about battering in general and the project in particular. Our data collection period coincided with the height of a national campaign on public education on this topic. We realized that it was virtually impossible to control or limit the amount and kind of information one received or was exposed to in the everyday world. This was particularly the case with respect to the battered women project because I and others were making many public appearances to advertise our work. Furthermore, it seemed detrimental to the development and training of undergraduate and graduate student interviewers to ask them not to read about the subject for which they were collecting data. Therefore, we decided to tackle this problem in several ways. First, we attempted to "standardize" the amount of information about battering that each interviewer had, by making sure they all received the same, though minimal, information about the project. Although the specific hypotheses were not discussed, a general outline of some major explanations for battering relationships was given. Aside from this, there was no control over how much information an interviewer obtained.

Development of a fairly structured questionnaire was a second way to control for potential bias. Forced choice questions were predominantly asked. Although there were a number of open-ended questions, some of which required the judgment of the interviewers (such as subjective evidence of learned helplessness), these proved too problematical to analyze and were not included in the final statistical design.

A related problem had to do with "informed" subjects. In the same way that interviewers get exposed to theories and explanations about battering, so did the subjects. In fact, many of our subjects called us as a result of having heard a speech on radio or a TV interview about battering which touched on or even fully exposed some of the theories we were testing. To provide at least a measure, and perhaps a way of controlling this, we asked the subjects to indicate what they'd heard about various theories. The list included some bogus theories (e.g., disassociation theory, marginal man theory) to measure the tendency to say "yes" to having heard all such theories. As the project continued, interviewers became more familiar with other checks and balances embedded within the interview design. The battered women we interviewed rarely exaggerated or gave phony responses that we could detect.

BURNOUT

A research project such as this one had dangers of burnout similar to those facing other human service workers in high stress positions (Freudenberger, 1975, 1980). In addition to the precautions already described regarding staff selection techniques, biweekly supervision groups, permission to advocate on behalf of the woman, and to provide referral sources, academic credit, and networking, we also permitted several interviewers to use some of our data for their own academic purposes. In fact, several were encouraged in this venture, and senior staff members helped them conceptualize their research problem. The reputation and prestige of this project was also an incentive for avoiding feelings of staff helplessness. During the last year and one-half, staff met weekly to discuss implications from the data analysis and to brainstorm new problem areas. While prevention of burnout was a high priority issue for the project, we did lose several staff members despite our efforts.

The Interview

INSTRUMENTS

It was originally proposed to collect data using an open-ended, unstructured interview which would be coded after administration. This procedure has provided the greatest flexibility and was used in earlier data collection efforts with battered women both in this country and Great Britain. Once underway, the senior administrative staff decided to construct a more structured questionnaire for a variety of reasons.

Preliminary interviews indicated that battered women who volunteer to be interviewed need to tell their stories in their own time. While they are sharing these important life details, they are also evaluating how much and what kind of information they can trust to the interviewer. Those who seem willing to spend unlimited time listening to women share their anguish, horror, and embarrassment are rewarded by getting rich information about the details of living with levels of violence heretofore unreported in the literature. The amounts and kinds of violence are truly staggering to those previously unexposed to battering in relationships.

Learning about the infinite varieties of violence can be difficult for interviewers when the informant is also the victim. Similarly, discussing emotionally laden details of their own battering can be difficult for the women. It makes it easier if the interviewer follows a format that has structure for objectivity and, at the same time, flexibility to allow the woman to give personalized information. We found that if we asked the woman to describe a battering incident, she typically minimized the violence sequence. For example, she might say, "He hit me and I got a black eye." But, when we asked for details, like, "Did he hit you with an open or closed hand?," or "How many times did he hit or punch you?," a more accurate description could be obtained. We found the use of both open-ended and forced-choice questions especially critical to accurate descriptions of physical and sexual assaults.

QUESTIONNAIRE

A 200-page questionnaire was developed specifically for this study. Questions were constructed by operationally defining the major variables. Four different forms were tried until a satisfactory interview schedule was finalized. All forms except for the first pretest were used in the final analysis, and the subsequent revisions were to shorten the interview. Those 20 pretests were sufficiently different to require major coding revisions, and it was more cost-efficient to eliminate them and collect new data.

Embedded in the questionnaire were several special scales such as the 25-item Attitudes Toward Women Scale (Spence et al., 1973) which the subject answered three different times: once as she thought her mother would respond, once for her father and, finally, as she thought her batterer would answer. If she reported on a nonbattering relationship, she also completed it for him. A semantic differential scale was designed to measure the woman's self-esteem, her perception of other women, and her perception of men. In addition to her own Attitudes Toward Women Scale, several series of items were designed to measure the woman's sex role stereotyped socialization patterns, childhood and present health, and critical periods in her life. These questions were designed to facilitate scale construction, if possible, during analysis. A series of items were also designed to measure previous physical and sexual assault in the woman's childhood. Some of the sexual assault items were adapted from Frieze's (1977) research instrument, during one of the revisions, as the original open-ended questions resulted in interviewers avoiding further problems due to their own hesitation in probing into this sensitive area.

The final questionnaire measured demographic and psychosocial variables from the subject's retrospective report. It contained both forced-choice and open-ended response categories. It was divided into several sections that included items about general demographic facts, the woman's childhood, the batterer and his childhood, and details about their relationship together. The final section included factual data about her current status and was structured to end the interview with less emotional data. If the woman had had a nonbattering relationship, the same data was collected for him as for the batterer. A special feature was the section requesting information about four specific battering incidents: the first, second, one of the worst, and the last incident prior to her coming to the interview. These details were part of the analysis for testing the Walker Cycle Theory of Violence. Following completion of the questionnaire, several standardized scales were administered. We evaluated the woman's current state on depression, attributional style, and attitudes toward women. Details of the scales used can be found in a later section.

ADMINISTRATION PROCEDURES

As this was considered a high-risk population, care was exercised in developing administration procedures that would not create additional trauma for the woman. This included strict adherence to the human rights assurances. Informed consent and confidentiality were given the highest priority. Special care was taken to lock up all sensitive material at the end of each day, and names or identifying information never appeared after the intake procedure was completed. Although the interview was taped, all tapes were stored apart from the questionnaire forms. A Certificate of Confidentiality was obtained from the U.S. Department of Justice to prevent the subpoena of any of our data in a court of law. Considering the expected legal difficulties of this sample, this certificate was additional protection of typical confidentiality procedures.

Interviews were administered in a routine procedure. All but a few of the Denver-based interviews were done at the Battered Women Research Center offices on the Colorado Women's College campus. The interview rooms were furnished with comfortable furniture to create a home like atmosphere, as contrasted with a business oriented atmosphere. Interviews began at approximately 9:00 in the morning. Coffee, soft drinks, and other refreshments were available for short breaks. Lunch in the college cafeteria was also provided. Sometimes, it was more appropriate to eat in the office building. The interviewer was responsible for accompanying her subject to lunch. The woman could choose if she wished to eat alone, with the interviewer, or join the rest of the staff and possibly other subjects if more than one interview was scheduled that day. Most chose to eat together with the entire staff.

A standard procedure was used to administer the various items. The appropriate materials were placed in a folder in order of administration. Each interviewer had her own set of materials. After consent was obtained, the questionnaire items were sequentially administered. The printed questionnaire was divided into several color-coded sections to provide ease in administration. The first section asked for simple factual data. As rapport was established, the material requested became more emotionally demanding. It closed with a section requiring fewer emotional facts. This took about 4 to 5 hours to complete. Then, each subject was given the paper and pencil schedules to complete. If she had difficulty understanding or reading, the interviewer was present to provide assistance. Although interviewers were responsible for checking each schedule before the woman left, they did not always do this properly, which sometimes resulted in missing data. The schedules were also administered in a standard order. They took between 1 and 2 hours to complete. While interviewers were fatigued afterwards, as predicted, the subjects were still ready to talk more. For most, this was the first place they had ever told their whole story without minimizing or leaving out details. It created a powerful bond between the subject and her interviewer.

QUALITY OF SELF-REPORT DATA

The quality of retrospective, self-report data from a self-referred and voluntary sample has long been understood to have limited generalizability by social science researchers. Despite the painstaking care we utilized, our data suffer from the same general criticisms. The major area of difficulty lies within the potential bias of not knowing how representative the sample is of the total population of battered women and how reliable the information is that they have reported. We have analyzed these problems and found that while there seem to be characteristics unique to the population of battered women, our data are as reliable as can be expected from a survey type of research.

SAMPLE REPRESENTATION

It is difficult to know how representative these women were of all battered women because of the voluntary and self-referred nature of the sample. Our recruitment efforts seem to have been successful when we compare the sample obtained with demographic characteristics of the regional population. It supports the contention that battered women are evenly distributed within the population at large. Comparisons with other kinds of research studies such as the Straus et al. (1980) epidemiological survey designed to measure the amount of violence in the general population and Frieze's (1980) study with a matched control group, lend confidence that our sample is not very skewed. However, we did have some difficulties in recruiting women still in the battering relationship, which leads us to be cautious in interpreting the results to the general population of battered women.

Frieze (1980) suggests that there may be two distinct subcategories of battered women distinguished by the severity of violence experienced and amount of relationship control or benefits the women received separate from the violence. While our data do not support two such distinct categories, our findings of progressive changes in the relationship as the violence continues over time could produce that same effect. Thus, Frieze's category of moderate violence victims could be the same as our victims at a middle point in the violence continuum of their relationship.

In any case, it is reasonable to speculate that our sample may be underrepresented in early violence victims or those for whom the violence begins at a low level and escalates slowly. We may also have an underrepresentation of those for whom the violence is not as much of a problem because they still have it under control. We can also assume we may not have reached the severely battered woman who is represented by the stereotype of passivity and lack of strength to acknowledge her situation or seek help. Therefore, our information on battered women may be skewed in that those in our sample are the self-selected survivors. Even if that is true, however, their survival has been at a great psychological cost and we've learned much from our data about the skills they needed to achieve it. Further, comparisons with clinical reports give reason to believe that other groups are not that different from our sample.

We do have a small subsample of women who may fall into the above-described categories because they needed our help with their legal difficulties, rather than because they self-identified as battered women. While most of these women had killed their batterer, some were involved in child custody, divorce issues, or other litigation. We have not been able to analyze this subsample for statistical differences but, qualitatively, they appeared to be similar but at a more violent end of the spectrum of such behavior. We have since completed about 50 more cases, usually at the request of attorneys. In most of the homicide cases, we do a psychological autopsy that suggests that the violence escalates to lethal proportions in a manner predictable and consistent with our data.

Clinical observations of couples who seek counseling at an early or previolence stage of their relationship also support the contention that if we are missing certain segments of the battered women population, it would not produce a bias which fundamentally changes the direction of our analyses. The issue of sample representation is important, as earlier studies overgeneralized findings from one particular subgroup (e.g., studies using police report data), leading to a misunderstanding of the battered women. We believe our sample is as representative as possible given the nature of battered women and the risk factors involved in such research.

RELIABILITY OF DATA

The second major question examined is the reliability of the self-reported information. Such reliability needs to be examined because much of the information is dependent upon the women's ability to recall facts and incidents that occurred over a long period of time. Further problems can be expected because we asked about events that had heightened emotional content when they were experienced. For our purposes, we accepted that the quality of our data would be impacted upon by these factors, but assumed that it would have a systematic bias experienced by all the battered women. Analysis shows this assumption to be valid. Battered women, in general, show some idiosyncratic response patterns rather than major individual response styles.

One of the most important and, in some ways, frustrating characteristics of the battered women's response style is their need to keep everything smooth. This leads to behavioral response styles that reflect approval-seeking, suggestibility, compliance, and indirect manipulation. While their compliant behavior, for example, facilitated completion of the long interview, the interviewer had to be alert for indirect signs of fatigue and discomfort which could spoil the data. Their need for interviewer's approval may have caused them to respond in ways they thought would please the interviewer or make her think more highly of them, again biasing the data. Such inconsistencies were sometimes seen. The best controls we had for this were the forced-choice sections of the questionnaire and careful monitoring of any potential bias from the interviewers.

There was a group of subjects for whom completion of the interview process was a difficult experience for the interviewer. They characterized their response style as one of passive-aggression. They would indicate compliance with a task and then do something different, indirectly expressing their anger. Others simply would not stick to the question-and-answer format of the interview, preferring to give the information in their own words. The flexibility of including portions where open-ended responses were appropriate helped resolve that difficulty. The most critical factor seemed to be the woman's perception that she was being believed. In fact, a matter-of-fact attitude on the part of the interviewer that these sorts of things could happen, accompanied with compassion for the woman's pain, was most helpful in eliciting accurate data.

The anticipation that battered women would not have difficulty in recalling details about the acute battering incidents was supported. Most of the women retold the violence in such complete detail that they appeared to be reexperiencing the entire incident, but this time as a spectator watching themselves and their batterers interact. This process of dissociation is thought to be an integral step in the recovery process (Walker, 1981a). Replaying the violent event helps the woman regain the control she didn't have during its actual occurrence. It is not known whether certain details may be distorted to facilitate this process, but literature on recovery of catastrophe victims who undergo a similar clinical recovery process would support its remarkable accuracy (Browne, 1980).

One way to regain self-control is to associate the violent incident with a cause, such as provocation. Thus, a higher incidence of self-blame or exaggeration of the importance of certain details triggering the event is expected. We found that our women did both, in a characteristic pattern. They assumed the responsibility for keeping the batterer's environment stress-free so he would not have the opportunity to get angry enough to trigger a violent explosion. However, they placed responsibility for his loss of control and subsequent violent reaction on him. Thus, if he got angry because of something they did or didn't do, it made the battering incident more understandable. This dual-level cognitive attribution could be overlooked without careful attention to such seeming inconsistencies.

Perhaps the richness of the data collected in this project, which came from the women's self-reports, occurred because of the clinical sensitivity of the entire project staff. Clinical experience indicates that battered women can be like chameleons, only giving enough information as they feel is safe. Since their survival often depends upon clear recognition of environmental clues that signal safety, these skills are already well developed. Thus, the more comfortable they feel in the interview situation, the more accurate information they could be expected to reveal. We paid careful attention to all details in data collection to control the environment for the subjects' maximum comfort. This included questionnaire design, design of furniture in the interview room, and staff rapport. The consistency of the data reported by the entire sample indicates we were successful in our goal. It is recommended that future researchers pay equal attention to such details as one measure of trust in the reliability of retrospective self-report data.

Standardized Scales

CES-D (Radloff, 1977). This inventory measures depression and was originally developed for the epidemiological survey of nonclinical populations. Radloff has reported high correlation with other major depression inventories including the Beck Depression Inventory originally proposed. The CES-D questions are not as clinically oriented, which was considered more appropriate for our population. It also has been used in other studies of learned helplessness and sex role socialization patterns in women.

Locus of Control Scale (Levenson, 1972). This scale was chosen, rather than the originally proposed scale by Rotter, because it added a second dimension to the external orientation, that of attribution of causation to presence of "powerful others," in addition to the usual "chance" scale. We anticipated that battered women would realistically perceive that "powerful others" (i.e., their batterers) were in control, and using the two subscales would refine our measure. The learned helplessness literature suggests that attributional style may be one of the identifying characteristics of learned helplessness (Seligman, 1975; Abramson et al., 1978).

Attitude Toward Women Scale (AWS) (Spence-Helmrich, 1972). This was used to measure each woman's own traditionality on sex roles for women as well as her perceptions of her father's, mother's, and batterer's attitudes. The original 55-item version was used for the subject's responses. A shorter, 25-question version (Spence et al., 1973) was embedded within the questionnaire to measure mothers', fathers', batterers', and nonbatterers' attitudes towards women.

PROPOSED BUT ELIMINATED

Marital Satisfaction Inventory (Weiss & Cerreto, 1975) and the *Marital Adjustment Test* (Locke-Wallace, 1959) were administered but not analyzed. As it was originally conceived, most subjects would have still been in the battering relationship at the time of the interview. These inventories should have been answered using a consistent time period for reference. Since our final samples were all at various points of the relationship, they had no consistent reference point. Therefore, these results were invalid.

Denver Community Health Questionnaire (Ciarlo & Reihman, 1977). This was chosen to measure the mental health of subjects. The results are presented in 13 scales that were developed by utilizing factor analytic techniques. The standardized norms provide for good comparison as these are norms for women in the region from which our sample was drawn. The first scale, labeled Psychological Distress, is sensitive to measuring changes that occur as a result of short-term therapeutic intervention. It is highly correlated with more well-known mental health measures such as MMPI. We administered the original version of this scale but were unable to complete the conversion to the new norms at this time.

Pleasers and Displeasers Cost Benefit Exchange (Weiss, 1976) was originally proposed. After administration of 25 schedules, it proved to be so time-consuming and problematic that a staff decision was made to eliminate it.

ADDED TO PRESENT EVALUATION

Minnesota Multiphasic Personality Inventory (MMPI) (now the MMPI-2) has been added as a mental health measure in current evaluations. The raw data are scored using the Harris-Lingoes subscales and compared to a battered woman population by Dr. Lynne Rosewater (1982, 1985).

Traumatic Stress Inventory (TSI) measures the various areas that trauma is known to affect in psychological functioning. A relatively new test (1996), it has been standardized by psychologist, John Briere.

Data Analysis

DATA REDUCTION

The data reduction process proceeded through the following steps: (1) coding, (2) cleaning and closing, (3) keypunching, (4) error estimates, (5) review and reduction of variables, and (6) computer editing. Each step is described below.

CODING

Our data were collected via lengthy interviews with battered women. Interviewers wrote out and circled the subjects' responses throughout the 200-page questionnaire. The interviewers were also required to edge-code the questionnaire after the interview. An extensive coding manual was developed for this purpose. The data were keypunched directly from the edge-codes in the questionnaire booklets, after cleaning and closing.

CLEANING AND CLOSING

The research assistants were responsible for cleaning the questionnaires after the interviewers had coded them. Cleaning the questionnaires involved double-checking the coding and completing the various revisions in edge-coding that evolved over time. The closing of open-ended questions was completed by the research assistants and sometimes by work-study students. Categories for closing these questions were developed, based on the most frequently occurring responses in a selected sample of initial interviews. Very few of the categories were used in these analyses as their reliability and validity were not yet ascertained.

KEYPUNCHING

Questionnaires were keypunched by a professional company. All keypunched cards were verified by a second round of keypunching, for greater accuracy.

ERROR ESTIMATES

Two types of error estimates were obtained. The first was an estimate of errors in cleaning and closing. The second was an estimate of errors in keypunching. For each error estimate, 10 interviews were randomly selected. Research assistants reviewed the cleaning and closing, listing any errors. They also checked each keypunched card against the edge codes. The error estimate for cleaning and closing was less than 1%. Many of the cleaning errors occurred in coding the "other" and missing values categories. These errors have been eliminated by deleting problematic variables and by recoding missing values. The error estimate for keypunching was 2.9 errors per questionnaire, and with 3,500 bits of data per questionnaire, this is an error rate of less than 0.1%. Both error rates were deemed to be acceptable, allowing us to proceed with data analysis.

REVIEW AND REDUCTION OF VARIABLES

Data reduction was completed by the principal investigator, the research psychologist, and the statistical consultants from the University of Denver during the last 18 months of the project. The new psychologist assumed many of the duties of the methodologist, following Dr. Joyce Nielsen's resignation. Consultants under the direction of Dr. Phil Shaver from the University of Denver were hired at that time to provide overall direction and supervision of data reduction and analysis. Working together, we carefully scrutinized all of the variables with the aim of eliminating those that had conceptual or methodological difficulties. A second aim was to specify the level of measurement of each variable (nominal, ordinal, interval), which would constrain our choice of appropriate statistics. A manual which listed variable names, location by computer card and column, questionnaire page, and the actual question-and-response categories was prepared and used for this purpose. Decisions to eliminate variables were also based on feedback from the interviewers who identified certain questions that did not appear to accurately measure the intended variables. Although this procedure was tedious and time-consuming, it gave us great confidence in the quality of the final data set.

Computer Editing

Data were put on the Burrough's computer at the University of Denver in a six-file system. Initial analyses were performed there until August, 1980 when the project exhausted its funds. Under a graduate student grant, our research associate, Angela Browne, was permitted to put these data on a larger archive file to be used to complete the analyses at the University of Colorado, Denver Center. Since UCD's new computer had MAXI-SPSS capability, the data were restructured to a new file. A new set of frequencies was generated and each variable was checked for consistency with the original set.

Preliminary analyses were begun to identify significance levels and trends in the data. Comparisons were looked at between the woman's self-report, her report on the batterer, and her report on the non-batterer. Subanalyses were also done comparing the responses of subjects with only a battering relationship to those subjects who reported on both a battering and a nonbattering relationship. A variable to discriminate those women who were in the abusive relationship at the time of our interview from those women who were out of the relationship was also constructed. Variables were chosen as measures of the theories of Learned Helplessness and the Cycle Theory of Violence, and more sophisticated analyses were conducted to test these theories.

References

Abel, G. G., Becker, J. V., Murphy, W. D., & Flanagan, B. (1981). Identifying dangerous child molesters. In R. B. Stuart (Ed.), *Violent behavior: Social learning approaches to prediction, management, and treatment* (pp. 116–137). New York: Brunner/Mazel.

Abel, G. G., Becker, J. V., & Skinner, L. J. (1980). *Aggressive behavior and sex.* Psychiatric Clinics of North America.

Abramson, L. Y., Seligman, M. E. P., & Teasdale, J. D. (1978). Learned helplessness in humans: Critique and reformulations. *Journal of Abnormal Psychology, 87,* 49–74.

Allen, C. M., & Straus, M. A. (1980). Resources, power, and husband-wife violence. In M. A. Straus & G. T. Hotaling (Eds.), *The social causes of husband and wife violence.* University of Minnesota Press.

American Medical Association. (1992). Diagnostic and treatment guidelines on domestic violence. *Archives of Family Medicine, 1,* 39–47.

American Psychiatric Association. (1994). *Diagnostic and statistical manual of mental disorders* (4th ed.). Washington, DC: Author.

American Psychological Association. (1995). *Issues and dilemmas in family violence from the APA Presidential Task Force on Violence and the Family.* Washington, DC: Author.

American Psychological Association. (1996a). *Report from the Presidential Task Force on Violence and the Family.* Washington, DC: Author.

American Psychological Association (1996b). *Final Report of the Working Group on Investigation of Memories of Childhood Abuse.* Washington, DC: Author..

American Psychological Association. (1997). *Potential problems for psychologists working with the area of interpersonal violence. Report of the ad hoc committee on legal and ethical issues in the treatment of interpersonal violence.* Washington, DC: Author.

America's Watch. (1991). Criminal injustice: Violence against women in Brazil. *Human Right's Watch. The Women's Rights Law Project.* New York: Author.

Antonopoulou, C. (1997). *Human sexuality.* Athens, Greece: University of Athens Press.

Antonopoulou, C. (1999). Domestic violence in Greece. *American Psychologist, 51.*

Bandura, A. (1973). *Aggression: A social learning analysis.* Englewood, NJ: Prentice Hall.

Bard, M., & Zacker, J. (1974). Assaultiveness and alcohol use in family disputes. *Criminology, 12,* 283–292.

Barnett, O. W., & LaViolette, A. (1993). *It could happen to anyone: Why do battered women stay.* Newbury Park, CA: Sage.

Barnett, O. W., Miller-Perrin, C. L., & Perrin, R. D. (1997). *Family violence across the lifespan.* Thousand Oaks, CA: Sage.

Barnett, O. W., & Pagan, R. W. (1993). Alcohol use in male spouse abusers and their female partners. *Journal of Family Violence, 8,* 1–25.

Barry, K. (1979). *Female sexual slavery.* New York: New York University Press.

Barry, K. (1992). *The Penn State Report: International meeting of experts on sexual exploitation, violence and prostitution.* State College, PA: UNESCO and Coalition Against Trafficking in Women.

Batres, G., & Claramunt, C. (1992). *La violencia contra la mujer en la familia Costra ricense: Un problema de salud Publica.* San Jose, Costa Rica: ILANUD.

Bauserman, R. (1989/1997). Man-boy relationships in a cross-cultural perspective. In J. Geraci (Ed.), *Dare to speak: Historical and contemporary perspective on boy-love* (pp. 120–137). England: Gay Man's Press. Originally published in 1989 in *Paedika, 2*(1) a Netherlands Journal edited by J. Geraci.

Beck, A. T. (1976). *Cognitive therapy and emotional disorders.* New York: International Universities Press.

Becker, J. M. (1990). Treating adolescent sex offenders. *Professional Psychology: Research and Practice, 21,* 362–365.

Bende, P. D. (1980). Prosecuting women who use force in self-defense: Investigative considerations. *Peace Officer Law Report: California Department of Justice,* 8–14.

Beneke, T. (1997). *Proving manhood: Reflections on men and sexism.* Berkeley: University of California Press.

Berk, R. A. (1993). What the scientific evidence shows: On the average, we can do no better than arrest. In R. J. Gelles & D. R. Loeske (Eds.), *Current controversies on family violence* (pp. 323–336). Newbury Park, CA: Sage.

Berk, R. A., Berk, S. F., Loeske, D., & Rauma, D. (1983). Mutual combat and other family violence myths. In D. Finkelhor, R. Gelles, C. Hotaling, & M. Straus (Eds.), *The dark side of families* (pp. 197–212). Beverly Hills, CA: Sage.

Berk, R. A., Newton, P. J., & Berk, S. F. (1986). What a difference a day makes: An empirical study of the impact of shelters for battered women. *Journal of Marriage and the Family, 48,* 481–490.

Berkowitz, L. (1962). *Aggression: A social psychological analysis.* New York: McGraw Hill.

Besharov, D. J. (1993). Overreporting and underreporting are twin problems. In R. J. Gelles & D. R. Loeske (Eds.), *Current controversies on family violence* (pp. 257–272). Newbury Park, CA: Sage.

Biden, J. R., Jr. (1993). Violence against women: The Congressional response. *American Psychologist, 48,* 1058–1060.

Blau, P. M. (1964). *Exchange and power in social life.* New York: Wiley.

Bowker, L. (1993). A battered woman's problems are social, not psychological. In R. J. Gelles & D. R. Loeske (Eds.), *Current controversies on family violence* (pp. 154–165). Newbury Park, CA: Sage.

Boyd, V. D. (1978). *Domestic violence: Treatment alternatives for the male batterer.* Paper presented at the meeting of the American Psychological Association, Toronto, Canada.

Brassard, M. R., Hart, S. N., & Hardy, D. B. (1993). The psychological maltreatment rating scales. *Child Abuse and Neglect, 17,* 715–730.

Briere, J. (1992). *Child abuse trauma: Theory and treatment of the lasting effects.* Sage: Newbury Park, CA.

Briere, J. (1995). Science versus politics in the delayed memory debate: A commentary. *Counseling Psychologist, 23,* 280–289.

Briere, J., & Elliott, D. M. (1997). Psychological assessment of interpersonal victimization effects in adults and children. *Psychotherapy, 34,* 353–364.

Brooks, G. (1996). *The centerfold psychology.* San Francisco, CA: Jossey-Bass.

Brooks, G. (1998). *A new psychotherapy for traditional men.* San Francisco, CA: Jossey-Bass.

Broverman, I. K., Broverman, D., Clarkson, F., Rosencrantz, P., & Vogel, S. (1970). Sex role stereotypes and clinical judgments of mental health. *Journal of Consulting and Clinical Psychology, 34,* 1–7.

Brown, L. S. (1992). A feminist critique of personality disorders. In L. S. Brown & M. Ballou (Eds.). *Personality and Psychopathology: Feminist reappraisals.* New York: Guilford Press.

Brown, L. S. (1994). *Subversive dialogues: Theory in feminist therapy.* New York: Basic.

Brown, L. S., & Ballou, M. (Eds.). (1992). *Personality and psychopathology: Feminist reappraisals.* New York: Guilford.

Browne, A. (1980, April). *Comparisons of victims' reactions across traumas.* Paper presented at the meeting of the Rocky Mountain Psychological Association, Tucson, AZ.

Browne, A. (1987). *When battered women kill.* New York: Free Press.

Browne, A. (1992). Violence against women: Relevance for medical practitioners (Report of the Council on Scientific Affairs, American Medical Association). *Journal of the American Medical Association, 267,* 3184–3189.

Browne, A. (1993). Violence against women by male partners. *American Psychologist, 48,* 1077–1087.

Browne, A., & Dutton, D. (1990). Escape from violence: Risks and alternatives for abused women—What do we currently know. In R. Roesch, D. G. Dutton, & V. F. Sacco (Eds.), *Family violence: Perspectives on treatment, research and policy* (pp. 67–91). Burnaby, BC, Canada: British Columbia Institute on Family Violence.

Browne, A., & Thyfault, R. (1981, August). *Battered women who kill: Interview techniques.* Symposium presented at annual conference of American Psychological Association, Los Angeles, CA.

Browne, A., & Williams, K. R. (1989). Exploring the effect of resource availability and the likelihood of female-perpetrated homicides. *Law and Society Review, 23,* 75–94.

Browne, A., & Williams, K. R. (1993). Gender, intimacy, and lethal violence. Trends from 1976–1987. *Gender & Society, 7,* 78–98.

Brownmiller, S. (1975). *Against our will: Women, men and rape.* New York: Simon & Schuster.

Brownmiller, S. (1988). *Waverly Place.* New York: Simon & Schuster.

Bureau of Justice Statistics. (1994a). *Selected findings: Violence between intimates* (NCJ-149259). Washington, DC: U.S. Department of Justice.

Bureau of Justice Statistics. (1994b). *Special report. Murder in families.* Washington, DC: U.S. Department of Justice.

Bureau of Justice Statistics (1995). *Violence against women: Estimates from the Redesigned Survey. Office of Justice Programs.* Washington, DC: U.S. Department of Justice.

Bureau of Justice Statistics. (1997). *Violence-related injuries treated in hospital emergency departments. Office of Justice Programs.* Washington, DC: U.S. Department of Justice.

Burgess, A. W., Baker, T., Greening, D., Hartman, C. R., Burgess, A. G., Douglas, J. E., & Halloran, R. (1997). Stalking behaviors within domestic violence. *Journal of Family Violence, 12,* 389–403.

Butler, S. (1978). *Conspiracy of silence: The trauma of incest.* San Francisco, CA: Bantam Books.

Buzawa, E. S., & Buzawa, C. G. (1993). The scientific evidence is not conclusive: Arrest is no panacea. In R. J. Gelles & D. R. Loeske (Eds.), *Current controversies on family violence* (pp. 337–356). Newbury Park, CA: Sage.

Cahn, N. R. (1991). Civil images of battered women: The impact of domestic violence on child custody decisions. *Vanderbilt Law Review, 44,* 1041–1097.

Calahan, D. (1970). *Problem drinkers: A national study of drinking behavior and attitudes.* San Francisco, CA: Jossey-Bass Ltd.

Cammaert, L. (1998). Non-offending mothers: A new conceptualization. In L. E. A. Walker (Ed.), *Handbook of child sexual abuse* (pp. 309–325). New York: Springer.

Campbell, J. C. (1981). Misogyny and homicide of women. *ANS: Women's Health. American Nursing Society,* 167–185.

Campbell, J. C. (1995). *Assessing dangerousness: Violence by sex offenders, batterers, and child abusers.* Thousand Oaks, CA: Sage.

Caplan, P. J. (1987). *The myth of women's masochism* (2nd ed.). New York: Signet.

Caplan, P. J. (1995). *They say you're crazy: How the world's most powerful psychiatrists decide who's normal.* Reading, MA: Addison-Wesley.

Caplan, P. J., & Caplan, J. B. (1994). *Thinking critically about research on sex and gender.* New York: Harper Collins.

Chalk, R., & King, P. A. (1998). Violence in families: Assessing prevention and treatment programs. *Committee on the Assessment of Family Violence Interventions. Board on Children, Youth and Families.* Washington, DC: National Academy Press.

Charney, D. S., Deutch, A. Y., Krystal, J. H., Southwick, S. M., & Davis, M. (1993). Psychobiological mechanisms of post-traumatic stress disorder. *Archives of General Psychiatry, 50,* 294–305.

Chimbos, P. D. (1978). *Marital violence: A study of interspousal homicide.* San Francisco, CA: R & E Research Associates.

Cohen, L. J. (1997). Meeting the challenge of the "junk science" defense in domestic violence litigation. *Psychotherapy, 34,* 397–409.

Coleman, D. H., & Straus, M. A. (1983). Alcohol abuse and family violence. In E. Gottheil, K. A. Druley, T. E. Skolada, & H. M. Waxman (Eds.), *Alcohol, drug abuse, and aggression* (pp. 104–124). Springfield, IL: C. W. Thomas.

Collins, J. J., & Messerschmidt, P. M. (1993). Epidemiology of alcohol-related violence. *Alcohol, Health and Research World: Special Issue on Alcohol, Aggression and Injury, 17,* 149–155.

Colorado Association for Aid to Battered Women. (1980). *A monograph on services to battered women. (DAMS Publication No. OHDS79-05708).* Washington, DC: Government Printing Office.

Comas-Díaz, L., & Greene, B. (1994). *Women of color: Integrating ethnic and gender identities in psychotherapy.* New York: Guilford Press.

Costello, C. C. (1978). A critical review of Seligman's laboratory experiments on learned helplessness and depression in humans. *Journal of Abnormal Psychology, 87* (1), 21–31.

Cotton, D. H. G. (1990). *Stress management: An integrated approach to therapy.* New York: Brunner/Mazel.

Courtois, C. A. (1988). *Healing the incest wound: Adult survivors in therapy.* New York: Norton.

Courtois, C. A. (1995). Scientist-practitioners and the delayed memory controversy: scientific standards and the need for collaboration. *Counseling Psychologist, 23,* 294–299.

Courtois, C. A. (1997). Delayed memories of child sexual abuse: critique of the controversy and clinical guidelines. In M. Conway (Ed.). *False and recovered memories* (pp. 206–229). Oxford, England: Oxford University Press.

Crowell, N. A., & Burgess, A. W. (1996). *Understanding violence against women.* Washington, DC: National Academy Press.

Cummings, E. M. (1998). Children exposed to marital conflict and violence: Conceptual and theoretical directions. In G. W. Holden, R. Geffner, & E. N. Jouriles (Eds.), *Children exposed to marital violence: Theory, research and applied issues* (pp. 55–93). Washington, DC: American Psychological Association.

Cummings, E. M., & Davies, P. T. (1994). Emotional security as a regulatory process in normal development and the development of pathology. *Development and Psychopathology, 8,* 123–139.

Davidson, T. (1979). *Conjugal crime: Understanding and changing the wife-beating pattern.* New York: Hawthorne.

DeBecker, G. (1997). *The gift of fear and other survival signals that protect us from violence.* New York: Dell.

Deed, M. (1991). Court-ordered child custody evaluations: Helping or victimizing vulnerable families. *Psychotherapy, 11,* 76–84.

Dobash, R. E., & Dobash R. P. (1981). *Violence against wives.* New York: MacMillan Free Press.

Dobash, R. P., & Dobash, R. E. (1983). The context specific approach to theoretical and methodological issues in researching violence against wives. In D. Finkelhor, R. Gelles, G. Hotaling, & M. Straus (Eds.), *The dark side of families* (pp. 261–276). Beverly Hills, CA: Sage.

Donnerstein, E. (1982). Aggressive-Erotica and violence against women. *Journal of Personality and Social Psychology, 39,* 269–277.

Doron, J. (1980). *Conflict and violence in intimate relationships: Focus on marital rape.* New York: American Sociological Association.

Douglas Dutton, M. A., & Walker, L. E. A. (Eds.). (1987). *Feminist Therapies: An integration of psychotherapeutic and feminist systems.* New Jersey: Ablex.

Dunford, F., Huizinga, D., & Elliot, D. (1990). The role of arrest in domestic assault: The Omaha Police experiment. *Criminology, 28,* 183–206.

Dutton, D. G. (1980). *Traumatic bonding.* Unpublished manuscript. University of British Columbia.

Dutton, D. G. (1988). *The domestic assault of women: Psychological and criminal justice perspective.* Boston: Allyn & Bacon.

Dutton, D. G. (1995). *The batterer: A psychological profile.* New York: Basic Books.

Dutton, M. A. (1992). *Empowering and healing the battered woman.* New York: Springer.

Dutton, M. A., & Goodman, L. S. (1994). Posttraumatic Stress Disorder among battered women: Analysis of legal implications. *Behavioral Sciences and the Law, 12,* 215–234.

Dutton, M. A., Honecker, L. C., Halle, P. M., & Burghardt, K. J. (1994). Traumatic responses among battered women who kill. *Journal of Traumatic Stress, 7,* 549–564.

Dweck, C. C., Goetz, T. E., & Strauss, N. L. (1980). Sex differences in learned helplessness: IV. An experimental and naturalistic study of failure generalization and its mediators. *Journal of Personality and Social Psychology, 38,* 441–455.

Eberle, P. (1982). Alcoholic abusers and non-users: A discriminate function analysis. *Journal of Health and Social Behavior, 23,* 260.

Edleson, J. L., & Grusznski, R. J. (1988). Treating men who batter: Four years of outcome data from the Domestic Abuse Project. *Journal of Social Service Research, 12,* 3-22.

Edwards, S. M. (1989). *Policing domestic violence: Women, the law and the state.* London: Sage.

Egeland, B. (1993). A history of abuse is a major risk factor for abusing the next generation. In R. J. Gelles & D. R. Loeske (Eds.), *Current controversies on family violence* (pp. 197–208). Newbury Park, CA: Sage.

Ellsberg, M., Caldera, T., Herrera, A., Winkvist, A., & Kullgren, G. (1999). Domestic violence and emotional distress among Nicaraguan women. *American Psychologist, 54,* 30–36.

Enns, C. Z., Campbell, J., & Courtois, C. A. (1997). Recommendations for working with domestic violence survivors, with special attention to memory issues and posttraumatic processes. *Psychotherapy, 34,* 459–477.

Enos, V. P. (1996). Prosecuting battered mothers: State laws' failure to protect battered women and abused children. *Harvard Women's Law Journal, 19,* 229–268.

Eron, L. D., Gentry, J. H., & Schlegel, P. (Eds.). (1994). *Reason to hope: A psychological perspective on violence and youth.* Washington, DC: American Psychological Association.

Eron, L. D., Huesman, L. R., & Zilli, A. (1991). The role of parental variables in the learning of aggression. In D. J. Pepler & H. Rubin (Eds.), *The development and treatment of child aggression* (pp. 169–188). Hillsdale, NJ: Erlbaum.

Ewing, C. P. (1987). *Battered women who kill.* Lexington, MA: Lexington Books.

Ewing, W., Lindsey, M., & Pomerantz, J. (1984). *Battering: An AMEND manual for helpers.* Denver, CO: AMEND (Abusive Men Exploring New Directions).

Fagan, J. A., Stewart, D. K., & Hansen, K. V. (1983). Violent men or violent husbands? Background factors and situational correlates of severity and location of violence. In D. Finkelhor, R. A. Gelles, G. Hotaling, & M. A. Straus (Eds.), *The dark side of families.* Beverly Hills, CA: Sage.

False Memory Syndrome Foundation (1992). *False memory syndrome* (brochure), Philadelphia.

Faludi, S. (1991). *Backlash.* New York: Crown.

Farley, M., & Barkan, H. (1998). Prostitution, violence and post-traumatic stress disorder. *Women & Health, 27,* 37–49.

Farley, M., Baral, I., Kiremire, M., & Sezgin, U. (1998). Prostitution in five countries: Violence and post-traumatic stress disorder. *Feminism & Psychology, 8,* 405–426.

Fawcett, G. M., Heise, L. L., Isita-Espejel, L., & Pick, S. (1999). Changing community responses to wife abuse: A research and demonstration project in Iztacalco, Mexico. *American Psychologist, 54,* 41–49.

Feher, L. (1982). *Comments concerning the victimology of alcoholism in Hungary.* Presented at the International Conference on Victimology, Sicily, Italy.

Fein, R. A., Vossekuil, B., & Holden, G. A. (1995). *Threat assessment: An approach to prevent targeted violence.* NIJ Research in Action. Washington, DC: U.S. Department of Justice.

Feldman-Summers, S., & Pope, K. S. (1994). The experience of "forgetting" childhood abuse: A national survey of psychologists. *Journal of Consulting and Clinical Psychology, 62,* 1–4.

Feshback, S., & Malamuth, N. M. (1978). Sex and aggression: Proving the link. *Psychology Today, 11,* 111–122.

Fields, M. D. (1994). The impact of spouse abuse on children and its relevance in custody and visitation decisions in New York State. *Cornell Journal of Law and Public Policy, 3,* 221–252.

Figley, C. R. (1985). *Trauma and its wake: The study and treatment of post-traumatic stress disorder.* New York: Brunner/Mazel.

Figley, C. R. (Ed.) (1995). *Compassion fatigue: Coping with secondary traumatic stress disorder in those who treat the traumatized.* New York: Brunner/Mazel.

Finkelhor, D. (1979). *Sexually victimized children.* New York: The Free Press.

Finkelhor, D. (1981). *Common features of family abuse.* Paper presented at the National Conference of Family Violence Researchers. Durham: University of New Hampshire.

Finkelhor, D. (1993). The main problem is still underreporting, not overreporting. In R. Gelles & D. R. Loeske (Eds.), *Current controversies on family violence* (pp. 273–287). Newbury Park, CA: Sage.

Finkelhor, D., & Yllo, K. (1985). *License to rape: Sexual abuse of wives.* New York: Holt, Rinehart & Winston.

Finkelhor, D., Gelles, R., Hotaling, G., & Straus, M. (Eds.). (1983). *The dark side of families.* Beverly Hills, CA: Sage.

Finkelhor, D., Hotaling, G. T., Lewis, I. A., & Smith, C. (1990). Sexual abuse in a national survey of adult men and women: Prevalence, characteristics, and risk factors. *Child Abuse and Neglect, 14,* 19–28.

Flanders, J. P. (1993). Alcohol and other drugs are key causal agents of violence. In R. J. Gelles & D. R. Loeske (Eds.), *Current controversies on family violence* (pp. 171–181). Newbury Park, CA: Sage.

Foa, E. B., Rothbaum, B. O., Riggs, D. S., & Murdock, T. B. (1991). Treatment of posttraumatic stress disorder in rape victims: A comparison between cognitive-behavioral procedures and counseling. *Journal of Consulting and Clinical Psychology, 59,* 715–723.

Frank, P. B., & Houghton, B. D. (1981). *Dealing with the batterer.* Report of the Domestic Violence Project of the Volunteer Counseling Service of Rockland County, Inc.

Freudenberger, H. (1975). The staff burn-out syndrome in alternative institutions. *Psychotherapy: Theory, Research, and Practice, 12* (1).

Freudenberger, H. (1979, September). *Children as victims: Prostitution and pornography.* Symposium presented at the annual meeting of the American Psychological Association, New York, NY.

Freudenberger, H. (1980). *Burn-out: The high cost of high achievement.* New York: Doubleday.

Freyd, J. (1994). Betrayal-trauma: Traumatic amnesia as an adaptive response to childhood abuse. *Ethics and Behavior, 4,* 304–309.

Freyd, J. J. (1996). *Betrayal trauma: The logic of forgetting child abuse.* Cambridge, MA: Harvard University Press.

Friedman, A. R. (1992). Rape and domestic violence: The experience of refuge women. *Women and Therapy, 13,* 65–78.

Frieze, I. H. (1977). *Rape within marriage: Rape as an aspect of wife battering.* (Supplement to Grant Proposal 1 RO1 MH 30193-01). Psychological factors in battered women.

Frieze, I. H. (1980). *Causes and consequences of marital rape.* Paper presented at the annual meeting of the American Psychological Association, Montreal, Canada.

Frieze, I. H., & Browne, A. (1989). Violence in marriage. In L. H. Ohlin & M. H. Tonrey (Eds.), *Crime and justice––An annual review of research: Family violence.* Chicago: University of Chicago Press.

Frieze, I. H., & Knoble, J. (1980). *The effects of alcohol on marital violence.* In Alcohol and Women's Lives. Symposium presented at the annual meeting of the American Psychological Association, Montreal, Canada.

Frieze, I. H., Knoble, J., Zomnir, C., & Washburn, C. (1980). *Types of battered women.* Paper presented at the annual research conference of the Association for Women in Psychology, Santa Monica, CA.

Ganley, A. (1981a). *The male offender examined.* Workshop conducted at the Violence in the Family: Spouse Abuse in Focus conference, Santa Barbara, CA.

Ganley, A. (1981b). *Participant and trainer's manual for working with men who batter.* Washington, DC: Center for Women Policy Studies.

Ganley, A., & Harris, L. (1978). *Domestic violence: Issues in designing and implementing programs for male batterers.* Presented at the annual meeting of the American Psychological Association, Toronto, Canada.

Garbarino, J., Gutterman, E., & Seeley, J. W. (1986). *The psychologically battered child: Strategies for identification, assessment, and intervention.* San Francisco, CA: Jossey-Bass.

Garbarino, J., Kostelny, K., & Dubrow, N. (1991). What children can tell us about living in danger. *American Psychologist, 46,* 376–382.

Gardner, R. (1987). *The parental alienation syndrome and the differentiation between fabrication and genuine child abuse.* Creskill, NJ: Creative Therapeutics.

Gardner, R. (1992). *True and false accusations of child sex abuse.* Creskill, NJ: Creative Therapeutics.

Garmezy, N. (1985). Stress resistant children: The search for protective factors. In J. E. Stevenson (Ed.), *Recent research in developmental psychology* (pp. 213–233). Oxford, England: Pergammon Press.

Gates, M. (1978). Introduction. In J. R. Chapman & M. Gates (Eds.), *The victimization of women. Vol. 3 Sage yearbooks policy studies of women.* Beverly Hills, CA: Sage.

Gauthier, L. M., & Levendosky, A. A. (1996). Assessment and treatment of couples with abusive male partners: Guidelines for therapists. *Psychotherapy, 33,* 403–417.

Geffner, R., Barrett, M. J., & Rossman, B. B. (1995). Domestic violence and sexual abuse: Multiple systems perspectives. In R. H. Mikesell, D. D. Lusterman, & S. H. McDaniel (Eds.), *Integrating family therapy: Handbook of family psychology and systems theory* (pp. 501–517). Washington, DC: American Psychological Association.

Gelles, R. J. (1972). *The violent home: A study of the physical aggression between husbands and wives.* Beverly Hills, CA: Sage

Gelles, R. J. (1975). Violence and pregnancy: A note on the extent of the problem and needed services. *Family Coordinator, 24,* 81–86.

Gelles, R. J. (1980). Violence in the family: A review of the research in the seventies. *Journal of Marriage and The Family, 42,* 873–885.

Gelles, R. J. (1983). An exchange/social control theory of intrafamily violence. In D. Finkelhor, R. Gelles, G. Hotaling, & M. Straus (Eds.), *The dark side of families* (pp. 151–164). Beverly Hills, CA: Sage.

Gelles, R. J. (1993a). Through a sociological lens: Social structure and family violence. In R. J. Gelles & D. R. Loseke (Eds.), *Current controversies on family violence* (pp. 31–46). Thousand Oaks, CA: Sage.

Gelles, R. J. (1993b). Alcohol and other drugs are associated with violence: They are not its cause. In R. J. Gelles & D. R. Loseke (Eds.), *Current controversies on family violence* (pp. 182–196). Newbury Park, CA: Sage.

Gelles, R. J., & Loseke, D. R. (Eds.). (1993). *Current controversies on family violence.* Newbury Park, CA: Sage.

Gelles, R. A., & Straus, M. A. (1988). *Intimate violence.* New York: Touchstone.

Gil, D. G. (1970). *Violence against children.* Cambridge, MA: Harvard University Press.

Gil, E. (1988). *Treatment of adult survivors of childhood abuse.* Walnut Creek, CA: Launch Press.

Gilbert, N. (1993). Examining the facts: Advocacy research overstates the incidence of date and acquaintance rapes. In R. J. Gelles & D. R. Loseke (Eds.), *Current controversies on family violence* (pp. 120–132). Newbury Park, CA: Sage.

Giles-Sims, J. (1983). *Wife battering: A systems theory approach.* New York: Guilford Press.

Gillespie, C. K. (1989). *Justifiable homicide.* Columbus, OH: Ohio State University Press.

Goetting, A. (1991). Female victims of homicide: A portrait of their killers and the circumstances of their death. *Violence and Victims, 6,* 159–168.

Goetting, A. (1989). Men who kill their mates: A profile. *Journal of Family Violence, 4,* 285–296.

Gold, S. N. (1997). Training professional psychologists to treat survivors of childhood sexual abuse. *Psychotherapy, 34,* (365–374).

Gold, S. N., Hughes, D. M., & Honecker, L. C. (1994). Degrees of repression of childhood sexual abuse memories. *American Psychologist, 48,* 441–447.

Goldberg, M. E. (1995). Substance-abusing women: False stereotypes and real needs. *Social Work, 40,* 789–798.

Golding, W. (1959). *Lord of the flies.* New York: Penguin Putnam.

Goldstein, H. H. (1975). Aggression and crimes of aggression. *Canadian Journal of Behavioral Science, 12,* 141–158.

Goleman, D. (1996). *Emotional intelligence.* New York: Bantam.

Goodwin, J. (1988). Post-traumatic symptoms in abused children. *Journal of Traumatic Stress, 1,* 475–488.

Gondolf, E. W., & Fisher, E. R. (1988). *Battered women as survivors: An alternative to treating learned helplessness.* Boston, MA: Lexington.

Goodman, L., Koss, M. P., Browne, A., Fitzgerald, L., Russo, N. F., Biden, J. R., & Keita, G. P. (1993). Psychology in the public forum. Male violence against women: Current research and future directions. *American Psychologist, 48,* 1054–1087.

Graham-Bermann, S. A. (1998). The impact of woman abuse on children's social development: Research and theoretical perspectives. In G. Holden, R. Geffner, & E. Jouriles (Eds.), *Children exposed to marital violence* (pp. 21–54). Washington, DC: American Psychological Association.

Greene, B., & Comas-Dias, L. (Eds.). (1994). *Women of color: Integrating ethnic and gender identities in psychotherapy.* New York: Guilford.

Gross, L. (1994). *To have or harm: True stories of stalkers and their victims.* New York: Time Warner Books.

Groth, A. N. (1979). *Men who rape: The psychology of the offender.* New York: Plenum Press.

Hageman-White, C. (1981, December). *Confronting violence against women in Germany.* Paper presented at the International Interdisciplinary Congress on Women, Haifa. Israel.

Hamberger, L. K. (1997). Research concerning wife abuse: Implications for physician training. *Journal of Aggression, Maltreatment, and Trauma, 1,* 81–96.

Hamberger, L. K., & Ambuel, B. (1997). Training psychology students and professionals to recognize and intervene into partner violence: Borrowing a page from medicine. *Psychotherapy, 34,* 375–385.

Hamberger, L. K., & Hastings, J. H. (1986). Personality correlates of men who abuse their partners: A cross validation study. *Journal of Family Violence, 1,* 323–341.

Hampton, R. L., & Gelles, R. J. (1994). Violence towards black women in a nationally representative sample of black families. *Journal of Comparative Family Studies, 25,* 105–119.

Hanneke, C. R., & Shields, N. M. (1981). *Patterns of family and non-family violence: An approach to the study of violent husbands.* Paper presented at National Conference of Family Violence Researchers, University of New Hampshire, Durham.

Hansen, J. C., & Barnhill, L. N. (Eds.). (1982). *Clinical approaches to family violence.* Rockville, MD: Aspen Systems Corporation

Hansen, M., & Harway, M. (Eds.). (1993). *Battering and family therapy: A feminist perspective.* Newbury Park, CA: Sage.

Hanson, R. F., Kilpatrick, D. G., Falasetti, S. A., & Resnick, H. S. (1995). Violent crime and mental health. In J. R. Freedy & S. E. Hobfoll (Eds.), *Traumatic stress: From theory to practice* (pp. 129–161). New York: Plenum.

Harrell, A. (1991). *Evaluation of court-ordered treatment for domestic violence offenders.* Washington, DC: The Urban Institute.

Hart, B. (1988). Beyond the "duty to warn": A therapist's "duty to protect" battered women and children. In K. Yllo & M. Bograd (Eds.), *Feminist perspectives on wife abuse* (pp. 234–248). Newbury Park, CA: Sage.

Harway, M., & Hansen, M. (1994). *Spouse abuse: Assessing and treating battered women, batterers, & their children.* Sarasota, FL: Professional Resource Press.

Hathaway-Clark, C. (1980). *Multidimensional locus of control in battered women.* Paper presented at the annual meeting of the Rocky Mountain Psychological Association, Tucson, AZ.

Heise, L. (1993). *Violence against women: The hidden health burden.* Washington, DC: World Bank.

Heise, L. (1996). Violence against women: Global organizing for change. In J. Edelson & Z. C. Eisikovits (Eds.). *Future interventions with battered women and their families* (pp. 7–33). Thousand Oaks, CA: Sage.

Heise, L. (1998). Violence against women: An integrated, ecological framework. *Journal of Violence Against Women, 4,* 262–290.

Helfer, E. R., & Kempe, C. H. (1974). *The battered child* (2nd ed.). Chicago: The University of Chicago Press.

Hendricks, M. (1985). Feminist spirituality. Feminist therapy: A coming of age. In L. B. Rosewater & L. E. A. Walker (Eds.), *Handbook of feminist therapy: Psychotherapy with women.* New York: Springer.

Herman, J. L. (1992). *Trauma and recovery.* New York: Basic Books.

Hilberman, E. (1980). Overview: The wifebeater's wife reconsidered. *American Journal of Psychiatry, 137,* 1336–1347.

Hilberman, E., & Munson, L. (1978). Sixty battered women. *Victimology: An International Journal, 2*(3–4), 460–471.

Hilton, N. Z. (Ed.). (1993). *Legal responses to wife assault: Current trends and evaluation.* Newbury Park, CA: Sage.

Hodges, W. F. (1986). *Interventions for children of divorce: Custody, access and psychotherapy.* New York: Wiley.

Holden, G. W., Geffner, R., & Jouriles, E. N. (Eds.). (1998). *Children exposed to marital violence: Theory, research, and applied issues.* Washington, DC: American Psychological Association.

Holmes, W. C., & Slap, G. B. (1998). Sexual abuse of boys: Definition, prevalence, correlates, sequelae, and management. *Journal of the American Medical Association, 280,* 1855–1862.

Holtzworth-Monroe, A., & Stuart, G. L. (1994). Typologies of male batterers: Three subtypes and the differences among them. *Psychological Bulletin, 116,* 476–497.

Horne, S. (1999). Domestic violence in Russia. *American Psychologist, 54,* 55–61.

Hotaling, G. T., & Sugarman, D. B. (1986). An analysis of risk markers in husband to wife violence: The current state of the knowledge. *Violence and Victims, 1,* 101–124.

Hughes, H. M. (1997). Research concerning children of battered women: Clinical implications. In R. Geffner, S. B. Sorenson, & P. K. Lundberg-Love (Eds.), *Violence and sexual abuse at home: Current issues, interventions, and research in spousal battering and child maltreatment* (pp. 225–244). Binghamton, NY: Haworth Maltreatment & Trauma Press.

Hughes, H. M., & Marshall, M. (1995). Advocacy for children of domestic violence: Helping the battered women with non-sexist child-rearing. In E. Peled, P. G. Jaffe, & J. L. Edleson (Eds.), *Ending the cycle of violence: Community responses to children of battered women* (pp. 97–105). Newbury Park, CA: Sage.

Hughes, H. M., & Barad, S. J. (in press). Psychological functioning of children in a battered women's shelter: A preliminary investigation. *Journal of Child Psychology and Psychiatry.*

Island, D., & Letelier, P. (1991). *Men who beat the men who love them: Battered gay men and domestic violence.* Binghamton, NY: Haworth.

Jacobson, N. S., & Gottman, J. M. (1998). *When men batter women: New insights into ending abusive relationships.* New York: Simon & Schuster.

Jaffe, P. G., & Geffner, R. (1998). Child custody disputes and domestic violence: Critical issues for mental health, social service, and legal professionals. In G. W. Holden, R. Geffner, & E. N. Jouriles (Eds.), *Children exposed to marital violence: Theory, research and applied issues.* (pp. 371–408). Washington, DC: American Psychological Association.

Jaffe, P. G., Wolfe, D. A., & Wilson, S. K. (1990). *Children of battered women.* Newbury Park, CA: Sage.

James, J. (1978). In J. R. Chapman & M. Gates (Eds.), *Victimization of women.* Beverly Hills, CA: Sage.

Janoff-Bulman, R. (1985). The aftermath of victimization: Rebuilding shattered assumptions. In C. Figley (Ed.), *Trauma and its wake.* New York: Brunner/Mazel.

Jens, K. (1979, September). *Assessing lethality in marital violence.* Paper presented at the Colorado Annual Mental Health Conference, Keystone, Colorado.

Jens, K. (1980, April). Depression in battered women. Paper presented at the annual meeting of the Rocky Mountain Psychological Association, Tucson, AZ.

Johnston, J. R., & Campbell, L. E. G. (1993). Parent-child relationships in domestic violence families disputing custody. *Family and Conciliation Courts Review, 31,* 282–298.

Jones, A. (1980). *Women who kill.* New York: Holt, Rinehart, & Winston.

Jones, A. (1994). *Next time she'll be dead: Battering and how to stop it.* Boston: Beacon Press.

Jones, A., & Schechter, S. (1992). *When love goes wrong: What to do when you can't do anything right.* New York: Harper/Collins.

Juvenile Justice Bulletin (JJB) (1998). *Juvenile arrests 1997.* Washington, DC: U. S. Department of Justice, Office of Juvenile Justice and Delinquency Prevention.

Kalichman, S. G. (1993). *Mandated reporting of suspected child abuse: Ethics, law and policy.* Washington, DC: American Psychological Association.

Kalmuss, D. S. (1984). The intergenerational transmission of marital aggression. *Journal of Marriage and the Family, 48,* 113–120.

Kanuha, V. (1990). Compounding the triple jeopardy: Battering in lesbian-of-color relationships. *Women and Therapy, 9,* 169–184.

Karr, P., Long, S. K., & Witte, A. D. (1981, July). *Family violence: A microeconomic approach.* Presented at the National Family Violence Researchers Conference, University of New Hampshire, Durham.

Kaslow, F. (Ed.) (1997). *Handbook of relational diagnosis.* New York: Wiley.

Kaufman, J., & Zigler, E. (1993). The intergenerational transmission of abuse is overstated. In R. J. Gelles & D. R. Loeske (Eds.), *Current controversies on family violence* (pp. 209–221). Newbury Park, CA: Sage.

Kiernan, J. E., & Taylor, V. L. (1990). Coercive sexual behavior among Mexican-American college students. *Journal of Sex and Marital Therapy, 16,* 44–50.

Kilpatrick, D. G., Saunders, B. E., Amick-McMullan, A. E., Best, C. L., Veronen, L. J., & Resick, H. S. (1989). Victim and crime factors associated with the development of crime-related post-traumatic stress disorder. *Behavior Therapy, 20,* 199–214.

Kilpatrick, D. G., & Resick, H. S. (1993). Posttraumatic stress disorder associated with exposure to criminal victimization in clinical and community populations. In J. R. T. Davidson & E. B. Foa (Eds.), *Posttraumatic stress disorder: DSM-IV and beyond* (pp. 113–143). Washington, DC: American Psychiatric Press.

King, D. F., & Straus, M. A. (1981, August). *When prohibition works: Alternatives to violence in the Odyssey House Youth program and in the family.* Paper presented at the annual meeting of the American Sociological Association, Toronto, Canada.

Kolodny, E. S. (1998). Cognitive therapy for trauma-related guilt. In V. M. Follette, J. I. Ruzek, & F. R. Abueg (Eds.), *Cognitive-Behavioral therapies for trauma.* New York: Guilford.

Koop, C. E. (1986). *Surgeon General's conference on violence and the family.* Washington, DC: National Institutes of Health.

Koss, M. P. (1990). The women's mental health research agenda. *American Psychologist, 45,* 374–380.

Koss, M. P., & Cook, S. L. (1993). Facing the facts: Date and acquaintance rape are significant problems for women. In R. J. Gelles & D. R. Loeske (Eds.), *Current controversies on family violence* (pp. 104–119). Newbury Park, CA: Sage.

Koss, M. P., & Haslet, L. (1992). Somatic consequences of violence against women. *Archives of Family Medicine, 1,* 53–59.

Koss, M. P., Ingram, M., & Pepper, S. (1997). Psychotherapists' role in the medical response to male-partner violence. *Psychotherapy, 34,* 386–396.

Koss, M. P., Goodman, L. A., Browne, A., Fitzgerald, L. F., Keita, G. P., & Russo, N. F. (1994). *No safe haven: Male violence against women at home, at work, and in the community.* Washington, DC: American Psychological Association.

Kozu, J. (1999). Domestic violence in Japan. *American Psychologist, 54,* 50–54.

Kubany, E. S. (1998). Cognitive therapy for trauma-related guilt. In V. M. Follette, J. L. Ruzek, & F. R. Abueg (Eds.), *Cognitive behavioral therapies for trauma.* New York: Guilford.

Kurz, D. (1993). Physical assaults by husbands: A major social problem. In R. J. Gelles & D. R. Loeske (Eds.), *Current controversies on family violence* (pp. 88–103). Newbury Park, CA: Sage.

Kutchins, H., & Kirk, S. A. (1997). *Making us crazy: DSM: The psychiatric bible and the creation of mental disorders.* New York: Free Press.

Labell, L. S. (1979). Wife abuse: A sociological study of battered women and their mates. *Victimology, 4,* 258–267.

Lang, A. R., Goeckner, D. J., Adesso, V. J., & Marlatt, G. A. (1975). Effect of alcohol on aggression in male social drinkers. *Journal of Abnormal Psychology, 84,* 508–518.

Laura X. Clearinghouse on Marital Rape (1981). Women's Herstory Research Center, 2325 Oak Str., Berkeley, CA 94708.

Lederer, L. (Ed.). (1980). *Take back the night: Women on pornography.* New York: William Morrow.

Leidig, M. W. (1981). Violence against women: A feminist-psychological analysis. In S. Cox (Ed.), *Female psychology: The emerging self* (2nd ed., pp. 190–205). New York: St. Martin's Press.

Lerman, H. (1996). *Pigeonholing women's misery.* New York: Basic Books.

Levant, R. F., & Pollack, W. S. (1993). *A new psychology of men.* New York: Basic Books.

Levenson, H. (1972). *Distinctions within the concept of internal-external control: Development of a new scale.* Proceedings of the 80th Annual Convention of the American Psychological Association, 261–262.

Levy, B. (1991). *Dating violence: Young women in danger.* Seattle, WA: Seal Press.

Lewinsohn, P. M. (1975). The behavioral study and treatment of depression. In M. Hersen, M. Eider, & P. M. Miller (Eds.), *Progress in behavioral modification.* New York: Academic Press.

Lewinsohn, P. M., Steinmetz, J. L., Larson, D. W., & Franklin, J. (1981). Depression and related cognitions: Antecedent or consequence? *Journal of Psychology, 90,* 213–219.

Lewis, E. M. (1980). *The effects of intensity and probability on the prefer-ence for immediate versus delayed aversive stimuli in women with various levels of interspousal conflict.* Unpublished manuscript, University of Illinois at Chicago Circle.

Lewis, E. M. (1981, July). *An experimental analogue of the spouse abuse cycle.* Paper presented at the National Conference for Family Violence Researcher, University of New Hampshire, Durham.

Lindsay, M., McBride, R., & Platt, C. (1992). *AMEND: Philosophy and cur-riculum for treating batterers.* Denver, CO: McBride.

Liss, M. & Stahly, G. (1993). Child custody and visitation issues for bat-tered women. In M. Hansen M. & Harway (Eds.), *Battering and family therapy: A feminist perspective.* Newbury Park, CA: Sage.

Lobel, K. (Ed.). (1986). *Naming the violence: Speaking out against les-bian battering.* Seattle, WA: Seal Press.

Loeske, D. R., & Berk, S. F. (1981, July). *Defining "Help": Initial encoun-ters between battered women and shelter staff.* Paper presented at the National Conference of Family Violence Researchers, University of New Hampshire, Durham.

Loftus, E. F. (1993). The reality of repressed memories. *American Psychologist, 48,* 518–537.

Loftus, E. F. with Ketcham, K. (1994). *The myth of repressed memory: False memories and allegations of abuse.* New York: St. Martin's Press.

Loving, N. (1981). Spouse abuse: A curriculum guide for police trainers. *Police Executive Research Forum.* Washington, DC.

Lystadt, M. H. (1975). Violence at home: A review of the literature. *American Journal of Orthopsychiatry, 45*(3), 328–345.

MacFarlane, K. (1977–1978). Sexual abuse of children. In J. R. Chapman & M. Gates (Eds.), *The victimization of women. Sage yearbooks in women's policy studies* (Vol. 3). Beverly Hills, CA: Sage.

MacKinnon, C. A. (1983). Feminism, Marxism, method and the state: Towards feminist jurisprudence. *Signs: Journal of Women in Culture and Society, 8,* 635–658.

Maguigan, H. (1991). Battered women and self-defense: Myths and mis-conceptions in current reform proposals. *University of Pennsylvania Law Review, 140,* 379–486.

Mahoney, M. R. (1991). Legal images of battered women: Redefining the issue of separation. *Michigan Law Review, 90,* 1–94.

Maiden, R. P. (1997). Alcohol dependence and domestic violence: Incidence and treatment implications. *Alcoholism Treatment Quarterly, 15,* 31–50.

Makepeace, J. (1981). Courtship. Violence among college students. *Family Relations, 30,* 97–102.

Malamuth, N. M. (in press). Rape proclivity among males. *Journal of Social Issues.*

Malamuth, N. M., & Check, J. V. P. (in press). The effects of mass media exposure on acceptance of violence against women: A field experiment. *Journal of Research in Personality.*

Margolin, G. (1979). Conjoint marital therapy to enhance anger management, and reduce spouse abuse. *American Journal of Family Therapy, 7,* 13–24.

Margolin, G. (1987). The multiple forms of aggressiveness between marital partners: How do we identify them? *Journal of Marital and Family Therapy, 13,* 77–84.

Martin, D. (1976). *Battered wives.* San Francisco, CA: Glide Publications.

Martin, V. (1982). Wife-beating: A product of socio-sexual development. In M. Kirkpatrick (Ed.), *Women's sexual experiences: Explorations of the dark continent* (pp. 247–261). New York: Plenum Press.

McCord, J. (1988). Parental aggressiveness and physical punishment in long term perspective. In G. Hotaling, D. Finkelhor, J. T. Kirkpatrick, & M. S. Straus (Eds.), *Family abuse and its consequences* (pp. 91–98). Newbury Park, CA: Sage.

McGrath, E., Keita, G. P., Strickland, B., & Russo, N. T. (Eds). (1990). *Women and depression: Risk factors and treatment issues. Final Report of the APA National Task force on Women and Depression.* Washington, DC: American psychological Association.

McWhirter, P. T. (1999). La violencia privada: Domestic violence in Chile. *American Psychologist, 54,* 37–40.

Meichenbaum, D. (1996). *Cognitive behavioral treatment with PTSD.*

Meloy, J. R. (1988). *The psychopathic mind.* Northvale, NJ: Aronson.

Meloy, J. R. (1992). *Violent attachments.* Northvale, N. J.: Aronson.

Meloy, J. R. (1995). Antisocial personality disorder. In G. Gabbard (Ed.). *Treatment of psychiatric disorders. Second Edition, Vol. 2.* (pp. 2273–2290). Washington, DC: American Psychiatric Press.

Meloy, J. R. (Ed.). (1998). *The psychology of stalking.* San Diego: Academic Press.

Meloy, J. R., Cowett, P. Y., Parker, S., Hofland, B., & Friedland, A. (1997). Domestic protection orders and the prediction of criminality and violence towards protectees. *Psychotherapy, 34.*

Miller, D., & Challas, G. (1981, July). *Abused children as adult parents: A twenty-five year longitudinal study.* Paper presented at the National Conference of Family Violence Researchers, University of New Hampshire, Durham.

Millon, T. (1991). *Toward a new personology: An evolutionary model.* New York: Wiley.

Monahan, L. (1981). *Predicting violent behavior: An assessment of clinical techniques.* Beverly Hills, CA: Sage.

Mones, P. A. (1991). *When a child kills: Abused children who kill their parents.* New York: Pocket Books.

Moore, D., & Pepitone-Rockwell, F. (1979). In D. Moore (Ed.), *Battered women.* Beverly Hills, CA: Sage.

Morris, G. W. (1985). *The kids next door: Sons and daughters who kill their parents.* New York: William Morrow.

Moss, L. E. (1985). Feminist body psychotherapy. In L. B. Rosewater & L. E. Walker (Eds.), *Handbook of feminist therapy.* New York: Springer.

Mott-MacDonald. (1979). *Report on Belmont Conference on spouse abusers.* Available from the Center for Women Policy Studies, Washington, DC.

Myers, T. (1982, January). *Wifebeaters' group through a women's center: Why and how.* Paper presented at the International Conference on Victimology, Sicily, Italy.

O'Leary, K. D. (1993). Through a psychological lens: Personality traits, personality disorders and levels of violence. In R. J. Gelles & D. R. Loeske (Eds.), *Current controversies on family violence* (pp. 7–30). Newbury Park, CA: Sage.

Oriel, K. A., & Fleming, M. F. (1998). Screening men for partner violence in a primary care setting: A new strategy for detecting domestic violence. *The Journal of Family Practice, 46,* 493–498.

Pagelow, M. D. (1993). Justice for victims of spouse abuse in divorce and child custody cases. *Violence and Victims, 8,* 69–83.

Parnell, T., & Day, D. (1998). *Munchausen by proxy syndrome: Misunderstood child abuse.* Thousand Oaks, CA: Sage.

Patterson, G. R. (1982). *Coercive family process.* Eugene, OR: Castalia Press.

Peled, E., Jaffe, P. G., & Edleson, J. L. (Eds.). (1995). *Ending the cycle of violence: Community responses to children of battered women.* Newbury Park, CA: Sage.

Peltoniemi, T. (1982, January). *The first 12 months of the Finnish shelters.* Paper presented at the International Conference on Victimology, Sicily, Italy.

Peltoniemi, T., & Aromaa, K. (1982, January). *Family violence studies and victimization surveys in Finland.* Paper presented at the International Conference on Victimology, Sicily, Italy.

Pence, E., & Paymar, M. (1993). *Education groups for men who batter: The Duluth model.* New York: Springer.

Perlman, L. A., & Saakvitne, K. (1995). *Trauma and the therapist:*

Countertransference and vicarious traumatization in psychotherapy with incest survivors. New York: Norton.

Peters, S., Wyatt, G., & Finkelhor, D. (1986). Prevalence. In D. Finkelhor & Associates (Eds.). *A sourcebook on child sexual abuse* (pp. 15–59). Beverly Hills, CA: Sage.

Pillemer, K. (1993). The abused offspring are dependent: Abuse is caused by the deviance and dependence of abusive caregivers. In R. J. Gelles & D. R. Loeske (Eds.), *Current controversies on family violence* (pp. 237–250). Newbury Park, CA: Sage.

Pillemer, K., & Finkelhor, D. (1988). The prevalence of elder abuse: A random sample survey. *The Gerontologist, 28,* 51–57.

Pizzey, E. (1974). *Scream quietly or the neighbors will hear.* London: Penguin.

Pleck, E. (1979). Wifebeating in nineteenth-century America. *ViCtl11iOtOg9: An International Journal, 4*(1), 60–74.

Plummer, C. A. (1993). Prevention is appropriate: Prevention is successful. In R. J. Gelles & D. R. Loeske (Eds.), *Current controversies on family violence* (pp. 288–305). Newbury Park, CA: Sage.

Pope, K. S. (1996). Memory, abuse and science: Questioning claims about the False Memory Syndrome epidemic. *American Psychologist, 51,* 957–974.

Pope, K. S. (1997). Science as careful questioning: Are claims of False Memory Syndrome epidemic based on empirical evidence? *American Psychologist, 52,* 997–1006.

Pope, K. S., & Brown, L. S. (1996). *Recovered memories of abuse: Assessment, therapy and forensics.*

Pope, K. S., Butcher, J., & Seelen, J. (1993). *The MMPI-1, MMPI-2, and MMPI-A in court: A practical guide for expert witnesses and attorneys.* Washington, DC: American Psychological Association Press.

Powers, R. J., & Kutash, I. L. (1978). Substance induced aggression. In I. L. Kutash, S. B. Kutash, & L. B. Schlessinger (Eds.), *Violence: Perspectives on murder and aggression.* San Francisco, CA: Jossey-Bass.

Pynoos, R. S. (1994). Traumatic stress and developmental psychopathology in children and adolescents. In R. S. Pynoos (Ed.), *Posttraumatic Stress Disorder: A clinical review* (pp. 65–98). Lutherville, MD: Sidran Press.

Radloff, L. S. (1975). Sex differences in depression: The effects of occupation and marital status. *Sex Roles, 1* (3), 249–265.

Radloff, L. S. (1977). The CES-D scale: A self-report depression scale for research in the general population. *Applied Psychological Measurement, 1* (3), 385–401.

Radloff, L. S. *Risk factors for depression: What do we learn from them? The mental health of women: Fact or fiction?* New York: Academic Press.

Radloff, L. S., & Cox, S. (1981). Sex differences in depression in relation to learned susceptibility. In S. Cox (Ed.), *Female psychology: The emerging self* (2nd ed.). New York: St. Martin's Press.

Radloff, L. S., & Monroe, M. K. (1978). Sex differences in helplessness— with implications for depression. In L. S. Hanson & R. S. Rapoza (Eds.), *Career development and counseling of women.* Springfield, IL: Charles C. Thomas.

Radloff, L. S., & Rae, D. S. (1979). Susceptibility and precipitating factors in depression: Sex differences and similarities. *Journal of Abnormal Psychology, 88*(2), 174–181.

Radloff, L. S., & Rae, D. S. (1981). Components of the sex difference in depression. *Research on Community Mental Health, 2,* 111–137.

Rave, E. (1985). Pornography: The leveler of women. In *Feminist therapy: A coming of age.* Selected proceedings from the Advanced Feminist Therapy Institute, Vail, Colorado, April 1982.

Reid, J. B., Taplin, P. S., & Lorber, R. (1981). A social interactional approach to the treatment of abusive families. In R. B. Stuart (Ed.), *Violent behavior: Social learning approaches to prediction, management, and treatment.* New York: Brunner/Mazel.

Renzetti, C. M. (1992). *Violent betrayal: Partner abuse in lesbian relationships.* Newbury Park, CA: Sage.

Reppucci, N. D., & Haugaard, J. J. (1993). Problems with child sexual abuse prevention programs. In R. J. Gelles & D. R. Loeske (Eds.), *Current controversies on family violence* (pp. 306–321). Newbury Park, CA: Sage.

Ressler, R. K., Burgess, A. W., & Douglas, J. E. (1988). *Sexual homicide: Patterns and motivation.* New York: Simon & Schuster.

Richardson, D. C., & Campbell, J. L. (1980). Alcohol and wife abuse: The effects of alcohol on attributions of blame for wife abuse. *Personality and Social Psychology Bulletin, 6,* 51–56.

Rind, B., Tromovitch, P., & Bauserman, R. (1998). A meta-analytic examination of assumed properties of child sexual assault using college samples. *Psychological Bulletin, 124,* 22–53.

Rizley, R. (1978). Depression and distortion in the attribution of causality. *Journal of Abnormal Psychology, 87*(1), 32–48.

Rhodes, N. R. (1992). Comparison of MMPI Psychopathic Deviate scores of battered and non-battered women. *Journal of Family Violence, 7,* 297–307.

Roberts, W. R., Penk, W. E., Gearing, M. L., Robinowitz, R., Dolan, M. P.,

& Patterson, E. T. (1982). Interpersonal problems of Vietnam combat veterans with Post-Traumatic Stress Disorder. *Journal of Abnormal Psychology, 91* (G), 444–450.

Root, M. P. P. (1992). Reconstructing the impact of trauma on personality. In L. Brown & M. Ballou (Eds.), *Personality and psychopathology: feminist reappraisals* (pp. 220–265). New York: Guilford.

Rosenberg, M. S. (1987). Children of battered women: The effects of witnessing violence on their social problem solving abilities. *Behavior Therapist, 10,* 85–89.

Rosenberg, M. S., & Rossman, B. B. R. (1990). The child witness to marital violence. In R. T. Ammerman & M. Hersen (Eds.), *Treatment of family violence* (pp. 183–210). New York: Wiley.

Rosewater, L. B. (1982). *An MMPI profile for battered women* (Doctoral dissertation, Union Graduate School, Ann Arbor, 1982). Dissertation Abstracts.

Rosewater, L. B. (1984). Feminist therapy. In L. E. Walker (Ed.), *Women and mental health policy.* Beverly Hills, CA: Sage.

Rosewater, L. B. (1985a). Schizophrenic or battered? In L. B. Rosewater & L. E. A. Walker (Eds.), *Handbook on feminist therapy: Psychotherapy with women.* New York: Springer.

Rosewater, L. B. (1985b). Feminist interpretations of traditional testing. In L. B. Rosewater & L. E. A. Walker (Eds.), *Handbook of feminist therapy* (pp. 266–273). New York: Springer.

Rosewater, L. B., & Walker, L. E. A. (1985). *Handbook of feminist therapy.* New York: Springer.

Rossman, B. B. R. (1998). Descartes' error and Post-traumatic Stress Disorder: Cognition and emotion in children who are exposed to parental violence. In G. W. Holden, R. Geffner, & E. N. Jouriles (Eds.), *Children exposed to marital violence: Theory, research and applied issues* (pp. 223–256). Washington, DC: American Psychological Association.

Rossman, B. B. R., & Rosenberg, M. S. (Eds.). (1998). *The multiple victimization of children: Conceptual, developmental, research, and clinical issues.* Binghamton, NY: Haworth Press.

Rotter, J. B. (1966). Generalized expectancies for internal versus external control of reinforcement. *Psychological Monographs (80),* 1.

Roy, M. (1978). *Battered women: A psychological study.* New York: Van Nostrand.

Russell, D. E. H. (1975). *The politics of rape.* New York: Stein & Day.

Russell, D. E. H. (1982). *Rape in marriage.* New York: Macmillan.

Russell, D. E. H. (1986). *The secret trauma: Incest in the lives of girls and women.* New York: Basic Books.

Russell, D. E. H., & Van der ven, L. (1976). *Crimes against women.* Millbrae, CA: Les Femmes.

Russo, N. F., Denious, J., Keita, G. P., & Koss, M. P. (1997). Intimate violence and black women's health. *Journal of Gender, Culture and Health, 3,* 315–348.

Saunders, D. G. (1982). Counseling the violent husband. In P. A. Keller & L. G. Ritt (Eds.), *Innovations in clinical practice: A source book,* (Vol. 1). Sarasota, FL: Professional Resource Exchange.

Saunders, D. G. (1986). When battered women use violence: Husband-abuse or self-defense? *Violence and Victims, 1,* 47–60.

Saunders, D. G. (1992). A typology of men who batter women: Three types derived from cluster analysis. *American Orthopsychiatry, 62,* 264–275.

Saunders, D. G., & Kindy, P. (1993). Predictors of physicians' response to woman abuse: The role of gender, background, and brief training. *Journal of General Internal Medicine, 8,* 606–609.

Schaum, M., & Parrish, K. (1995). *Stalked: Breaking the silence on the crime of stalking in America.* New York: Pocket Books.

Schechter, S. (1982). *Women and male violence: The visions and struggles of the battered women's movement.* Boston: South End Press.

Schmidt, J. D., & Sherman, L. W. (1993). Does arrest deter domestic violence? *American Behavioral Scientist, 36,* 601–609.

Schneider, E. (1980). Equal rights to trial for women: Sex bias in the law for self-defense. *Harvard Civil Rights—Civil Liberties Law Review, 5*(3), 623–647.

Schneider, E. (1986). Describing and changing: Women's self defense work and the problem of expert testimony on battering. *Women's Rights Law Reporter, 9,* 195–222.

Schuller, R. A. (1992). The impact of battered woman syndrome evidence on jury decision processes. *Law and Human Behavior, 16,* 597–619.

Schuller, R. A., & Hastings, P. A. (1996). Trials of battered women who kill: The impact of alternative forms of expert evidence. *Law and Human Behavior, 20,* 167–187.

Schuller, R. A., & Cripps, J. (1998). Expert evidence pertaining to battered women: The impact of gender of expert and timing of testimony. *Law and Human Behavior, 22,* 17–31.

Sedlak, A. (1991). *Study findings: Study of national incidence and prevalence of child abuse and neglect 1988.* Washington, DC: U. S. Department of Health and Human Services.

Seligman, M. E. P. (1975). *Helplessness: On depression, development, and death.* San Francisco, CA: W. H. Freeman.

Seligman, M. E. P. (1978). Comment and integration. *Journal of Abnormal Psychology, 87,* 165–179.

Seligman, M. E. P. (1991). *Learned optimism.* New York: Alfred A. Knopf.

Seligman, M. E. P. (1994). *What you can change and what you can't: The complete guide to successful self-improvement.* New York: Alfred A. Knopf.

Seligman, M. E. P. (1997). *The optimistic child.* New York: Alfred A. Knopf.

Seligson, M. R., & Bernas, R. J. (1997). Battered women and AIDS: Assessment and treatment from a psychosocial-educational perspective. *Psychotherapy, 34,* 509–515.

Shainess, N. (1979). Vulnerability to violence: Masochism as a process. *American Journal of Psychotherapy, 33,* 174–189.

Shainess, N. (1985). *Sweet suffering: Women as victim.* New York: Pocket Books.

Shapiro, F., & Forrest, M. S. (1997). *Eye Movement Desensitization Reprocessing (EMDR): The breakthrough psychotherapy for overcoming stress and trauma.* New York: Basic Books.

Sherman, L. W. (1992). *Policing domestic violence: Experiments and dilemmas.* New York: Free Press.

Sherman, L. W., & Berk, R. A. (1984). The specific deterrent effects of arrest for domestic assault. *American Sociological Review, 49,* 261–271.

Shields, H., & Hanneke, C. (1983). Battered wives reaction to marital rape. In D. Finkelhor, R. J. Gelles, G. Hotaling, & M. Straus (Eds.), *The dark side of families* (pp. 132–148). Beverly Hills, CA: Sage.

Snell, J. E., Rosenwald, R. J., & Robey, A. (1964). The wifebeater's wife: A study of family interaction. *Archives of General Psychiatry, 2,* 107–112.

Sonkin, D. J. (1998). Internet Web Site.

Sonkin, D. J. (1986). Clairvoyance vs. common sense: Therapist's duty to warn and protect. *Violence and Victims, 1,* 7–22.

Sonkin, D. J. (Ed.). (1987). *Domestic violence on trial: Psychological and legal dimensions of family violence.* New York: Springer.

Sonkin, D. J. (1994). *Wounded boys: Heroic men: A man's guide to recovering from child abuse.* Stamford, CT: Longmeadow Press.

Sonkin, D. J. (1995). *Counselors' guide to learning to live without violence.* Volcano, CA: Volcano Press.

Sonkin, D. J., & Durphy, M. (1982). *Learning to live without violence: A book for men.* San Francisco, CA: Volcano Press.

Sonkin, D. J., & Liebert, D. (1998). Legal and ethical issues in the treatment of multiple victimization of children. In B. R. Rossman & M. S.

Rosenberg (Eds.), *Multiple victimization of children: Conceptual, developmental, research, and treatment issues.* New York: Haworth Press.

Sonkin, D. J., Martin, D., & Walker, L. E. (1985). *The male batterer: A treatment approach.* New York: Springer.

Sonkin, D. J., & Walker, L. E. A. (1995). *Juris Monitor stabilization and empowerment programs.* Denver, CO: Endolor Communications.

Spence, J. T., & Helmreich, R. (1972). The attitude toward women scale: An objective instrument to measure attitudes towards the rights and roles of women in contemporary society. *JSAS, Catalog of Selected Documents in Psychology, 2*(66), 1–51.

Spence, J. T., Helmreich, R., & Stapp, J. (1973). A short version of the attitudes toward women scale (AWS). *Bulletin of the Psychonomic Society, 2*(4), 219–220.

Srole, L. (1956). Social integration and certain corollaries. *American View, 21,* 709–716.

Stark, E., & Flitcraft, A. (1983). Social knowledge, social policy and the abuse of women: The case against patriarchal benevolence. In D. Finkelhor, R. J. Gelles, G. Hotaling, & M. Straus (Eds.), *The dark side of families* (pp. 330–348). Beverly Hills, CA: Sage.

Stark, E., & Flitcraft, A. (1988). Violence among intimates: An epidemiological review. In V. Van Hasselt, R. Morrison, A. Bellak, & M. Hersen (Eds.), *Handbook of family related violence* (pp. 293–317). New York: Plenum.

Stark, E., Flitcraft, A., & Frazier, W. (1979). Medicine and patriarchal violence: The social construction of a "private" event. *International Journal of Health Services, 9,* 461–493.

Starr, B. (1978). Comparing battered and non-battered women. *Victimology: An International Journal, 3*(1–2), 37–44.

Steiner, Y. (1999). Prevention and intervention for high risk girls in Israel and the Arab sectors. *American Psychologist, 54*(1), 64–65.

Steinmetz, S. (1978). The battered husband syndrome. *Victimology: An International Journal, 2*(3–4), 499–509.

Steinmetz, S. (1993). The abused elderly are dependent: Abuse is caused by the perception of stress associated with providing care. In R. J. Gelles & D. R. Loeske (Eds.), *Current controversies on family violence* (pp. 222–236). Newbury Park, CA: Sage.

Sternberg, K. J., Lamb, M. E., & Daawud-Noursi, S. (1998). Using multiple informants to understand domestic violence and its effects. In G. W. Holden, R. Geffner, & E. N. Jouriles (Eds.), *Children exposed to marital violence: Theory, research and applied issues* (pp. 121–156). Washington, DC: American Psychological Association.

Stone, M. (1976). *When God was a woman.* New York: Harcourt, Brace, Jovanovich.

Straus, M. A., Gelles, R. J., & Steinmetz, S. K. (1980). *Behind closed doors: Violence in the American family.* Garden City, NY: Anchor/ Doubleday.

Straus, M. A. (1993a). Physical assaults by wives: A major social problem. In R. J. Gelles & D. R. Loeske (Eds.), *Current controversies on family violence* (pp. 67–87). Newbury Park, CA: Sage.

Straus, M. A. (1993b). Identifying offenders in criminal justice research on domestic assault. *American Behavioral Scientist, 36,* 587–600.

Straus, M. A., & Gelles, R. J. (1990). How violent are American families? Estimates from the National Family Violence Research Resurvey and other studies. In M. A. Straus & R. J. Gelles (Eds.), *Physical violence in American families* (pp. 95–112). New Brunswick, NJ: Transaction.

Swenson, R. A., Nash, D. L., & Ross, D. C. (1984). Source credibility and perceived expertness of testimony in a simulated child-custody case. *Professional Psychology: Research and Practice, 15,* 891–898.

Taylor, S. P., & Gammon, C. B. (1975). Effects of type and dose of alcohol on human physical aggression. *Journal of Personality and Social Psychology, 32,* 169–175.

Terr, L. (1990). *Too scared to cry.* New York: Harper & Row.

Thoennes, N., & Tjaden, P. (1990). The extent, nature, and validity of sexual abuse allegations in custody/visitation disputes. *Child Abuse & Neglect, 14,* 151–163.

Thyfault, R. (1980a, April). *Sexual abuse in the battering relationship.* Paper presented at the annual meeting of the Rocky Mountain Psychological Conference, Tucson, Arizona.

Thyfault, R. (1980b, October). *Childhood sexual abuse, marital rape, and battered women: Implications for mental health workers.* Paper presented at the Annual Meeting of the Colorado Mental Health Conference, Keystone.

Tolman, R. M. (1989). The development of a measure of psychological maltreatment of women by their male partners. *Violence and Victims, 3,* 159–178.

Toomey, T. C., Hernandez, J. T., Gittleman, D. F., & Hulka, J. F. (1993). Relationship of sexual and physical abuse to pain and psychological assessment variables in chronic-pain patients. *Pain, 53,* 105–109.

Totman, J. (1978). *The murderers: A psychological study of criminal homicide.* San Francisco, CA: R & E Research Associates.

Unger, R. K. (1979). Toward a redefinition of sex and gender. *American Psychologist, 34* (11), 1088–1094.

U.S. House of Representatives, Subcommittee on Domestic and International Scientific Planning, Analysis, and Cooperation. *Proceedings of hearings on research into domestic violence,* February 14, 1978.

Van der Kolk, B. (1988). The trauma spectrum: The interactions of biological and social events in the genesis of the trauma response. *Journal of Traumatic Stress, 1,* 273–290.

Van der Kolk, B. (1994). The body keeps score: Memory and the evolving psychobiology of posttraumatic stress. *Harvard Review of Psychiatry, 1,* 253–265.

Van Hasselt, V., Morrison, R., Bellak, A. (1985). Alcohol use in wife abusers and their spouses. *Addictive Behavior, 10,* 137–135.

Vega, W., Kolody, B., Hwang, J., & Noble, A. (1993). Prevalence and magnitude of perinatal substance exposure in California. *New England Journal of Medicine, 329,* 850–854.

Veltkamp, L. J., & Miller, T. W. (1994). *Clinical handbook of child abuse and neglect.* Madison, CT: International Universities Press.

Viano, E. C. (1992). *Critical issues in victimology: International perspectives.* New York: Springer.

Walker, L. E. (1977–1978). Battered women and learned helplessness. *Victimology: An International Journal, 2,* 525–534.

Walker, L. E. (1978). Treatment alternatives for battered women. In J. R. Chapman & M. Gates (Eds.), *The victimization of women, Sage yearbooks in women's policy studies,* (Vol. 3). Beverly Hills, CA: Sage.

Walker, L. E. (1979). *The battered woman.* New York: Harper & Row.

Walker, L. E. (1980a, April). *The battered woman syndrome study.* Paper presented at the annual meeting of the Rocky Mountain Psychological Conference, Tucson, AZ.

Walker, L. E. (1980b, October). *Clinical aspects of the battered woman syndrome study.* Paper presented at the annual meeting of the Colorado Mental Health Conference, Keystone, CO.

Walker, L. E. (1980c). Battered women. In A. Brodsky & R. Hare-Mustin (Eds.), *Women and psychotherapy.* New York: Guilford

Walker, L. E. (1981a). Battered women: Sex roles and clinical issues. *Professional Psychology, 12,* 81–91.

Walker, L. E. (1981b). *The battered woman syndrome study: Final report submitted to the National Institute of Mental Health.*

Walker, L. E. (1981c). A feminist perspective of domestic violence. In R. Stuart (Ed.), *Violent behavior: Social learning approaches to prediction, management, and treatment* (pp. 102–115). New York: Brunner/Mazel.

Walker, L. E. (1983). Battered woman syndrome study: Results and discussion. In D. Finkelhor, R. J. Gelles, G. Hotaling, & M. Straus (Eds.), *The dark side of families* (pp. 31–48). Beverly Hills, CA: Sage.

Walker, L. E. (Ed.). (1984). *Women and mental health policy.* Beverly Hills, CA: Sage.

Walker, L. E. (1985a). Feminist forensic psychology. In L. B. Rosewater & L. E. Walker (Eds.), *Handbook on feminist therapy: Psychotherapy with women.* New York: Springer.

Walker, L. E. (1985b). Feminist therapy with victims/survivors of interpersonal violence. In L. B. Rosewater & L. E. Walker (Eds.), *Handbook on feminist therapy: Psychotherapy with women.* New York: Springer.

Walker, L. E. A. (1989a). *Terrifying love: Why battered women kill and how society responds.* New York: Harper Collins.

Walker, L. E. A. (1989b). Psychology and domestic violence. *American Psychologist, 44,* 695–702.

Walker, L. E. A. (1991). Abused women, infants, and substance abuse: Psychological consequences of failure to protect. In P. R. McGrab & D. M. Doherty (Eds.), *Mothers, infants and substance abuse: Proceedings of the APA Division 12, Midwinter Meeting,* Scottsdale, AZ, January 19–20.

Walker, L. E. A. (1993a). The battered woman syndrome is a consequence of abuse. In R. J. Gelles & D. R. Loeske (Eds.), *Current controversies on family violence* (pp. 133–153). Newbury Park, CA: Sage.

Walker, L. E. A. (1993b). Are personality disorders gender biased? Yes! In S. A. Kirk and S. D. Einbinder (Eds.), *Controversial issues in mental health.* New York: Allyn and Bacon.

Walker, L. E. A. (1994). *Abused women and survivor therapy: A practical guide for the psychotherapist.* Washington, DC: American Psychological Association.

Walker, L. E. A. (1996a). Assessment of abusive spousal relationships. In F. Kaslow (Ed.), *Handbook of relational diagnosis.* New York: Wiley.

Walker, L. E. A. (1996b). *Survivor therapy with abused women video series.* New York: Newbridge Communications.

Walker, L. E. A. (1997). Domestic violence: Theory, policy and intervention in the Americas. Invited Address at Congreso Regional de Psicologia para Professionals en America: Entrelazando la Ciencia y la Practica en la Psicologia. Ciudad de Mexico, 27 de Julio al 2 de Agosto de 1997.

Walker, L. E. A. (1998). *Feminist therapy: Psychotherapy with the experts video series.* Needham Heights, MA: Allyn & Bacon.

Walker, L. E. A. (1999). Domestic violence around the world. *American Psychologist, 54,* 21–29.

Walker, L. E. A., & Corriere, S. (1991). Domestic violence: International perspectives on social change. In E. Viano (Ed.), *Victim's rights and legal reforms: International perspectives. Proceedings of the Sixth International Institute on Victimology, Onati Proceedings, No. 9* (pp. 135–150). Onati, Spain: University of Onati Institute on Sociology and the Law.

Walker, L. E. A., Gold S., & Lucenko, B. (Eds.). (in press). *Handbook on child sexual abuse* (2nd ed.). New York: Springer.

Walker, L. E. A., & Meloy, J. R. (1998). Stalking and domestic violence. In J. R. Meloy (Ed.), *The psychology of stalking: Clinical and forensic perspectives* (pp. 139–162). San Diego, CA: Academic Press.

Walker, L. E. A., Stokes, L., & Monroe-DeVita, M. (in preparation). Battered women in prison: A study of the long term women offenders in the Colorado prison system.

Walker, L. E., Thyfault, R. K., & Browne, A. (1981). Beyond the jurors ken: Battered women. *Vermont Law Review.*

Wardell, L., Gillespie, D. L., & Leffler, A. (1983). Science and violence against wives. In D. Finkelhor, R. Gelles, G. Hotaling, & M. Straus (Eds.), *The dark side of families* (pp. 69–84). Beverly Hills, CA: Sage.

Warsaw, C. (1989). Violence against women. *Gender and Society, 3,* 506–517.

Washburn, C., & Frieze, I. H. (1980, March). *Methodological issues in studying battered women.* Paper presented at the meeting of the Association for Women in Psychology, Santa Monica, California.

Washburne, C. K. (1983). A feminist analysis of child abuse and neglect. In D. Finkelhor, R. J. Gelles, C. Hotaling, & M. Straus (Eds.), *The dark side of families* (pp. 289–292). Beverly Hills, CA: Sage.

Weiss, R. L., Hops, H., & Patterson, C. R. (1973). A framework for conceptualizing marital conflict, a technology for altering it, and some data for evaluating it. In L. A. Hamerlynck, L. C. Handy, & E. J. Mash (Eds.), *Behavior change: Methodology, concepts, and practices.* Champaign, IL: Research Press.

Weiss, R. L., & Cerreto, M. (1975). *Marital Status Inventory (MSI).*

Weissman, M. M., & Klerman, C. L. (1977). Sex differences and the epidemiology of depression. *Archives of General Psychiatry, 34,* 98–111.

White, J. W., & Koss, M. P. (1991). Courtship violence: Incidence in a national sample of higher education students. *Violence and Victims, 6,* 247–256.

Wolfgang, M. E. (1968). *Studies in homicide.* New York: Harper & Row.

Wright, J. A., Burgess, A. G., Burgess, A. W., Laszlo, A. T., McCrary, G. O., & Douglas, J. E. (1996). A typology of interpersonal stalking. *Journal of Interpersonal Violence, 11,* 487–502.

Wyatt, G. E. (1985). The sexual abuse of Afro-American and White American women in childhood. *Child Abuse and Neglect, 9,* 507–519.

Yllo, K. (1981, July). *Types of marital rape: Three case studies.* Paper presented at the national conference for Family Violence Researchers, University of New Hampshire, Durham.

Yllo, K. A. (1993). Through a feminist lens: Gender, power and violence. In R. J. Gelles & D. R. Loeske (Eds.), *Current controversies on family violence* (pp. 47–62). Newbury Park, CA: Sage.

Zeichner, A., & Pihl, R. O. (1979). Effects of alcohol and behavior contingencies on human aggression. *Journal of Abnormal Psychology, 88* (2), 156–160.

Zorza, J. (1995). How abused women can use the law to help protect their children. In E. Peled, P. G. Jaffe, & J. L. Edelson (Eds.), *Ending the cycle of violence: Community responses to children of battered women* (pp. 147–169). Thousand Oaks, CA: Sage.

Index

$\boxed{\text{S}}$ *Springer Publishing Company*

Crisis Intervention and Trauma Response
Theory and Practice
Barbara R. Wainrib, EdD and Ellin L. Bloch, PhD

"The authors have eminently succeeded in developing effective and well-grounded theoretical approaches towards helping people in crisis situations...an important contribution to the field of crisis intervention...actively helps restore the feeling of self that has been damaged by trauma. I highly recommend this book."

-**Martin Symonds,** MD Deputy Chief Surgeon (Psychiatrist),
New York City Police Department
Clinical Associate Professor of Psychiatry,
New York University-School of Medicine

"This book is very special in its integration of solid conceptualization and compassionate practice. Covering an unusually wide spectrum of crisis and traumas, it places them in a context well-suited for the practice-oriented student. Through the use of well-integrated exercises and introspections, it successfully conveys the message that "helping" is a personal - not just an academic- experience."

-**John A. Clizbe,** PhD
Management and Consulting Psychologist

Written in a lively and informative style, the book presents a successful general crisis response model for intervention. Using real-life case examples and exercises to develop techniques for building verbal and nonverbal skills, the authors encourage therapists to help clients cope by focusing on clients' inner strengths rather than on pathologies that need to be fixed.

The authors' down-to-earth approach to this topic will appeal to crisis intervention professionals, teachers, students, and volunteer workers.

1998   224pp.   soft   0-8261-1175-0 $31.95 (outside U.S . $35.80)

536 Broadway, New York, NY 10012-3955 • (212) 431-4370 • Fax (212) 941-7842